Theophilus Hunter
Holmes

For DAVID Bagan

Wal Hildmih

Dec 21st, 2014

Theophilus Hunter Holmes

A North Carolina General in the Civil War

WALTER C. HILDERMAN III

McFarland & Company, Inc., Publishers

Jefferson, North Carolina, and London

LIBRARY OF CONGRESS CATALOGUING-IN-PUBLICATION DATA

Hilderman, Walter Carrington.
Theophilus Hunter Holmes : a North Carolina general in
the Civil War / Walter C. Hilderman III.
p.   cm.
Includes bibliographical references and index.

ISBN 978-0-7864-7310-6

softcover : acid free paper ∞

1. Holmes, T. H. (Theophilus Hunter), 1804–1880.   2. Generals—Confederate
States of America—Biography.   3. United States—History—Civil War,
1861–1865—Biography.   4. North Carolina—History—Civil War,
1861–1865—Biography.   I. Title.
E467.1.H576H55 2014   355.0092—dc23   [B]   2013033487

BRITISH LIBRARY CATALOGUING DATA ARE AVAILABLE

On the cover: Model 1850 U.S. Army infantry officer's
sword that Lt. Gen. Holmes carried (courtesy
Ted Spilman); Lt. Gen. Theophilus Hunter
Holmes, CSA (Library of Congress)

Manufactured in the United States of America

*McFarland & Company, Inc., Publishers
Box 611, Jefferson, North Carolina 28640
www.mcfarlandpub.com*

To the memory of
Laura W. Holmes,
a soldier's wife.

Table of Contents

Acknowledgments

In 2005, I met Louis and Mary Spilman, of Fayetteville, North Carolina. Mrs. Spilman is General Holmes's great-granddaughter. The Spilmans' research on Holmes's military career dates back to the 1960s when Mr. Spilman wrote a college paper on the general's life. Descendants of General Holmes now living in Texas, Beth Lawrence, Dwain Holmes, and Harrison Holmes Wright, provided valuable information. The Spilman and Holmes families gave their blessing to a biography of General Holmes and helped with advice, family records, and encouragement throughout the project.

In writing this biography, I needed to research parts of American history that had escaped my attention as a student of the American Civil War in the East. The Confederate Trans-Mississippi, Indian removal, the Seminole Wars, and the U.S.–Mexican War were beyond my usual field of study. My research on these topics led me to contact a number of individuals who were kind enough to critique my work and render additional guidance.

Among those who were most helpful are Chris Kimbal of Naples, Florida, who advised me on the Seminole Wars. Historian and author Dr. Timothy D. Johnson assisted me with the U.S.–Mexican War. Doyle Taylor of White Hall, Arkansas, and Clifton Shultz of Coldspring, Texas, helped with the Civil War in Arkansas, the Trans-Mississippi, and the Battle of Helena. Robert E. L. Krick, Chief Historian, Richmond National Battlefield Park, assisted with the Peninsular Campaign. Paul Troutman, Hugh Harkey, Donny Taylor, Larry Walker, Harriet Little, Charles Howell, and my wife, Pat, provided other assistance. Joe Long of the Confederate Relic Room in Columbia, South Carolina, Bill Brasington, Bob Seigler, and Fred Knudsen, also of South Carolina, assisted in estimating the number of South Carolina's Junior and Senior Reserves. Matthew Brown of the North Carolina Department of Cultural Resources provided information on the North Carolina Reserves. Mike Purdy and Alan Pitts assisted with information on Georgia Reserve soldiers. Brian Basore of the Oklahoma Historical Society kindly provided copies of entries from the Fort Gibson letter book. Prominent American Civil War historian and author Chris Fonvielle gave generously of his time and expertise.

The gentlemen at the Orangeburg, South Carolina, Public Library's reference desk, Ken Coleman, Keith Byers, and Capers Bull, handled scores of interlibrary loan requests. Teresa Roan and John Coski at the Museum of the Confederacy, Richmond, Virginia, provided advice and copies of documents from the museum's collection. Jack House at the National Archives and researcher Patrick Funiciello made possible my access to National Archives documents. Bill Hall, of Eutawville, South Carolina, provided technical assistance with the illustrations.

Dozens of web sites maintained by universities, museums, historical societies, historical sites, and individuals provided additional information and help. Many of these web sites are listed in the bibliography. These full and part-time historians dedicate untold hours to researching and sharing with the world through the Internet. They are the great underpinning for the documentation of American history. Without their help this work would not have been possible.

Preface

The rise of military professionalism in the first half of the 19th century profoundly influenced the American Civil War. As an 1829 graduate of the United States Military Academy, Theophilus Hunter Holmes was among America's first generation of officers trained at West Point. As lieutenants and captains, these men served on the frontier and fought wars in Florida and Mexico. These conflicts were practice fields for junior officers who became senior commanders in the American Civil War. The war with Mexico has been aptly described as a dress rehearsal for the larger conflict that came only thirteen years later. Many officers who developed their skills on these earlier battlefields would be Holmes's commanders, subordinates, and adversaries in the years that followed.

Nineteenth-century military troop strength reports can be confusing. United States and Confederate States reporting formats usually distinguished between "Absent," "Present for duty," "Aggregate present and absent," etc. Typically, the number of troops "present for duty" was one-half to two-thirds of the "aggregate" number. The aggregate number included all officers and enlisted men assigned to a division, district, brigade, etc., whether they were physically present in camp, in the hospital, home on leave, temporarily assigned to other duty, or absent without leave. The "present for duty" strength is the number of soldiers who were physically present, whether they were sufficiently armed and equipped. This is a particularly significant consideration in the Confederacy's Trans-Mississippi department.

Confederate soldiers in that region suffered, more than their Eastern counterparts, from shortages of food, weapons, ammunition, tents, shoes, clothing, and transportation resources. These shortages had no effect on their "present for duty" numbers, but significantly reduced the number of troops that were considered to be "effective," i.e., prepared for a campaign. This consideration also had significant impact on the ability of Trans-Mississippi Confederate armies to remain in the field for extended periods.

This work often quotes directly from primary sources. Original spelling and word usage remain unaltered unless doing so would be confusing to the reader. Brackets are used to indicate the changes in those instances.

Introduction

When asked, "Who was Lieutenant General Theophilus Hunter Holmes?" most students of the American Civil War respond with a blank stare. Historian and editor Clay Williams has said that when historians write about the Civil War, "Holmes's name is either forgotten or ridiculed."[1]

Holmes came from a prominent and politically connected North Carolina family. He attended the United States Military Academy at West Point with such notables as Robert E. Lee, Jefferson Davis, and Joseph E. Johnston. He served on the western frontier, fought the Seminoles in Florida, and was breveted to the rank of major for his service during the war with Mexico. He became the United States Army's chief recruiting officer in 1859, but resigned only days before the war began and cast his lot with the Confederacy.

He led a brigade at First Manassas and a division during the Peninsular Campaign. From August 1862 through April 1863, he commanded armies in the Department of the Trans-Mississippi, one-half of the Confederacy's territory. In July 1863, he led seven thousand soldiers in a determined but ill-fated attack on Helena, Arkansas, recklessly exposing himself to enemy fire. During the last year of the war he was responsible for the conscription of more than ten thousand Junior and Senior Reserve soldiers in North Carolina. His prominence in American Civil War history should have been assured, but such was not his destiny.

I became aware of General Holmes while doing research for my first book, *They Went Into the Fight Cheering! Confederate Conscription in North Carolina.* The universal condemnation by historians of Holmes's role in the American Civil War was not consistent with the information I had discovered. My research indicated that Holmes had done a commendable job of organizing North Carolina's Junior and Senior Reserve regiments and overseeing conscription in the state during the last year of the war.

No books have been written about Holmes. He left no memoirs and few letters. He appears briefly in Civil War books and articles as a detached, almost sinister figure in North Carolina, the Peninsular Campaign, and the Trans-Mississippi. Historians refer to him as "weak, vacillating, and totally devoid of energy." A Confederate surgeon accused him as having "softening of the brain."[2] The accusation has been made that, prior to his resignation from the United States Army, Holmes was a spy for the Confederacy and warned Charleston, South Carolina, of Union attempts to reinforce Fort Sumter. While criticizing Holmes, however, his contemporary detractors frequently remarked that he was patriotic, courageous, and a man of excellent heart and kind disposition.[3]

3

In the Trans-Mississippi, Holmes's soldiers derisively referred to him as "Granny," a term also applied to Robert E. Lee early in the war. The most common observation made by historians about Holmes's attack at Malvern Hill during the Peninsular Campaign is that he "made a feeble attempt to turn the Union left." He has been described as "sickly." Like many veterans of the Seminole and Mexican wars, Holmes may have suffered from recurring bouts of malaria. His service record indicates that he was often listed as "present, sick" or "absent, sick."

Holmes was noticeably hard of hearing. He may have taken quinine, which was commonly available after the 1830s, for recurring fevers caused by malaria. Deafness, tinnitus, and headaches are side effects of quinine. His deafness, which worsened over the years, likely contributed to the perception that he was inattentive or aloof.

By 1861, at the age of fifty-six, Theophilus Holmes had spent thirty-six years in the United States Army. In the twilight of his career, rather than planning for retirement, he was forced to make a decision that would draw him into America's bloodiest war as an enemy of the nation he had sworn to serve. He avoided making the decision to resign from the United States Army for as long as he could. Throughout his career he had watched the growing schism between North and South. Like his native state, while other Southern states seceded from the Union, Holmes waited. He was an experienced combat officer, a capable administrator, and a responsible soldier. He could not avoid the war no matter which path he chose. He was expected to take up the sword against the South or resign from the army. When he was convinced that war would come and North Carolina would secede, Holmes offered his services to his lifelong friend, Jefferson Davis. By then, North Carolinians had spent months preparing for war.

In 1862, President Davis promoted Holmes to lieutenant general. Of the eighteen Confederate generals who attained that rank, Holmes was one of only two North Carolinians.[4] (Holmes and Leonidas Polk were promoted to lieutenant general on the same date. Braxton Bragg was a full general. The appointment of Daniel Harvey Hill to lieutenant general was never approved by the Confederate senate.)

A devoted family man with deep religious convictions, Holmes, the man and the soldier, possessed the traits of both triumph and tragedy.

1

A First Family
of North Carolina

The Holmes family migrated from Ireland to America in the late 17th century. By the early 18th century, part of the family had moved from Boston, Massachusetts, through Virginia, and were substantial land owners in northeastern North Carolina. Gabriel Holmes Sr. (1719–1788) of Edgecombe County and his wife, Mary Caison Holmes, settled during the 1750s at Gilmore Swamp, now Sampson County. Their son Gabriel Holmes Jr. (1769–1829) was the youngest of seven children. His parents' prosperity and influence afforded him opportunities that were rare in eastern North Carolina. He attended school in Fayetteville and at the Zion Parnassus Academy in Iredell County. He attended Harvard University for three years and studied law under John Louis Taylor, the first chief justice of the North Carolina Supreme Court.[1]

Gabriel Holmes Jr. married Mary Smith Hunter in Raleigh on January 7, 1795. They lived on a thirty-four-hundred-acre plantation on the Little Coharie River near Roseboro in Sampson County. Mary's father was Colonel Theophilus Hunter Sr. of Wake County. Gabriel Holmes served in the state's General Assembly on four occasions between 1793 and 1813. He was on the board of trustees of the University of North Carolina from 1801 to 1804 and again from 1817 to 1829. He was governor of North Carolina from 1821 to 1824. After the governorship, he was a U.S. congressman until his death in 1829. He was distinguished, cultured and "fitted to move in the highest circles of society, where he was ever welcome."[2] Gabriel and Mary Holmes raised six children, four girls and two boys. Two other children died in infancy. Their youngest son, Theophilus Hunter Holmes, was born on November 11, 1804.[3]

Theophilus Holmes attended local schools in Sampson County and a private academy in Fayetteville. As a young man, he half-heartedly tried his hand at farming, but he had neither the talent nor the inclination for plantation life. While his father was governor, Holmes decided on a career in the army, but his choice of vocation was not popular with his family. In remarking on his decision against managing his father's plantation, a family member described young Holmes as "indolent."[4]

North Carolina adjutant general Beverly W. Daniel contacted Secretary of War John C. Calhoun in mid–1824 and requested an appointment for the governor's son to the United States Military Academy. Daniel stated that young Holmes was of "excellent character and of a good disposition; his qualifications in other respects are such as will be perceived without doubt sufficient to bring him within the rules of the Institution."[5]

Several months later, the governor and Theophilus were notified that the appointment had been approved by President James Monroe. Governor Holmes accepted the appointment on behalf of his son (as was required) on December 6, 1824. He wrote, "I hereby express my appreciation and agreement to any obligation or arrangement my son Theophilus H. Holmes may enter into with the officers of the Military Academy at West Point." In a separate letter written the same day, Theophilus advised Secretary Calhoun that he would "report myself at the time, and in the manner specified in the notice."[6]

Holmes began his military career as a West Point cadet on September 1, 1825, two months before his twenty-first birthday. He was older than many of his classmates. Of those who would graduate with him four years later, his youngest classmate was Joseph A. Smith, who entered the academy at the age of fifteen years and four months. His oldest classmate was Miner Knowlton, almost twenty-two years old. Two of his classmates were Joseph E. Johnston and Robert E. Lee. One year behind him were future Confederate generals William Pendleton and John Bankhead Magruder. Holmes's closest friend during his West Point years was upperclassman Jefferson Davis, future president of the Confederacy.[7] (The academic year at the United States Military Academy started on July 1 of each year, but, as was the case with Holmes, it was common for incoming cadets to report for duty after that date. Cadet Jefferson Davis had arrived several weeks late the previous year.)

The academy was located near the small town of West Point, New York, on the Hudson River. Upon arriving, Holmes was greeted by a lone sentinel who recorded his name on a slate, as was required for all persons arriving or departing the area. Holmes proceeded toward town. His baggage was carried by an old, one-armed soldier, the only person authorized to carry such items to the academy. From nearby Gridley's Hotel, Holmes could see the two largest buildings on campus, North and South barracks. Most of the incoming cadets stayed at Gridley's until they were assigned to their quarters in South Barracks.[8]

On the appointed day, Holmes lined up with other new cadets near South Barracks and took his oath: "I, [Theophilus H. Holmes], a cadet born in the state of North Carolina, aged [twenty years and ten months], do hereby acknowledge to have this day voluntarily engaged with the consent of my mother to serve in the Army of the United States for the period of five years." The cadets were issued (at their own expense) clothing consisting of the regulation gray uniform, a tall cap with a leather visor, a blue work uniform, and four pairs of white pants.[9] Each cadet was introduced, very briefly, to the superintendent, Lieutenant Colonel Sylvanus Thayer, and then escorted to South Barracks by an orderly.

"South" was a three-story stone structure with long hallways separating rooms on either side of the building. Holmes was introduced to an upperclassman, the "officer of new cadets," who assigned him to his room and introduced his roommates.[10] The barracks rooms were small, approximately eleven feet on a side. Each room accommodated three cadets. Cadets provided their own furniture and a pitcher, mirror, water pan, night pot, and mattresses. No beds were allowed. Each cadet was responsible for keeping the room clean for a week at a time using the broom, scrub brush, and bucket the academy required in each room. Firewood was carried to the room for the open hearth that provided the only source of heat in the cold New York winters. Water was carried to the rooms in buckets from an outside well until 1827, when a water system was installed. During the summer, cadets bathed in the Hudson River.[11]

The threat of fire was always present, and the cadet fire company drilled frequently. There were a number of small room fires each year, which were usually extinguished quickly. Cadets were disciplined for leaving their rooms without placing a metal "bumper" in front of the hearth. While Holmes was at West Point, the post artillery quarters (the "Bombardier Barracks") burned to the ground.[12]

Cadets were paid twenty-eight dollars each month, which included twelve dollars for expenses. They were not allowed to receive money from any other source.[13] Holmes learned that as a first-year cadet he was referred to as a "plebe." Once settled in their rooms, plebes were expected to "fall in" at the very next formation whether or not they knew what the command "Fall in!" meant. There was a great deal of confusion and stumbling around, accompanied by the shouts of upperclassmen who served as drill instructors.[14]

Each day at the academy began at dawn with a cannon blast, the "sunrise gun." Cadet Holmes rose with his roommates, washed up, got his mattress off the floor, dressed in his uniform, and answered at roll call. Thirty minutes after the sunrise gun, each room was inspected. Plebes studied mathematics until breakfast, which began at promptly at 7:00 A.M. and ended thirty minutes later. They sat on wooden benches and stared across the tables at each other during meals. Idle conversation was discouraged. After breakfast, the cadets were lined up on the parade ground and marched to mathematics class, where they took instruction until 11:00 A.M. They returned to their barracks and studied until noon. They were allowed one hour for their midday meal, which began at 1:00 P.M. They reformed their ranks on the parade ground and marched to Claudius Berard's two-hour French language class.[15]

Nineteenth century American society and academic communities, including the military, considered France to be the cultural and educational center of Western civilization. Consequently, many of the textbooks at West Point were written in French. Well-educated young men of the day were expected to have some knowledge of the language. French classes focused on reading and understanding French rather than social conversation.[16]

From 4:00 P.M. until dusk, cadets practiced military formations, the manual of arms, and drill maneuvers. After the evening meal, they returned to their quarters and studied until the nine-thirty roll call. All cadets were to be in bed at 10 P.M. The library was open for two hours each Saturday afternoon, and cadets were encouraged to check out books and study quietly in their rooms. No non-academic reading material was allowed in the barracks except one magazine approved by the academy.[17]

Cadet Holmes and his classmates were subject to rules of personal conduct that reflected early 19th century standards for young gentlemen. All cadets were required to take dance lessons. They were expected to be neatly groomed and to make no unnecessary noise, and were forbidden from spitting on the floor. Card playing, the use of tobacco, and drinking "spiritous beverages" were strictly forbidden.[18]

The corps of cadets was divided into two companies for administrative purposes and military formations. Discipline was enforced by the cadets themselves. As each class rose in seniority from year to year, cadets who impressed the superintendent and commandant were selected to assume additional responsibilities. Cadet captains, lieutenants, and orderly sergeants were taken from the "first class," those in their final year. Sergeants and corporals came from the "second class," the third year cadets. Second-year students and the "plebes" were at the bottom of the rank structure along with cadets in the upper classes who had not been promoted. They were the "privates" in formations. Cadets could expect little leniency from the upperclassmen who had been appointed to enforce academy rules.[19]

Cadets inclined toward mischief stole away during their free time and went to the local "public houses," Benny Haven's or North's Tavern. They did so at great risk. Being caught drinking was a serious offense. Jefferson Davis was court-martialed and nearly expelled from the academy after he was caught in Benny Haven's tavern.[20]

Of the one hundred eight cadets who entered West Point in 1825, only forty-six graduated in 1829. Among those completing their studies, Holmes did not distinguish himself academically. He graduated forty-fourth, well behind Lee at second and Joseph E. Johnston at thirteenth. Holmes accumulated one hundred thirty-six demerits during his four years at "the Point," which ranked him at thirty-fourth on the Merit in Conduct list. His classmate Albert D. Blanchard earned more than three hundred demerits.[21]

Upon graduating on July 1, 1829, Holmes was commissioned as a 2nd lieutenant and assigned to the 7th U.S. Infantry regiment. The assignment would shape Holmes's military experience for the next twenty-five years. While serving in this regiment, he would fight in two wars and participate in the expansion of America's frontiers. In 1829, the 7th Infantry was already one of America's premier fighting regiments.

A regiment designated the "7th Infantry" had been organized in 1798 in preparation for a land war with France that never occurred. The regiment was disbanded two years later. During the War of 1812, a reorganized 7th Infantry played a leading role in the battle of New Orleans, fought on January 8, 1815. During one part of the campaign, American infantry and artillery fired from behind breastworks constructed of cotton bales. After New Orleans, the 7th U.S. Infantry would be forever known as the "Cottonbalers." With the end of the war in 1815, a reorganization of the United States Army resulted in a consolidation of regiments. A new 7th Infantry was made of three older units, the 8th, 24th and 39th regiments.[22]

With the army's reorganization complete, the U.S. government focused its military attention on securing the nation's borders. In June 1816, the army established Camp Crawford in the southwest corner of Georgia at the confluence of the Chattahoochee and Flint rivers. The wooden stockade, later named Fort Scott, was intended to confront former British allies in nearby Spanish Florida: Seminoles, Choctaws, and "Red Stick" Creeks, so called for their red-colored war clubs and religious objects. This diverse native population had been migrating to Florida from Alabama and Georgia since 1750.[23] Many of them occupied an abandoned British military installation on the Apalachicola River.

The fort, referred to as the "Negro Fort," bristled with artillery left behind by the British and was a gathering place for hundreds of free African Americans and runaway slaves. They and their native allies established a farming community surrounding the fort. Soon, Georgia settlers and backwoodsmen began raiding into Florida. They stole Seminole livestock and abducted anyone suspected of being a runaway slave. The Seminoles and African Americans had been conducting cross-border raids of their own. The Spanish still owned Florida but were unable to keep the peace.[24]

Raids from Negro Fort and its appeal to slaves seeking freedom became such a nuisance that the army launched a campaign to destroy the settlement. On July 27, after several skirmishes, a duel between the fort's cannons and U.S. artillery ended with the explosion of Negro Fort's powder magazine. Two hundred seventy of the fort's defenders and their dependents were killed. The sixty survivors were returned to Georgia as slaves. With the end of the campaign in late 1816, Fort Scott was abandoned by the U.S. Army, but it reopened the following spring. Seminole attacks in Georgia had increased with the approach of good weather. The U.S. Army needed the fort to use as a base for a campaign against the raiders.[25]

The First Seminole War, or Creek War, began when the Creeks refused to leave their lands as required by the Treaty of Fort Jackson (1814). Troops from Fort Scott attacked a Creek village, Fowltown, in November 1817. In retaliation, the Creeks allied with the Seminoles and attacked an army boat on the Chattahoochee River on November 30, killing approximately thirty men, women, and children.[26] They also attacked Fort Scott in December, but in January 1818, a severe winter brought hostilities to a halt.

General Andrew Jackson arrived in the spring of 1818 and reinforced Fort Scott. His one thousand men, augmented by native allies, included the 7th U.S. Infantry. The 7th participated in the campaign that defeated the Seminoles and Creeks and went on to capture Spanish settlements in Florida.[27] By 1821, when the United States acquired Florida from Spain, the 7th Infantry had become one of the young nation's best known and hardest fighting regiments.

For the next several decades, the U.S. Army's responsibility was to implement United States policy in dealing with the "Indian problem." The "problem" was to devise and execute a plan to relocate Eastern tribes, Cherokee, Chickasaw, Choctaw, Creek, and Seminole (referred to as the Five Civilized Tribes or the Five Nations), to lands west of the Mississippi River. Friction between tribes native to the West and those arriving from the East was inevitable. Fort Smith, Arkansas Territory, became an early focal point of the forced migration, which would come to be called "The Trail of Tears."

During Theophilus Holmes's teenage years, the 7th Infantry remained in Georgia at Fort Scott. Surrounded by the advantages of his parents' wealth and political influence in North Carolina, Holmes had little knowledge of the social and military events that were shaping his future. Like most youngsters of the era, he came of age aware that military service to his state was an expected part of life. Dating back to Colonial times, most men had been required to join the militia. Holmes's maternal grandfather, Theophilus Hunter Sr., had been a North Carolina militia officer from 1771 to 1776. One of Holmes's grandfathers had been a soldier in the American Revolution. His uncle, Hardy Holmes, had been an officer in the 1st North Carolina Regiment, rising to the rank of captain before being wounded at the battle of Eutaw Springs, South Carolina, in 1781.[28]

The 7th Infantry regiment was divided into two battalions in 1822 and sent to the western frontier. Lieutenant Colonel Zachary Taylor and four companies of the 7th, one hundred forty-four officers and enlisted men, were sent to Louisiana, where they established Cantonment Jesup (later named Fort Jesup) near Natchitoches. The remaining companies, under the regiment's commander, Colonel Matthew Arbuckle, were sent to Fort Smith in Arkansas Territory. Disease haunted Arbuckle's column, making their journey from Georgia torturous. Only one hundred thirty-nine of the two hundred fifty soldiers who left Fort Scott survived the trip.[29]

Fort Smith had been built in 1817 to protect white settlers and ensure peace between the local Osage tribe and the displaced Eastern tribes. The fort was located on a fifty-foot rise, overlooking the Arkansas and Poteau rivers, and measured one hundred thirty-two feet on each side with stockade walls ten feet tall. The stockade protected log barracks, officer's quarters, offices, a hospital, and two blockhouses at diagonal corners.[30] When combined with Fort Smith's existing garrison, Major Bradford's rifle regiment, Arbuckle's force was sufficient to maintain peace among the tribes in the area and prevent white homesteaders from settling on land reserved for the Osages and Cherokees. In July 1822, a peace treaty was signed by the two tribes. For the next several years, the 7th Infantry policed the region, maintained the peace, and chased away white trespassers.[31]

By the time Theophilus Holmes entered West Point, life at Fort Smith was peaceful and routine. Military families had arrived and small farms surrounded the fort. Merchants sold goods to soldiers, Native Americans, and civilians. Peaceful conditions around Fort Smith signified that the "Indian problem" had been pushed farther west. The stability brought by Fort Smith soon made the fort unnecessary.[32]

This pattern was repeated all along the western frontier, from Fort Snelling in the Northwest Territory, southward past Fort Smith, down to Fort Jesup, Louisiana. Towns grew up around military posts, and the need for a local military presence diminished. As the edge of the frontier stabilized, forts had to send their patrols farther and farther west to be effective. Local tribes and those resettled from the East were pushed together and ever westward as a rising tide of white settlers arrived. Keeping peace among the tribes and guarding their lands against encroachment by settlers came to be the military's secondary mission. Facilitating the migration of white settlers and keeping peace between them and native populations became the army's primary task. The term "Manifest Destiny" was not coined until 1845, but it identified a philosophy and a process that had been evolving for thirty years. In 1830, social and political pressure created by Manifest Destiny would result in the passage of the Indian Removal Act.

In the spring of 1824, Colonel Arbuckle and five companies of the 7th Infantry left Fort Smith. They built Fort Gibson approximately eighty miles away on the banks of the Grand River, near its confluence with the Arkansas and Verdigris rivers. Arbuckle's soldiers resumed peace-keeping between the tribes and white settlers.[33] The ten companies of the 7th Infantry did not serve together during these years. Various companies were divided among Fort Smith in Arkansas Territory; Fort Gibson, Indian Territory (northeast Oklahoma); and Fort Jesup.

The military needed good roads for supply and communication within the network of forts. Planning began for roads between Little Rock (Arkansas Territory), Fort Smith, and Fort Gibson. For the next several years, construction projects, patrols, and occasional clashes between the tribes broke the monotony of army life on the frontier. Fresh out of the academy, 2nd Lieutenant Theophilus Holmes arrived at Fort Jesup, Louisiana, in 1830.

2

The Indian Removal

Holmes was glad to leave his classroom life behind and was excited about his assignment. Fort Jesup was the largest military post in Louisiana, consisting of several buildings and a nearby supporting outpost called Cantonment Taylor. He was at the forefront of America's western expansion, and his regiment was one of the oldest and most famous units in the army. Many of his countrymen and fellow officers had come to believe that America's expansion should end only at the Pacific Ocean. European powers feared that Mexico and even Canada were regarded by Americans as components of their national destiny.[1]

On May 28, 1830, President Andrew Jackson signed the Indian Removal Act. American whites, particularly in the South, favored moving the Seminoles, Creeks, Cherokees, Choctaws, and Chickasaws west, beyond the Mississippi River. The state of Georgia, in particular, had been in conflict with the Cherokees for years over land ownership. Bands of several southern tribes had already gone west while others, like the Seminoles in Florida, were resisting pressure to give up their land.[2]

Treaties signed under the Indian Removal Act induced tribes to exchange their land in the east for land in the "Indian Territory." Agreements usually included payment to the tribes and transportation. Tribal chiefs got the best terms possible, but they were often coerced or bribed into signing treaties. They had no choice. In 1831, the U.S. Supreme Court ruled that the Cherokees in Georgia had a right to self rule, but President Jackson refused to enforce the decision, and the state of Georgia simply ignored it. The chiefs knew their tribes had to cooperate with the Indian Removal Act or suffer the inevitable consequences of losing their land at gunpoint and without compensation. Eastern tribes were also concerned about the reception they would receive in the new lands.[3]

After touring the American West in 1832, Washington Irving described Indian Territory as "great grassy plains, interspersed with forests and groves, and clumps of trees, and watered by the Arkansas, the grand Canadian, the Red River, and all their tributary streams." Of the inhabitants he wrote, "the Osage, the Creek, the Delaware and other tribes ... live within the vicinity of white settlements.... Pawnees, Comanches, and other fierce, and as yet independent tribes" roamed freely, following the herds of elk, buffalo, and wild horses. These regions, Irving wrote, form a "debatable ground of these warring and vindictive tribes."[4] The arrival of additional tribes from the East was sure to bring conflict to the area. There were also competing international agendas in the region.

The U.S. government's policy of moving Eastern tribes westward, while supporting white settlers also moving west, was colliding with Mexico's desire to maintain control over Texas. The situation was further complicated by bands of Pawnees and Comanches whose presence was tolerated by the U.S. government in some areas but violated treaties in others. The 7th Infantry and other military units operating in the area were ordered to begin negotiations with some natives and push others farther west. All sides were attempting to gain influence, stake out territory, and build infrastructure to further their interests. Political intrigue and manipulation were practiced by all participants, from the local tribes to the nation states.

Lieutenant Holmes had been settled at Fort Jesup for about a year when his commanding officer, Lieutenant Colonel James B. Many, was ordered to take four companies to Fort Gibson and join the rest of the 7th Infantry. Once united, the regiment was to provide labor and protection for road construction between Fort Smith and Fort Towson on the Red River. Colonel Many's companies left Fort Jesup in late October 1831 and proceeded overland to Natchitoches, Louisiana. The troops boarded the steamboat *Enterprise* and traveled down the Red River to the Mississippi River, up the Mississippi to the Arkansas River, then on to Little Rock. They changed to smaller boats and arrived at Fort Gibson in February 1832. By this time, Fort Gibson was the 7th Infantry's headquarters.[5] Second Lieutenant Holmes was assigned to Company B of the regiment under the command of 1st Lieutenant Macomb and Captain Bonneville.

The road construction plan had been approved by the secretary of war and was designed to support the forts and facilitate the relocation of displaced Eastern tribes. Additionally, the Mexican army was planning to build a fort on the south side of the Red River. A U.S. Army road terminating nearby could be useful if troops were needed to confront Mexico in the future. The Mexicans had allied themselves with some of the Cherokees who had been relocated to the area several years earlier. Territorial quarrels between tribes under the protection of the United States were in Mexico's interests. The conflicts threatened the tribes' local sovereignty and the stability sought by the U.S. government. The governor of Arkansas also opposed having a Mexican fort in the region.[6]

Colonel Many assumed command of Fort Gibson (the post commander, Colonel Matthew Arbuckle, was absent) and began to organize the road construction project. The existing route was a series of foot and horse paths that had been in use for many years. The trails crossed prairies, forests, streams, and areas strewn with large boulders. Bridges and passages wide enough for wagons that would permit the movement of displaced tribes (and, perhaps, military columns with artillery moving toward Texas) were needed all along the route. Surveys by a variety of individuals and agencies had been made, giving some idea of the obstacles to be overcome. The Cherokee Agent at Fort Smith contacted Colonel Many in March. He described the background of the project and suggested that one hundred fifty miles of road work should be completed before summer heat made the labor much more difficult.[7]

Construction, under the supervision of Captain John Stuart, 7th Infantry Regiment, began in May. The work was grueling. The project was marred by a lack of coordination between government agents, civilian contractors, and the military. There were shortages of food and tools for the work parties. An insufficient number of draft animals and wagons were provided. The threat of attack by Pawnees became a possibility toward the end of the project. Soldiers labored with their weapons nearby and under the watchful eyes of their comrades acting as scouts and guards.[8]

The work ended on June 19, and the soldiers made preparations to return to their posts. Native travelers and civilians began using sections of the road before the project was finished.[9] Everybody involved was glad to have the arduous episode at an end. While this kind of assignment was becoming common for soldiers on the frontier, it is unlikely that Theophilus Holmes had road construction in mind when he applied to West Point seven years earlier. Soldiers stationed at frontier posts did so many construction projects during this period that their "fatigue" uniforms wore out quickly. Often, they had to supply additional work clothes at their own expense.[10]

Army life at Fort Gibson during the 1830s was harsh. Enlisted men died at a frightful rate from disease and accidents. Even among officers, the death toll was high. In 1831, Holmes's fellow lieutenants in the 7th Infantry, John W. Murray and Frederick Thomas, were buried at the fort. Thomas drowned in the Arkansas River. Murray was thrown from a horse. A former Arkansas militia general and sutler at the fort, John Nicks, died at the end of 1831. Lieutenant Benjamin Kinsman, also of the 7th Regiment, died at the post in 1832.[11]

Holmes was given a sixty-day furlough on June 23, 1832, but did not return to Fort Gibson until January 1833. When his leave expired and he did not report to the post, he was listed as "absent without leave." His continued absence through December, perhaps due to illness or some other emergency, was later approved by a series of extensions granted by the army.[12] Holmes and Company B remained at Fort Gibson for the next several months. During this time, 1st Lieutenant Macomb was assigned to recruiting duty and sent to New York City. In November, Captain Bonneville deserted from the regiment. As the only company officer present, Holmes commanded the company through March 1834.[13]

In late March, Lieutenant Holmes was briefly assigned to the 1st Regiment of Dragoons (mounted infantry) for another construction project. He was placed in command of two companies and ordered to proceed from Fort Gibson to a point along the "Big Osage War and Hunting Trail." His assignment was to build a fort near the mouth of the Little River. The fort was to be large enough to garrison the troops under his command, "fifty to seventy men ... eighty yards square," with blockhouses at diagonal corners, stone foundations, a wooden stockade, and clapboard buildings with stone chimneys. Construction on Camp Canadian began on June 21 and continued through the summer.[14] During the project, Holmes was offered a permanent assignment with the 1st Dragoon regiment but declined the appointment.

Army patrols began using Camp Canadian as a stopover during the construction. As part of a larger expedition under the 1st Dragoons' commander, Colonel Dodge, lieutenants T. B. Wheelock and Jefferson Davis arrived at the camp on July 25, 1834. The expedition was scouting the region, building temporary camps, and making contact with local tribes. Daily temperatures of one hundred degrees had dogged the column since its departure from Camp Rendezvous. Fatigue, dysentery, and heat stroke were crippling the expedition. Wheelock left twenty-seven of his men at Camp Canadian to be cared for by the surgeon serving with Holmes. Wheelock observed that Holmes's men were cutting trees, laying foundations, and building chimneys. On his return trip, after making contact with Comanches, Kiowas, and Washitas, Wheelock reported that Lieutenant Holmes was "well advanced with his buildings; one block house, and quarters for one company erected."[15]

Wheelock also reported sickness among Holmes's soldiers at the construction site. Holmes's choice of locations for the fort turned out to be near a "malaria-ridden marshland." At times during the project, as many as fifty of his soldiers were sick.[16] Holmes became ill and did not fully recover until the following February. Once Camp Canadian was completed, he remained in command at the post, later named Fort Holmes, for a year, until the need for an army post in the area ended. The frontier was always moving.

At the closing of his fort, Lieutenant Holmes and his men were ordered back to Fort Gibson. He was promoted to 1st Lieutenant on March 26, 1835, and transferred to Company E in May. He was put in charge of another construction project in early October and spent that month with Companies A and E repairing the road between Fort Gibson and Fort Coffee. He remained at Gibson until March 10, 1836, when he was assigned to recruiting duties. Assignments to recruiting service were an indication of career potential and much sought after. After serving for several years on the frontier, young officers were anxious to spend time in the East. Holmes's capabilities were being noticed by his superiors.

He was sent to his hometown, Fayetteville, North Carolina, to gather recruits for the 7th Infantry. He remained there for a year, until March 1837, when he returned to Fort Gibson. While he was away, Company E got a new captain, Dixon S. Miles. Miles was sent to Philadelphia, Pennsylvania, on recruiting service the same month that Holmes returned. Holmes commanded Company E through July 1838, when he was given an additional assignment as the regiment's adjutant.[17] The regimental adjutant writes daily orders for the colonel's signature, conducts morning and evening formations, maintains personnel records, and serves as the colonel's contact with company officers, government agents, and other military posts. As an adjutant, Holmes was developing the administrative skills needed for further advancement in the army.

Colonel Arbuckle, breveted to the rank of general, commanded the 7th Regiment during this period. Major William Whistler of the 2nd Infantry was promoted to lieutenant colonel and transferred to the 7th Infantry. He became Arbuckle's second in command. Like many married soldiers, particularly officers, Whistler's family moved from one post to another as his career advanced. When his family arrived at Fort Gibson, they had to be quartered in a log house outside the fort. The military and civilian population had outgrown the fort's barracks and officers' quarters.[18]

As living conditions became less harsh around Fort Gibson, other problems arose. Boredom among the troops, drunkenness among the officers and enlisted men, and disease took a toll. The delivery of supplies and military equipment was often delayed for many weeks while river levels were too low to allow the passage of transport vessels. In a November 11, 1834, report to the adjutant general in Washington, D.C., General Arbuckle stated that the number of sick personnel in his command stood at one hundred twenty-three officers and men. Of that number, a full third were in the 7th Infantry. He expected that "eight or ten will die before the end of the next month." He also complained that uniforms and other clothing needed by the 1st Dragoons and the 7th Infantry had not arrived.[19]

That same week, General Arbuckle dealt with problems created by alcohol abuse by one of his officers. Assistant Quartermaster Lt. Thomas Johnston had been sent to New Orleans with U.S. Treasury drafts. His orders were to cash the drafts and return to Fort Gibson. Arbuckle had been informed that the trip was being unnecessarily delayed by Lieutenant Johnston's drunkenness. Fearing the loss of his command's payroll, Arbuckle sent Capt. David Perkins of the dragoons to locate Johnston, arrest him if necessary, take possession of the bank drafts, and complete the assignment. In the event of Johnston's arrest, Perkins was to hand him a letter from Arbuckle. The letter recited Arbuckle's orders for Johnston's arrest and the reasons for such action, "in the event you should be so intemperate in the use of ardent spirits or wines, as to be found intoxicated or may by other irregular habits endanger the safety of the public money in your hands."[20]

Disciplinary matters involving officers occurred with some frequency. Routinely, officers were required to serve on courts-martial to determine guilt and punishment, often in cases involving close friends. A series of courts-martial was empaneled at Fort Gibson in February 1835. In one trial, lieutenants Holmes, fellow North Carolinian Richard C. Gatlin, and Jefferson Davis were among officers ordered to serve on the court-martial of Lt. Lucius B. Northrop. Northrop was charged with "disobedience of orders," "breach of arrest," and "conduct unbecoming an officer and a gentleman." Holmes, Northrop, and Davis had been together as cadets at West Point. Davis managed to get excused from the trial, but Holmes remained on the panel. After twenty-two days of testimony, Northrop was convicted and sentenced to be "cashiered" from the army. The court, however, recommended to have the sentence set aside.[21] (Years later, Davis would appoint Northrop as the Confederacy's commissary general.) That same month, Davis was court-martialed as well. The court, including Holmes and Gatlin, exonerated Davis of "conduct subversive of good order and Military discipline."[22] Davis, however, resigned from the army that same year.[23]

In the mid–1830s, the United States intensified efforts to move Creek tribes from Alabama and Georgia to Indian Territory just west of Fort Gibson. Resettling Eastern tribes on land already occupied by other Native Americans would intensify pre-existing conflicts in the region. Recalling his 1832 tour through the area, Washington Irving wrote that when "the Pawnees, the Comanches, and other fierce, and as yet independent tribes ... in their excursions, meet the hunters of an adverse tribe, savage conflicts take place."[24]

In Alabama and Georgia, the Creeks had been negotiating land exchange treaties with the government since 1831. They were hoping to get the best agreements possible before being forced out by the increasingly hostile white population. On several occasions, large native bands were prepared to leave, but lack of coordination by the government, broken financial agreements, and lawsuits delayed the plans. Often, Creeks sold their land, crops, and all but a few personal belongings in preparation for the long journey, only to be told that transportation and provisions for the trip were not available. Some groups of Creeks, after having prepared for the journey, were placed under the control of civilian guides contracted by the government, who had already swindled them in a variety of schemes. The Creeks refused to begin the journey until someone they trusted was appointed to conduct them westward.[25]

Large groups of Creeks, homeless and huddled in makeshift camps awaiting transportation, fell prey to whiskey peddlers and unscrupulous businessmen who charged them inflated prices. Often, lawyers accepted money from Creek families, promised to file lawsuits on their behalf, then did nothing. The Creeks were being abused and swindled out of their land, money, and dignity in every conceivable manner.[26]

In 1836, friction between Creeks and whites resulted in serious violence on the Alabama and Georgia border near the Coosa River. A company of Georgia militiamen killed several Creeks on the Georgia side of the border and drove the rest into Alabama. In May, fighting broke out in Alabama as frustrated and destitute Creeks began attacking and robbing the white population. The situation was so serious that the secretary of war ordered General Thomas S. Jesup to end the violence and transport the Creek population to Indian Territory under guard. General Jesup utilized more than eleven thousand troops, including eighteen hundred friendly Creek warriors, to suppress the uprising. By midsummer, the hostile Creek factions were defeated.[27]

In July, eight hundred warriors in chains and seventeen hundred women, children, and elderly Creeks were transported down the Alabama River to Mobile and on to New Orleans. Many of them were sick and starving. At New Orleans, they were crowded into a makeshift camp and suffered through three days of torrential rain. The Creeks and their guards were then loaded aboard the steamships *Lamplighter*, *Majestic*, and *Revenue* and transported up the Mississippi and White rivers to Rock Row, Arkansas. They waited at Rock Row for eight days while the army and civilian authorities gathered enough wagons, provisions, and draft animals to take them to Fort Gibson. The overland portion of the journey began in early August. The weather was extremely hot, forcing the wagon train to travel only at night. Twenty wagons carried the sick, elderly, and children, while the rest of the party walked. They arrived at Fort Gibson on September 3 and camped on the west bank of the Verdigris River. Eighty-one Creeks died during the journey.[28]

Lieutenant Holmes was on recruiting service when the pathetic column arrived at Fort Gibson. His fellow officers in the 7th Infantry were appalled at the condition of

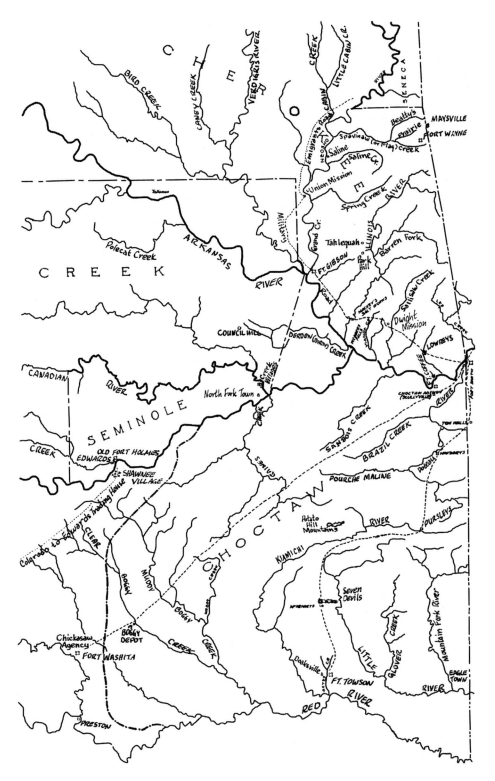

Indian Territory, 1842. Tribal boundaries, Fort Gibson, Fort Washita, and Camp Canadian (old Fort Holmes) (Grant Foreman, *The Five Civilized Tribes*, 1934, courtesy of University of Oklahoma Press).

the refugees. Captain Armstrong observed that he had "never seen so wretched and poor a body of Indians as this party of Creeks; they have really nothing." Armstrong and General Arbuckle arranged meetings between the recently arrived Creeks and Creek tribal leaders who were already settled in the area. Arbuckle forced the new arrivals to submit to the rule of the U.S. government and the local chiefs by threatening to withhold government money and supplies. The immigrants, destitute and exhausted, had no option but to comply.[29]

Additional bands of Creeks, all in the same deplorable condition, came to Fort Gibson in the following weeks. Approximately thirty-two hundred arrived in December. Throughout November and December 1836, roads between Little Rock and Fort Gibson were traveled by perhaps as many as fourteen thousand members of the Creek nation. Many of them had walked from southeast Alabama to Memphis, Tennessee, and were then transported to Little Rock on boats. Hundreds of them died along the way. Clouds of vultures circled the columns as they moved west. By the spring of 1837, more than fifteen thousand Creeks lived near Fort Gibson.[30]

The Chickasaw nation began moving from Mississippi and northern Georgia in 1837. The United States government had failed to honor treaties that protected the tribe from abuses of state law. As was the custom, the government agreed to "pay the expense of their removal," support them for twelve months after they arrived, and give them tracts of land in the Indian Territory, where they could live for "as long as the grass grows, or the water runs."[31] The years 1833 through 1836 passed while the government and the Chickasaws tried to find land in the West that was agreeable to both parties. In the meantime, white settlers were moving onto Chickasaw land in Mississippi and Alabama. The Chickasaw people, like the Creeks before them, fell prey to whisky peddlers and con men. The state governments failed to protect the tribe from these abuses.

In early 1837, several hundred Chickasaws headed west. This small group did not reach their destination near Fort Coffee (present-day Oklahoma) until August 2, 1837.[32] As with the earlier migrations, the column left a wake of sick and starving Native Americans along the trail. In November, another four thousand Chickasaws were gathered at Memphis, Tennessee, and began moving in small groups by steamboat. By January 1838, approximately thirty-five hundred Chickasaws had arrived at Fort Coffee, and others were en route. Compared with the removal of other tribes, the Chickasaw removal was smaller and more orderly, although they too were subjected to bad weather, transportation delays, disease, and death along the way.[33]

Professional army officers, including Holmes, found themselves torn between their duty as soldiers and the sympathy they felt for Native Americans during the Removal. The forced emigration of the Creek, Seminole, and Chickasaw nations, and that of the Cherokees yet to come, was a wretched chapter in their careers and had a lasting effect on their attitudes toward the military profession. Holmes never forgot what he saw on the frontier. Nearly twenty-five years and three wars later, he would speak of Native Americans with respect and sympathy.

By mid–1838, Fort Gibson had become the hub of military and political activity in the region and was designated "Headquarters of the Southwestern Frontier." The 1st Dragoon regiment was divided between forts Gibson and Leavenworth to extend the army's reach. Expeditions from the forts established contact with the Plains Indians and arranged treaties between them and the tribes that were being removed from the East.

The most infamous forced emigration of Native Americans was the Cherokee removal. The principal routes taken by the Cherokee nation started in Tennessee, Georgia, and North Carolina. Prior to that, Cherokees in Georgia began moving "voluntarily" after the state seized their lands and deprived them of most of their legal rights. (If a Cherokee's land was stolen, the Cherokee was not allowed to testify in court if the defendant was white.) Prominent Cherokees arranged for and led the early groups westward, often being well paid by other Cherokees or the government for their services. By 1838 only about two thousand Cherokees had gone to Indian Territory in this manner. Another fifteen thousand remained in the East, clinging to the hope that the government would not forcibly remove them. General Winfield Scott and seven thousand U.S. soldiers and state militiamen were given the assignment to get the Cherokees moving.

Years later, Scott would write, the "Cherokees were an interesting people." More than half of them were Christians. They occupied land in western North Carolina, Georgia, Alabama, and Tennessee. According to Scott, most of their leaders were educated and "possessed much ability." A considerable number of Cherokee men had large tracts of land with "good houses" and owned "negro slaves." North Carolinians and Tennesseans "were kindly disposed towards their red brethren," and intermarriages between the two races were frequent. Scott, however, observed that years of land disputes between Cherokees and the Alabamians and Georgians had fostered deep hatred on both sides. More than half of the army that Scott used to remove the Cherokees was made up of Georgia militiamen who denied "that a Cherokee was a human being."[34] Abandoned by the rule of law and facing Scott's soldiers, Cherokee leaders mounted no organized resistance. Families were dragged from their homes and imprisoned in stockades. This process continued through the last half of 1838. Approximately seventeen thousand Cherokees and members of other tribes were imprisoned, often under deplorable conditions.[35]

The Cherokees traveled a longer distance overland than the other tribes. Two land routes began in Tennessee and went through Kentucky and into southern Illinois. From Illinois, the Cherokees either crossed Missouri and went south into Indian Territory or were led further south out of Missouri and across northern Arkansas. The third route was mostly by water and took them from Georgia and North Carolina, up the Tennessee River, down the Mississippi River, then along the Arkansas River to Fort Smith and Fort Gibson.[36] More than four thousand Cherokees died during their removal from the East.[37]

Through the late 1830s and beyond, "Indian commissioners" (agents appointed by the government) held negotiations with the native tribes in the region around Fort Gibson and the newly arriving tribes. Lieutenant Holmes and other officers led patrols, monitored white immigration, and settled local disputes over hunting lands. They dealt with complaints of thievery and trespassing and tried to foster good will among the tribes and between the tribes and the U.S. government. The army also kept a close watch on the Mexican army in Texas.

Mexico had no intention of abandoning Texas or allowing American settlers, "Texicans," to develop their own national identity or to ally themselves with the United States. In 1836, rumors were circulating that Mexico had sent twelve thousand soldiers into Texas. The reports were determined to be false, but only after several companies of the 7th Infantry were sent to Fort Jesup and became part of an army that General Edmond P. Gaines was assembling. The combined force marched several hundred miles in the summer heat before Gaines realized that he was chasing rumors. The troops returned to Fort Gibson in early January 1837.[38] Within ten years, United States expansionism and Mexico's determination to retain control of Texas (as well as territory from Texas to California) would lead to war between the two nations.

While the U.S. government dealt with increasingly volatile conditions on the western frontier, relations with the Florida Seminoles worsened. Between 1812 and 1820, additional Seminoles and African Americans migrated to Florida from Georgia and Alabama. Beginning in the 1820s, the United States pressured the Seminoles to abandon the African Americans (some of whom were slaves owned by the Seminoles) and move to a reservation in central Florida, there to be protected and supported by the government. Spain ceded Florida to the United States in 1819, effective in 1821. White settlers were moving into Florida, and land disputes resulted in violence. Without a treaty restricting white migration and designating certain areas for the Seminoles, there could be no peace. [39]

The Treaty of Moultrie Creek was signed in 1823. Some Seminole bands agreed to relinquish their land except four million acres in the center of Florida. In return, the government would provide the tribe with farm tools, livestock, compensation for traveling to the reservation, and food for the first year until their crops could be harvested.[40] Implementation of the treaty agreements was slow. After a year of further negotiations, coercion, and threats of war, the Seminoles reluctantly began moving to the reservation. The peace lasted for five years, but demands for the complete removal of the Seminoles to beyond the Mississippi River grew louder. The Seminole reservation became a popular destination for slaves who escaped from Florida plantations.[41]

With the passage of the Indian Removal Act in 1830, the United States made clear its intention to send the Seminoles west with the other Eastern tribes. In 1832, several Seminole bands agreed to move within three years. By 1835, some of them had left Florida. Other chiefs and their bands still refused to leave. Osceola, an emerging Seminole leader, was particularly hostile to the treaties. In claiming that the United States was trying to enslave his people, he said, "The white man shall not make me black. I will make the white man red with blood and then blacken him in the sun."[42]

In the atmosphere of escalating tension, both sides were preparing for war. Late that year, Seminoles began raiding plantations. Local militia and regular army units were sent to defend the civilians. On December 28, 1835, Maj. Francis Dade of the 4th

Infantry regiment and more than one hundred of his soldiers were killed in a single ambush. With this battle, the Second Seminole War began. It spread quickly throughout Florida.[43]

In the military, support was not universal for the government's treatment of the Seminoles and prosecution of the war. One soldier, Major Ethan Allen Hitchcock, wrote, "The government is in the wrong, and this is the chief cause of the persevering opposition of the Indians, who have nobly defended their country against our attempt to enforce a fraudulent treaty. The natives used every means to avoid a war, but were forced into it by the tyranny of our government."[44] The continuing draw of runaway slaves to Florida generated a demand for action among slave-holding states. Many civilians and career army officers were bothered by this aspect of the conflict.

The Second Seminole War went badly for the army through most of 1836. General Gaines brought eleven hundred soldiers from New Orleans in February, but was out-maneuvered, and his force was briefly put under siege. General Winfield Scott brought another five thousand men to the campaign in March, but was unsuccessful in fighting against Seminole guerrilla war tactics.[45]

In late 1836, Major General Thomas Jesup took command of U.S. forces in Florida. Rather than trying to draw the Seminoles into large battles, Jesup began a war of attrition. He ultimately built his army to nine thousand men, including the regular army, volunteers, and militia. Jesup hounded the Seminoles and kept them on the move. The next two years saw the capture or killing of important Seminole leaders, including Osceola, and victory by U.S. forces in several large skirmishes. Various warrior groups began making overtures about restoring the peace. By then, the United States military presence in Florida had grown beyond all expectations. Perhaps as much as half of the nation's army was tied up in the conflict. Congress and the public were growing weary of the expensive and seemingly endless fighting.[46]

In his final report, Jesup said, "[the] villages of the Indians have all been destroyed; and their cattle, horses, and other stock, with nearly all their other property, taken or destroyed.... The small bands who remain ... have nothing of value left but their rifles." Jesup was a good soldier. He fought the Seminoles as hard and as well as he could, but like so many of his fellow officers, he could see no end to the war. In a letter to the *Army and Navy Chronicle*, he questioned the morality of what he considered to be a pointless war and stated, "The war will continue for years to come, and at constantly accumulating cost."[47]

General Jesup was replaced by Zachary Taylor in May 1838. Taylor's plan was to stabilize Florida by dividing the state into military districts, each of approximately four hundred square miles. The army built forts in each district and connected them with good roads, also built by Taylor's soldiers. The strategy was to use the forts as bases for small raids and defeat the Seminoles piecemeal in their hideouts. From their posts in Indian Territory, Holmes and the 7th Infantry watched the war through newspapers and other publications. They knew that if the fighting continued, sooner or later they would be part of it.

Taylor's new tactics were implemented in early 1839. Within months, additional native chiefs realized that winning the war was not possible. War weariness was beginning to settle in among their people. The only time the chiefs could regroup their tribes was during the summer months when the U.S. Army was hampered by the rain, heat, and disease that made conventional military operations nearly impossible. The American public's displeasure with the war, and a growing sense that the Seminoles had earned the right to stay on their land, made negotiations possible. In May 1839, through the efforts of Commanding General of the Army Alexander Macomb, two Seminole chiefs informally agreed to end the fighting and settle on land in southern Florida. Other native leaders did not participate in the arrangement. That same month, General Taylor was replaced, at his own request, by Gen. Walker K. Armistead.[48]

The Seminoles did not trust the American government to keep its promises. Slave hunters' attempts to capture "black Seminoles" and return them to their owners continued to inflame the situation. The peace lasted until July, when a native force attacked a trading and army post on the Caloosahatchee River. Most of the soldiers and several civilians were killed. With the outbreak of new hostilities, the U.S. Army looked westward for fresh troops to send to the endless war. Armistead wanted to fight his enemy year-round, even in the summer.[49]

At Fort Gibson on May 1, 1837, while the Seminole war dragged on in Florida, Lieutenant Holmes participated in the signing of a peace treaty between the United States and several native tribes. The treaty was fashioned after an earlier treaty involving the Comanches, Cherokees, Choctaws, Osages, Senecas, and others. Two commissioners of Indian treaties, Montford Stokes and A. P. Chouteau, signed for the U.S. government. Native American leaders signed for their tribes. The signature "T. H. Holmes, First Lieutenant, 7th Infantry" appears on the treaty, along with fourteen other military and civilian witnesses.[50]

The treaty provided for "perpetual peace and friendship" between the United States and the tribes, safety for anyone passing through tribal lands en route to Texas and Mexico, and compensation for stolen horses and other property. The treaty proclaimed that there should be no interruption in the tribes' tradition of hunting in the "Republics of Mexico and Texas" and that the "United States desire that perfect peace shall exist between the tribes and said Republics."[51] This and other treaties created more peaceful conditions in Fort Gibson's southwestern frontier territory. By December 1838, the worsening situation in Florida made the 7th Infantry a logical choice for transfer to that conflict.

Holmes was promoted to captain on December 9 after having served as the 7th Infantry's regimental adjutant for four months.[52] He was assigned to command Company C of the regiment. Lieutenant Richard Gatlin replaced Holmes as the adjutant. (Gatlin's brother, Dr. John Gatlin, had been killed in Florida with Major Dade in December 1835.) These and other personnel changes were made to prepare the regiment for its transfer to Florida. After two decades on the western frontier, the 7th Infantry was ordered back to the East.

3

Two Wars

The 7th Infantry left Fort Gibson on March 1, 1839, en route to Fort Smith. When the river rose sufficiently, the regiment departed by boat from Fort Smith and arrived at Little Rock. From Little Rock, the soldiers were towed in keel boats by a steamship to New Orleans and on to Tampa Bay, Florida. Many of the 7th's officers had never served anywhere but in Arkansas and the Indian Territory. According to a New Orleans newspaper article, some of them had never seen a railroad or a canal.[1]

Several of the 7th's officers were opposed to the move to Florida. At least one of them wrote anonymous letters, published in the *Army and Navy Chronicle*, criticizing the conduct of the Florida war. Their attitudes reflected increasing public and military opposition to the war. They also felt they were being transferred from one dangerous and thankless assignment to another. In the Indian Territory, they could see the frontier slowly moving westward. In Florida, there was no end in sight. From newspaper reports and the military rumor mill, they were aware that the war was being mishandled. Officers and enlisted men knew that mismanagement by politicians and generals would mean hardship and casualties for them.[2]

Under the command of Lieutenant Colonel William Whistler, Fort Micanopy in north central Florida became the 7th Regiment's headquarters in April 1840. By May of that year, the 7th Infantry had been building and manning small forts and conducting local patrols in the area for a year. In November, the regiment reported eighteen officers and three hundred seventy-three enlisted men on the roster. Consistent with General Armistead's tactics, the regiment's companies were scattered over a wide area and conducted year-round independent raids and ambushes. Captain Holmes's Company C was garrisoned at Fort Russell from May 1839 through May 1840. During this time, three companies of the regiment, E, F, and I, remained at Fort Micanopy. On February 1, while leading a patrol, Holmes and his men were ambushed near Fort No. 5. One of his soldiers was killed and two were wounded.[3]

Companies A, B, and D were stationed at forts King and Brooks, and Fort No.10, respectively. Captain Holmes and his company remained at Fort Russell.[4] On April 28, Capt. Gabriel Rains and part of Company A were involved in a skirmish that was typical of Seminole guerrilla warfare. Rains led a sixteen-man patrol out of Fort King. Two miles from the fort, the patrol was ambushed by a large war party. When the Seminoles opened fire, Rains realized that his company was nearly surrounded. He ordered his men to fix bayonets and charge first one enemy position, then another. The soldiers

Seminole War, 1835

Florida during the Second Seminole War (Florida Center for Instructional Technology, University of South Florida).

and warriors fought hand-to-hand until Rains saw that part of the Seminole band had gotten between him and the fort in an effort to block his retreat.[5]

Rains ordered his men to form a line, charge through the warriors, and keep going until they reached Fort King. As the Seminoles broke under the onslaught, Rains's soldiers dashed toward the fort, stopping only to shoot at their pursuers and gather wounded comrades. When their chief was shot dead by one of Rains's corporals, the Seminoles slowed their pursuit. As the soldiers neared the fort, the warriors retreated. Captain Rains was wounded, two enlisted men were killed, and two others seriously wounded. One of Rains's men counted ninety-three Seminole warriors accompanied by fifteen women and four African Americans. The women and African Americans carried dead and wounded warriors away from the fight.[6]

Holmes and his men conducted similar scouting missions during June. In July his company was sent to garrison Fort Wheelock, but Holmes took a two-month leave of absence beginning July 13. Summer weather conditions and sickness were still keeping the soldiers close to their forts. Dysentery, yellow fever, and malaria often thinned company ranks by more than fifty percent. So many sick soldiers were being sent in from outlying forts that a new hospital was built at Fort Micanopy.[7]

Sutlers set up small shops around Micanopy and other forts. They sold clothes, food, and other necessities to the soldiers, as well as large amounts of liquor. Officers tried to keep their men busy, but drunkenness and misconduct kept the guardhouse full. As a result of the conditions he found at Micanopy, one army inspecting officer recommended that the fort should be closed. Fort Micanopy was the centerpiece of the 7th Infantry's operation in Florida. All of the satellite forts were supplied and reinforced through Micanopy. The army ignored the inspector's recommendation.[8]

Under the watchful eyes of their officers, most soldiers maintained some semblance of discipline in their off-duty time. They tended gardens and raised livestock to supplement their rations. When weather permitted, soldiers built roads and bridges so the forts could reinforce each other quickly. When native camps were located, the army raided them, burning crops that the Seminoles would need during the winter.[9]

As cooler weather approached, a significant skirmish was fought by members of the 7th Infantry. On September 6, 1840, thirty-five soldiers of Company B, under the command of Lt. W. K. Hanson, were conducting a patrol eight miles from Fort Micanopy, near Fort Wacahoota. Approximately one hundred warriors attacked without warning. Hanson's men counterattacked, defeated them, and drove the survivors from the field.[10] Captain Holmes rejoined his company at Fort Wheelock on October 10. In November, he and the company were sent to Fort Micanopy, where they remained into the new year.[11]

A particularly tragic incident involving the 7th Infantry occurred on December 28. Elizabeth Montgomery, wife of one of Captain Holmes's lieutenants, Alexander Montgomery, was traveling with thirteen mounted soldiers from Fort Micanopy to Fort Wacahoota. They spotted Seminole warriors hiding along the trail. As the soldiers tried to dismount to fight on foot, the warriors opened fire and closed in on the party. Mrs.

Montgomery was attempting to hide in the supply wagon when she and four soldiers were shot down. One soldier, Pvt. Lansing Burlington, stood his ground and defended the dying woman, trying to protect her from the rape and mutilation he knew were sure to occur. The warriors knew the sound of gunfire would bring reinforcements from Fort Micanopy. Quickly, they scalped several dead soldiers and departed.[12]

When soldiers from the fort, including Lieutenant Montgomery, reached the scene, they found Private Burlington, fatality wounded, lying beside Mrs. Montgomery's body. Before he died, Burlington expressed regret to the lieutenant for not having been able to save his wife. Burlington's last words were, "I did my duty."[13] The murder of Mrs. Montgomery ended a difficult year for Holmes's regiment. Twenty-three soldiers had died of disease, twenty-four had been killed in combat, and three had died in accidents. Twenty-three soldiers had deserted from the regiment, but eighteen of them were quickly captured.[14]

Captain Holmes's company remained at Fort Micanopy for the entire year of 1841. He and other officers led their soldiers on frequent raids and ambushes. The area around the fort came to be regarded as one of the most dangerous assignments in Florida. Holmes began another furlough on May 27. He traveled to Fayetteville, North Carolina, where on June 6, he married Laura Wetmore. The newlyweds remained together until September, when Holmes's furlough expired and he returned to Fort Micanopy. Mindful of Mrs. Montgomery's death, the couple decided that Laura would remain in North Carolina.[15]

While Holmes was absent from his regiment, the Florida army got a new commander. On August 31, General Armistead was replaced by Col. William Jenkins Worth. The forty-seven-year-old Worth was not West Point educated. He had fought as a militia officer in the War of 1812 and had been seriously wounded in 1813. He was held in high regard by the U.S. military and accepted a commission when it was offered. He was promoted to major in 1820. Worth served as the superintendent of the U.S. Military Academy for eight years until 1828 and was there for most of Holmes's time as a cadet.[16]

The autumn of 1841 saw the resumption of small raids and ambushes. When the year ended, the 7th Infantry reported fifty-five deaths. Eight men in Holmes's company had died. The bad conditions at Fort Micanopy kept the desertion rate high. Twenty-seven soldiers had deserted from the regiment's various forts. Micanopy accounted for all but six of them.[17]

In January 1842, Colonel Whistler took five companies of the 7th Infantry, including Holmes's Company C, into the Wahoo Swamp and conducted a two-month search-and-destroy mission from Camp Stephenson. Whistler reported good morale among his officers and men during the campaign. Holmes's company returned to Fort Micanopy in February and conducted another mission in March. In April, General Worth led elements of the 2nd, 4th, and 8th U.S. Infantry regiments and the 2nd Dragoons into central Florida. They attacked and defeated a band of about forty warriors. This was the last major engagement of the Second Seminole War. Most of the surviving Seminoles and their allies had been shipped west to Indian Territory. Only about three hundred warriors remained.[18]

General Worth spent the summer talking the Seminoles and the United States government into ending the war. He and his army knew the Seminoles were beaten, and some regiments would soon be leaving Florida. In August, Worth arranged for the few surviving Seminoles to live in remote areas. The government agreed to leave them alone. The United States declared the war to be at an end on August 14, 1842.[19] Prior to that, the 7th Infantry had been ordered to abandon some of its forts and was preparing to leave. Companies E and F stayed in Florida at Fort Brooks. Company K remained at Fort Pickens. Six companies, including Holmes's Company C, left Florida for Louisiana and Alabama.[20] Although the 7th Infantry had come late to the fight in Florida, the regiment suffered more than its share of casualties. During three years of duty, the regiment lost two officers and twenty-eight enlisted men in battle. One hundred sixteen enlisted men and two officers died of disease or by accident.[21]

No one will ever know how many Seminoles and their allies were killed, died of disease, or starved to death in Florida.[22] After years of fighting, the war of attrition had worn down both sides. The U.S. government spent approximately forty million dollars. Forty thousand regular troops, militiamen, and volunteers participated, and fifteen hundred of them died, most from disease. General Taylor reported that 2,833 Seminoles had been removed from Florida and shipped to Indian Territory. They arrived in the same wretched condition as the other Eastern tribes. Most Seminoles settled in the area around Fort Gibson and on the nearby Canadian River.[23]

The 7th Regiment's new headquarters was established at New Orleans Barracks. Captain Holmes visited North Carolina in July and met his daughter, Elizabeth Wetmore Holmes, who had been born on May 18. He and his wife, Laura, were happy that his company had been assigned to New Orleans. The family could live there for the foreseeable future.

The companies of the 7th Infantry that sailed from Florida were sent to various posts, including forts Ward and Pike in Louisiana and Fort Morgan in Alabama. Company I went to New Orleans, along with Company C. The companies remained scattered at these posts through June 1844, except when Captain Holmes's company and Company I spent the summer of 1843 "in camp at Pass Christian," Mississippi.[24] Holmes was uneasy at being away from New Orleans for so long. Laura had told him in the spring that she was carrying their second child. Fortunately, he was able to return to New Orleans in October. He was with Laura when the baby was born on Christmas day. Mary Maria Holmes lived only three days. Her grieving parents buried her at the barracks cemetery.[25] Except for an occasional month's assignment at other posts, Holmes and his company stayed at New Orleans for the next year.

New Orleans Barracks was one of the best assignments in the army. During an inspection tour in May 1844, Colonel George Croghan visited the post and remarked, "There is perhaps no post in the country at which soldiers live better. They have a pretty good garden of their own" and "opportunities for exchanging with the market people their rations of rice, salt beef, or pork, for every variety of vegetables and fruits that they may desire."[26]

Laura was pregnant in the spring of 1844 and was again likely to deliver her baby in December. Like the previous year, Holmes was away at Pass Christian for two months, but was back at New Orleans Barracks in October. On December 17, Theophilus Hunter Holmes Jr. was born. Captain Holmes stayed with Laura, Elizabeth, and Theo through July 1845, except for a brief "special assignment" in Key West, Florida, in March. He also did a month of duty with his company at Pass Christian in June. During the summer, he told Laura and the children that his regiment would soon leave New Orleans. War with Mexico was looming.[27]

While much of the United States's military resources were tied up in Florida, conflict between the United States and Texas with Mexico continued to escalate. Once part of Spain's empire, Mexicans had fought for nearly three decades to win their independence in 1821. American settlers began arriving in Texas in 1822. Mexican leaders (most notably, President Antonio López de Santa Anna) tried to centralize the Mexican government and hold on to the region north of the Rio Grande up to the Neuces River.[28]

As Mexico tried to tighten its grip on Texas, more American settlers moved into the area with the encouragement of the United States government. Friction between Mexico and pro–United States, independence-minded Texicans was the inevitable result. Santa Anna suspected that the United States was fomenting revolution in the region. His increasingly brutal treatment of Texicans, culminating in 1836 with massacres at the Alamo and Goliad, set the stage for the battle of San Jacinto and Texas independence.[29]

Sam Houston became the first president of the Republic of Texas. He favored annexation by the United States. Still at issue was the border between Mexico and Texas. The Mexican government recognized the Neuces River as the border. Texas (and later the United States) recognized the Rio Grande, well south of the Neuces. At stake was one-half of Mexico's territory, land that would become the American Southwest, and the deep-water ports on California's coast.[30] Sporadic fighting between Mexico and Texas continued for the next several years.

Attempts to make Texas part of the United States began in 1827, but fear of igniting war with Mexico and the political climate in the U.S. Congress delayed the union. In 1845, after Santa Ana was replaced by José Herrera as Mexico's leader, President James K. Polk offered to buy California and the disputed land between the Rio Grande and the Neuces River. Mexico refused. Herrera exiled Santa Anna to Cuba in April.

United States Army units began repositioning for war in early summer, 1845. Captain Holmes was on leave from his company from June 28 until July 9. (He was likely making arrangements for Laura and the children to travel back to North Carolina.) The 7th Regiment boarded transport vessels at New Orleans in August and sailed for the Texas coast. Other regiments received their orders as well. By fall, Gen. Zachary Taylor had the 3rd, 4th, 5th, 7th, and 8th U.S. Infantry regiments camped near Corpus Christi. He also had twelve artillery companies, including Major Samuel B. Ringgold's three batteries of light artillery. Taylor's force was strengthened with seven companies of the 2nd Dragoons and four companies of artillery soldiers serving as infantry. On paper, Taylor's army consisted of approximately four thousand men, but this number was steadily reduced by sickness while the army waited for marching orders.[31]

The United States officially inherited the border dispute with Mexico in December 1845, when Texas became the twenty-eighth state. The Mexican population was enraged by Texas statehood. Both nations prepared for war by accelerating their build-up of forces.[32] If diplomacy failed, General Taylor was prepared to march overland from Corpus Christi to the Rio Grande near Matamoros, Mexico. In that event, he would secure that part of the river and build a fort for use as an anchor for an invasion of Mexico. He could use the nearby port city of Point Isabel to keep his army supplied. If Mexico would not negotiate to resolve the dispute, President Polk intended to take the territory by force. The Mexican government rejected President Polk's emissary, John Slidell, in early 1846.

While Taylor assembled his army, negotiations between the United States and Mexico continued to be deadlocked. President Polk decided to send the army to the Rio Grande and test Mexico's resolve. Instructions from the secretary of war gave General Taylor wide latitude. He was warned not to treat Mexico as an enemy nation, "but should [Mexico] assume that character by a declaration of war or any open act of hostility ... you will not act merely on the defensive if your relative means enable you to do otherwise."[33] During the second week of March 1846, Taylor divided his army into three brigades and marched away from Corpus Christi. Matamoros was nearly two hundred miles distant. The army and its three hundred supply wagons moved at a leisurely pace the first four days and arrived at a supply depot Taylor had established fifty miles south of Corpus Christi. The soldiers were re-supplied with food and continued their journey.[34]

Two weeks later, after establishing a supply depot at the port city of Point Isabel, Taylor reached the Rio Grande across from Matamoros. His army numbered approximately three thousand men. Most of Matamoros's twenty thousand citizens fled at the approach of the U.S. Army. General Francisco Mejía and his five thousand soldiers defended the town. Mejía sent messages to Taylor, protesting the presence of the American army on Mexican soil, but Taylor insisted that his side of the river was United States territory. Both generals established picket outposts and sent out cavalry patrols. General Mariano Arista arrived and assumed command of the Mexican force. He considered Matamoros too difficult to defend. Instead of waiting for Taylor to move, Arista considered crossing the river and attacking. For the next several weeks, the armies probed each other's positions and strengthened their own defenses. General Taylor ordered his troops to build "Fort Texas" near the river, across from Matamoros, while he waited for word from his government about negotiations with Mexico.[35]

While the armies glared at each other across the Rio Grande, generals Mejía, Arista, and Pedro Ampudia tried to convince U.S. Catholic soldiers to change sides. Mexico was a Catholic nation. The Mexican generals knew there were large numbers of European Catholics serving in U.S. Army regiments. Many of these soldiers had joined the army shortly after their arrival in America. Arista and Ampudia reasoned that Catholicism might be more firmly set in these men than loyalty to the United States. The Mexican army circulated notices offering land bounties and other enticements to prospective deserters. Some U.S. Catholic soldiers deserted, crossed the river, and went into the Mexican lines. They joined several hundred German and Irish Catholics, and others, and fought for Mexico as Saint Patrick's Battalion, but the Mexican generals were largely disappointed with the recruiting effort.

Most of the U.S. Army's Catholics were angered and embarrassed by the public attempt at bribery. There was also a significant deterrent provided by their own army. Desertion in the presence of the enemy was a serious offense. Guards were placed at the river's edge where deserters might cross. They had orders to shoot anyone who tried to swim to the Mexican side.[36] By April 6, thirty deserters had gotten across the river and entered Mexican lines. Four had drowned, and two more had been shot by Taylor's guards.[37]

In April, Mexican and U.S. cavalry patrols collided. The Mexicans trapped sixty-three U.S. dragoons, killing eleven and capturing most of the rest. Those who escaped notified General Taylor, who in turn notified the president. As a result of the incident, the United States Congress passed a declaration of war.[38] Before Taylor was notified that war had been declared, the Mexican army forced him to act.

One of Taylor's cavalry patrols, under the command of Texas Ranger Sam Walker, brought news that General Arista, with six thousand men, was crossing the Rio Grande east of Matamoros. Arista's move threatened the vital supply line between Point Isabel on the coast and Taylor's army at Fort Texas. Should that link be cut, or worse, should the Mexicans seize the supply depot at Point Isabel, Taylor's army would be cut off and deprived of the means to stay in the field. Both Arista and Taylor knew that the American army would have to leave Fort Texas and fight the Mexican army somewhere along the road to Point Isabel.[39]

On May 1, General Taylor divided his force. He left the 7th Infantry under Maj. Jacob Brown with two companies of artillery at Fort Texas, a total of five hundred men. With approximately twenty-five hundred soldiers and the rest of his artillery, Taylor started the twenty-six-mile march to Point Isabel. Major Brown was ordered to finish construction on the earthen walls and hold the fort against Mexican forces who were sure to attack. The fort's perimeter was eight hundred yards, with walls fifteen feet thick at the base and nine feet in height. The structure was surrounded by a wide trench, twelve feet deep. In addition to infantry and artillery soldiers in the fort, there were approximately one hundred non-combatants: women, children, captured Mexicans, and sick U.S. soldiers.[40] After nearly twenty-four hours on the road, Taylor's army arrived at Point Isabel. Hard marching by U.S. soldiers and a slow river crossing by the Mexicans had put Taylor's army ahead in the race to the coast.[41]

At dawn on May 3, Mexican artillery began bombarding Fort Texas. The fort's four 18-pounder cannons returned fire and quickly demonstrated the superiority of American artillery. Two Mexican cannons were promptly destroyed, and several batteries were forced to withdraw. During the artillery duel, the fort's 6-pounder cannons, under the command of Lt. Braxton Bragg, were found to be ineffective at the distances involved. Major Brown ordered them to be repositioned to cover the rear of the fort in case Mexican infantry crossed the river and attacked. As a diversion, Brown tried to set fire to Matamoros by having "hot shot" fired into the town, but the cannon balls could not be heated sufficiently.[42]

Soon after the siege began, soldiers in the fort realized that the garrison's flag was not flying. The flagpole stood naked on the parade ground approximately one hundred yards from the fort. Major Brown was a fifty-eight-year-old veteran of the War of 1812. He had started his military career as an enlisted man and won his officer's commission on the battlefield. Determined to have the colors raised, he called for volunteers. Future Confederate general Earl Van Dorn, a lieutenant in the 7th Infantry, and another man stepped forward. The two soldiers dodged cannon balls as they sprinted across the open field. They raised the U.S. flag and returned safely to the fort.[43] At 10:00 P.M., Brown ordered his artillery to cease fire. The Mexicans silenced their guns at about the same time "but recommenced, and continued at intervals until 12 o'clock at night."[44]

The Mexican artillery renewed the contest at dawn, but with a slower rate of fire. The American artillerists slowed their return fire to conserve ammunition. Most of the Mexican shells passed over the fort or fell short. Those that landed on the walls or inside the works usually buried themselves in the earth and exploded, causing little damage. Some bounced and rolled along the ground for several feet, their fuses smoking, before detonating. Captain Holmes and other soldiers who were digging bombproof shelters had time to scatter and take cover before the shells exploded. Two U.S. soldiers were killed by artillery fire on May 4.[45]

The artillery contest could be heard by General Taylor and his army on the coast. Taylor sent mounted scouts to ascertain the garrison's condition. Captain Sam Walker brought back news that the fort's walls were withstanding the bombardment well.[46] Taylor knew the fort had plenty of food on hand, but the artillery ammunition would soon be expended. He needed to quickly strengthen Point Isabel, load the supply wagons, and start back toward Fort Texas. As long as he could hear the distant rumbling of artillery, he knew the fort was holding its own.

On May 5, Mexican infantry and cavalry patrols were spotted around Fort Texas at a range of eight hundred yards. Mexican artillerists crossed the river and positioned one of their batteries behind the fort. By late in the day, the garrison was taking fire from three sides. Mexican infantry had arrived and was firing on the fort as well. While the fight continued, Major Brown kept his men at work repairing earthworks and digging bombproof shelters. At noon, while Brown was inspecting one of the bombproofs, a shell landed only a few feet away and exploded immediately. Shrapnel tore into his right leg above the knee. He was carried into the fort's magazine, where his shattered leg was amputated.[47] Captain Edgar S. Hawkins assumed command of the fort.

On May 6, General Arista suspended his bombardment and sent a message demanding the fort's surrender. Captain Hawkins called Holmes and the other officers to a meeting. They voted to reject the surrender demand. After an hour's cease-fire, the cannonading resumed.[48] General Arista sent his infantry close to the fort, but they were spotted by the sentries. Braxton Bragg's light artillery battery opened an accurate fire and drove them back. Arista realized that his men would be slaughtered by Bragg's artillery if he tried a direct assault. The siege continued unabated through May 7.[49] That night, Captain Hawkins sent an army engineer, Captain Mansfield, and a squad outside the fort to clear away obstructions. Hawkins was still expecting an infantry attack at any time.[50] The U.S. flag on the parade ground was removed and brought into the fort.

By the morning of May 8, the Mexicans had improved their artillery fire. Most of their shells were landing within the fort. One shell exploded in front of a tent filled with army band instruments and destroyed everything but the drums. The fort's makeshift hospital suffered more hits and near misses than any other part of the works.[51] A soldier in the 7th Regiment lost an arm when he was struck by a cannonball. Two Mexican prisoners were injured by shell fragments. Several of Lieutenant Bragg's artillery horses were killed. His men had to shoot horses that were seriously wounded.

The rate of fire from the Mexican guns slowed intermittently, but only to allow the cannon barrels to cool.[52] The garrison was running dangerously low on artillery ammunition, some of which had to be saved in case of an infantry attack. Captain Holmes and his men looked and listened anxiously toward the east. They were hoping for some indication of Taylor's return.

General Taylor completed loading his supply wagons on May 7. Reinforcements had arrived, and Point Isabel was safe. With twenty-three hundred soldiers, his artillery, and two hundred fifty supply wagons, Taylor headed back toward Fort Texas. His troops would soon collide with General Arista's army, which had finally crossed the river. Arista and more than four thousand soldiers were waiting for Taylor on a muddy, grass-covered rolling plain known as Palo Alto.

Taylor's soldiers marched seven miles and halted for the night. They marched eight more miles the next day and approached the Mexican position. Arista's army was drawn up in a battle line just south of the road, approximately eight miles from Fort Texas and Matamoros. Taylor halted about a mile from the Mexicans and deployed his troops for battle. Incredibly, General Arista did not take this opportunity to attack, politely allowing Taylor to prepare for the engagement. The U.S. soldiers even had time to rest and refill their canteens at nearby ponds.[53]

When General Taylor was satisfied with his troop disposition, he ordered his army forward to within eight hundred yards of his foe, well beyond musket range but within range of the Arista's artillery. He stopped and waited for Arista to make the next move. The two armies glared silently at each other across the field for nearly two hours. At 2:00 P.M., the Mexican artillery opened fire, but with little effect because of the distance and the poor quality of their cannon powder. Ulysses S. Grant, serving in Taylor's army, later wrote that the slow-moving Mexican cannon balls "would strike the ground long before they reached our line, and ricocheted through the tall grass so slowly that the men would see them and open ranks and let them pass."[54]

The U.S. artillery, positioned in front of Taylor's infantry, returned fire immediately. General Arista watched as American 18-pounder guns and light artillery tore gaping holes in the closely stacked ranks of his infantry. His soldiers bravely stood their ground. General Taylor initially had planned to follow up his artillery barrage with an infantry attack and settle the matter at bayonet point. After seeing the unequal artillery exchange, Taylor decided to hold his infantry in place. He allowed the artillery to continue pounding Arista's troops. After an hour of punishment, Arista's officers and men began shouting at their general. They wanted to attack or be withdrawn.[55] Back at Fort Texas, captains Hawkins and Holmes, and their men could hear a distant rumbling. They hoped it was Taylor's artillery and not thunder.

General Arista realized that an attack with his infantry against Taylor's artillery would result in slaughter. He decided to use his elite cavalry, the lancers, to turn Taylor's right flank and destroy the American supply wagons. As the eight hundred lancers charged forward, their horses were slowed by the muddy terrain and shoulder-high grass. Taylor's flank regiment, the 5th U.S. Infantry, fixed bayonets and marched toward the struggling Mexicans. The 5th formed a hollow square and opened fire from all four sides as the frustrated Mexican cavalrymen struggled through the mud to ride around them. Artillery officers Samuel French and Randolph Ridgely, of Sam Ringgold's Light Artillery, rushed two horse-drawn 12-pounders to the flank. They fired into the confused Mexican horsemen and broke the attack.[56]

During the next several hours, each army tried to strike the other's flanks. Ringgold's fast-moving artillery repeatedly out-maneuvered the slower Mexican guns and blunted attacks by Mexican cavalry. Most of the infantry on both sides was never aggressively engaged. They stood in battle lines watching the artillery and cavalry fight the battle. During the latter part of the fight, Major Ringgold and his horse, "Old Branch," were struck by a 6-pounder cannonball. The shot passed through both of Ringgold's thighs, inflicting a mortal wound, and killed his horse instantly.[57]

The battle lasted from 2:30 P.M. until nearly dark. Late in the afternoon, the grassy fields were set on fire by burning cannon wadding. With most of the battlefield obscured by smoke for both armies, the fighting ended. General Taylor ordered no final infantry attack to drive his enemy from the field, choosing instead to remain close to his slow-moving wagon train of supplies.[58] His soldiers searched the battlefield for wounded comrades and prepared to camp for the night. They collected wounded Mexican soldiers and buried the dead. Ringgold was put into a wagon and sent to Point Isabel. He died several days later, never knowing that General Taylor would credit him with the victory at Palo Alto.[59]

Losses for Taylor's army were light: five men killed and forty-three wounded. Four hundred Mexican soldiers were killed outright. It is likely that four or five times that many were wounded. Early the next morning, Arista quietly moved his army away from Palo Alto and headed in the direction of Matamoros and Fort Texas. He was looking for a defensive position that would be impregnable. He had been taught a costly lesson about the U.S. Army at Palo Alto, but he was still willing to fight.[60]

When General Taylor was informed that Arista's army was retreating, he ordered several hundred of his troops and the wagon train to remain at Palo Alto and build earthen defenses for protection against Mexican cavalry. He sent his cavalry and a light infantry battalion to maintain contact with Arista's rear guard and to see where the Mexicans would make their next stand. The rest of the army, approximately eighteen hundred men, would pursue Arista as soon as they could get moving.[61]

General Arista marched his army five miles to an area called Resaca de la Palma. He decided to make a stand on the road where it crossed a *resaca*, a dry river channel. The resaca was two miles long and two hundred yards wide, with low muddy areas. The deepest parts of the riverbed were twelve feet below the surrounding countryside, offering protection for Arista's troops from American artillery. The area on each side of the resaca, particularly along the American army's approach, was covered with trees and an almost impenetrable *chaparral*, tangled undergrowth. Arista had chosen the spot well. It was a natural defensive position. Taylor's cavalry, artillery, and infantry would have difficulty maneuvering anywhere but along the road. At Resaca de la Palma, the Mexican army was only two miles from Fort Texas.[62]

Arista sent messengers to his infantry and cavalry at Fort Texas. He wanted them to abandon the siege and join him for the fight against Taylor.[63] He ordered Mexican artillery to stay at the fort and continue the bombardment. When Captain Holmes saw Mexican infantry units withdrawing toward the east, he knew Taylor was winning and the siege might soon end.

Once Taylor was satisfied that his wagon train was safe, he left Palo Alto and followed the retreating Mexicans. His army had gone only a few miles when he was informed by his cavalry scouts that Arista would likely make a stand at Resaca de la Palma. Taylor halted his army and deployed skirmishers for several hundred yards in the thick brush on both sides of the Matamoros road. The skirmishers were ordered to advance until they made contact with the Mexican pickets. When Arista's pickets, approximately one hundred yards in front of the resaca, heard Taylor's skirmishers struggling through the undergrowth, they opened fire. When Taylor heard the firing, he brought the rest of the army up the road and deployed. He placed Lieutenant Ridgely's artillery on the road and infantry regiments on either side.[64]

Taylor's advancing skirmishers, backed up by infantry regiments, slowly pushed the Mexican pickets back toward the resaca. The American advance became an unco-ordinated, small-unit effort as the difficult terrain broke the regiments into companies and companies into squads, most of which lost contact with each other. Mexican pickets retreated and took cover in the resaca with the rest of their army. As the broken American line approached through the woods, Mexican infantry opened fire. Taylor's attack stalled.[65]

Sensing an opportunity, Arista ordered a cavalry charge on Ridgely's battery posted in the road. Ridgley's fast-firing gunners beat back the assault with loads of canister but then came under fire from Mexican artillery. Ridgely sent word to Taylor that he was being shelled by a battery that was only one hundred yards away and directly in

35

front of him. Taylor sent forward his cavalry, the dragoons. The hard-charging horsemen swept down the road and through the Mexican cannons. Arista's artillerymen scattered, but quickly regrouped when the dragoons galloped past the guns and down into the resaca. The dragoons found themselves in the middle of the Mexican army, where they came under heavy fire from three sides. They turned and made a mad dash back up the road, but not before capturing a Mexican general.[66]

Taylor realized that nothing but a determined infantry assault would end the stalemate. He ordered the 5th U.S. Infantry (including future Confederate General Edmund Kirby Smith) forward, toward Arista's right, and brought the 8th Infantry up from his reserves. The two regiments fought their way through the underbrush, flanked the Mexican artillery, and attacked the resaca near the road. The right flank of Arista's battle line began to crumble.[67]

As the attack on the Mexican right made progress, the 4th U.S. Infantry, on the opposite side of the battlefield, found a path through the tangled terrain. They crossed the resaca and marched toward the Mexican army's left flank. Arista launched two unsuccessful counterattacks against them. His army was exhausted and demoralized. After seeing both flanks of their army turned, Mexican soldiers began a retreat that quickly turned into a two-mile rout all the way to the Rio Grande near Fort Texas.[68]

The garrison at Fort Texas had been under siege for seven nerve-racking days. In that time, Mexican artillery fired twenty-seven hundred shells at the fort. The 7th Infantry's popular and respected field commander, Major Jacob Brown, died just hours before Arista's panicked soldiers appeared on the road. When the fort's defenders saw the helpless Mexicans fleeing toward the river, they opened fire on them with artillery.[69] The Mexicans found two boats at the river's edge and fought each other to get on board. Many of them drowned while trying to swim across the river. When General Taylor's lead troops approached the fort, they were greeted by hundreds of U.S. soldiers standing on the fort's walls and cheering wildly. After the battle, Fort Texas was renamed Fort Brown.[70]

For the Mexicans, Resaca de la Palma was a disaster. After trying to rally his troops, General Arista abandoned his headquarters and all of his personal belongings, and fled. He lost between six hundred and twelve hundred men killed, wounded, captured, and missing. Taylor reported thirty-three of his soldiers dead and eighty-nine wounded. Arista made his way to Matamoros. Several days later, he contacted Taylor to arrange an armistice. Taylor refused and threatened to destroy the town. American troops crossed the river on May 18 and found that Arista had evacuated his army, leaving four hundred wounded soldiers behind.[71]

Taylor spent the next several months strengthening his army and establishing the area around Matamoros for use as a base of operations for a campaign deeper into Mexico. The 7th Infantry was reorganized from ten companies to six and placed under the command of Captain Dixon S. Miles. Captain Holmes remained in command of one of the reorganized companies. Taylor's victories at Palo Alto and Resaca de la Palma, and the valiant defense of Fort Texas were widely reported in the American press. He and his army became national heroes. Patriotism and newfound enthusiasm for the war with Mexico infected much of the country, particularly in the South.[72]

Because a formal state of war existed between the United States and Mexico, state militias were called upon for volunteers. Taylor's army grew by several thousand men, but most of them were poorly trained and equipped. En route to Mexico, some of the militia regiments gathered at New Orleans. Many of them camped on the battlefield made famous by Andrew Jackson and the 7th Infantry during the War of 1812. The camps were squalid, overcrowded, and mosquito infested. Inevitably, "camp sickness" (diseases common at most crowded military camps) swept through the bivouacs and killed scores of soldiers. When passage was arranged, the soldiers were loaded on troop transport vessels and sailed to Corpus Christi, then on to Point Isabel. Other militia units marched through southern Texas, rendezvoused at San Antonio, and went on to Matamoros. It was a grueling journey in the summer heat, made worse by inadequate provisions, shelter, and water.[73]

Militia units from Mississippi, Louisiana, Alabama, Tennessee, Kentucky, Illinois, Indiana, Georgia, Missouri, Maryland, and Texas set up camps along the Rio Grande. By late July, General Taylor's hybrid army of novices and battle-tested regulars had grown to fourteen thousand troops, but he was having serious problems keeping them supplied. He was also coming under political pressure to move deeper into Mexico. President Polk and Secretary of War William Marcy were considering ordering Taylor, now a major general, to march his army south and capture Mexico City.[74]

Rather than seeking to conquer and occupy all of Mexico, the objective of the U.S. government was to force Mexico to recognize U.S. control (by virtue of Texas statehood) of the land between the Neuces River and the Rio Grande, plus regions further west. To accomplish this goal, the government wanted to apply just enough pressure to bring Mexico to the bargaining table and force concessions. Taylor's victories had not induced Mexico to negotiate. The capture of the Mexican capital would assure that result.[75]

General Taylor's extended occupation of Matamoros without beginning a new campaign, plus the U.S. government's repeated calls for negotiations, clearly indicated to Mexico the United States's limited objectives. But President Polk knew that public and political support for the war was soft. The addition of thousands of militia troops sent to Taylor's army, all of whom had to be paid, equipped, and fed by the U.S. government, meant that a protracted conflict would be expensive. The war was unpopular with President Polk's opposition party, the Whigs. Even when no battles were being fought, the cost of the war and the alarming death rate from disease among American troops could be expected to erode support for the war.[76]

General Taylor was reluctant to take his army to Mexico City. He did not want to march his soldiers, the majority of whom were untried volunteers, nearly one thousand miles through the summer desert to attack a strongly fortified national capital. If forced to lay siege to Mexico City, he could be trapped hundreds of miles from any source of supply by converging Mexican armies. Taylor was being mentioned as a possible presidential candidate for the Whig Party. He had not commented on the matter, but if his army suffered a catastrophic defeat in Mexico, his political future would end before it could begin.[77] Taylor proposed that he should, instead, strike at Monterrey, to his southwest. President Polk agreed to the plan.

During the summer of 1846, Taylor began repositioning his army. Part of his force would remain at Matamoros, Point Isabel, and along the Rio Grande, guarding his supply line. He moved most of his troops two hundred fifty miles upstream to Camargo. Several regular army regiments steamed up river on troop transports, beginning in July. The 7th Infantry and division commander Gen. William Jenkins Worth were the first to arrive, on July 14. Captain Holmes's regiment and the 5th Infantry were fortunate in not having to make the overland march. The boat ride was a refreshing change. Other army and militia units moved along the Rio Grande, some by boat, others marching by a shorter route south of the river. Most of the militia units took the land route, but they suffered from heat and thirst when their line of march turned away from the river.[78]

Taylor's choice of Camargo as his Monterrey campaign staging area could not have been worse. The camps were situated in a hot, rocky dust-bowl, where temperatures reached one hundred degrees Fahrenheit daily. Soldiers were tormented by tarantulas, scorpions, snakes, and the relentless wind-driven sand. Disease spread through the bivouac, particularly the militia camps, killing fifteen hundred soldiers.[79]

Taylor realized that he would have to reduce the number of troops that would take part in the march to Monterrey. Many of his volunteer militia regiments had proved to be incapable of the hard marching and discipline needed by an army in the field. Illness had already diminished the army's effective force by one-third, but he sent many of his militiamen home. When his force left Camargo for Monterrey in mid–August, Taylor had 6,000 men under his command; roughly half were his trusted regular army regiments.[80]

General Worth's division, including the 5th, 7th, and 8th Infantry regiments, was the first to leave Camargo. It was followed by General David Twiggs's division of regulars and the militia division commanded by Gen. William O. Butler. Captain Holmes and his company were glad to be on the move, but they had to march over rock-strewn roads for seven long days before reaching the town of Cerralvo and the first fresh water they had seen in a week. By then, the heat of summer had broken. The troops noticed a definite cooling of the temperatures, particularly at night, as they marched into the mountains surrounding Monterrey.[81] The army reached a position only a few miles from the city on September 19. General Taylor, his staff (including future Union general Lieutenant George Gordon Meade) and a party of Texas Rangers rode ahead of the column to conduct a reconnaissance. Mexican artillery fired on them as they probed approaches to the town and its defenses. The sound of cannon fire in the distance told Holmes that the advanced units were within sight of their goal.[82]

General Ampudia had approximately ten thousand troops and ample artillery, but he fortified Monterrey in an unorthodox manner. Rather than having his strongest defenses on the hilltops and in the intervening valleys leading toward town, he placed relatively light fortifications and few troops in those areas. He used the majority of his

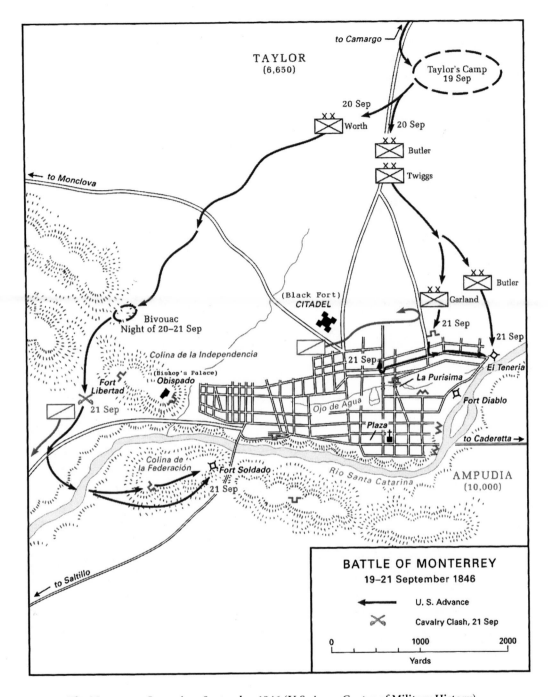

The Monterrey Campaign, September 1846 (U.S. Army Center of Military History).

artillery (perhaps as many as forty guns), troops and construction efforts to heavily fortify a building known as the Citadel, or Black Fort, and the interior approaches to the city's central square. Trenches were dug, streets were barricaded, and key intersections were defended with artillery. Mexican soldiers turned houses, shops, government buildings, and even churches into fortresses.[83] Ampudia had plenty of ammunition and food for his garrison. He wanted to wear down American soldiers with house-to-house fighting, forcing Taylor to lay siege to the city until Mexican reinforcements arrived. General Ampudia underestimated both Taylor and his army.

Taylor's army halted for a day at Walnut Springs, a "beautiful grove of Lofty Timber" approximately three miles from the city.[84] Reconnaissance missions by Texas Rangers and army engineers told Taylor that the hilltop fortifications near the Saltillo Road should be taken first. Securing this southwestern approach would block Mexican reinforcements coming from Saltillo and provide an excellent position to launch the attack against Monterrey.

Taylor ordered General Worth to march southwest with the Louisiana Volunteers, an artillery battalion, the 5th, 7th, and 8th Infantry regiments, and five hundred mounted Texas Rangers. The rangers, led by Col. Jack Hays, were often described as the "Cossacks of the Army." They wore red or blue shirts, buckskin coats, and straw hats or Mexican sombreros. Each man carried a Bowie knife, a Colt revolver, and a musket or rifle. One of their captains was the fearless Ben McCulloch, a famous "Indian fighter" and friend of the late Davy Crockett. McCulloch would survive the war with Mexico to become a Confederate general in 1861.[85]

General Worth's assignment was to reach the Saltillo Road, seven miles distant, and attack the two fortified ridges nearby, Federación and Independencia. Taylor and the rest of the army would create a diversion with a simultaneous attack on the northeast side of the city.[86]

On September 20, Worth's division took a circuitous route around Monterrey, bypassed the Black Fort, and halted for the night near the ruins of a building called Obispado or "Bishop's Palace." They were within range of Mexican artillery stationed in the palace, but were not fired upon during the cold, rainy night. On the 21st, the division moved out at dawn and came under artillery fire from Independencia Ridge after marching only a mile. A large force of Mexican lancers attacked the column as well but was driven off. The division continued working its way through the hills until it reached the intersection of Saltillo and Monterrey roads. They again came under artillery fire, this time from Federación Ridge. After moving his troops out of range, Worth ordered the regiments to form a line of battle, stack arms, and rest. His division was now in a position to attack the first objective, Federación Ridge.[87]

After thirty minutes of rest, the 7th Infantry was ordered to advance toward Federación in support of five companies of dismounted Texas Rangers and the artillery battalion which was serving as infantry. Federación had two hilltops. An entrenched artillery position rested on one peak and a larger fort, El Soldado, crowned the second. Nine hundred yards across the valley from Federación stood Bishop's Palace on the eastern slope of Independencia.[88] A fortress on the peak of Independencia, Fort Libertad, was heavily fortified with artillery and infantry, as was the palace below. From Monterrey, General Ampudia was reinforcing the forts on both ridges and ordered his regiment of lancers to remain nearby.

The 7th Infantry moved three-quarters of a mile before coming under artillery fire from the ridge above. The firing intensified as the soldiers approached Santa Catarina River (a tributary of the San Juan River), which flowed between the two ridges nearest to the base of Federación. The regiment arrived at the river's steep banks and prepared to wade through the waist-deep water. The soldiers held their muskets and cartridge boxes high over their heads as they slid down the bank and into the water. They struggled against the current, slipping on smooth stones that covered the river bottom, often sinking up to their necks. Mexican artillery and infantry on the hills above kept up a lively fire, but no one was wounded during the crossing. On reaching the far side of the river, most of the regiment took shelter under an outcropping of rock where they were safe from the Mexican fire. The soldiers cleaned and dried their muskets and waited for orders.[89]

The enlisted men soon tired of hiding while the Mexicans poured musket and cannon fire around them. Captain Holmes and the other company commanders had to forbid their men to attack up the hill until the Texas Rangers and artillerymen were in position. The frustration was relieved briefly when a detachment of the 7th was sent up the hill and skirmished with Mexican soldiers who were positioning themselves to attack while the regiment was pinned down. The fight ended after about twenty minutes, when the Mexicans withdrew back up the hill toward their fort.[90]

Two hundred Texas Rangers were ordered to lead the attack. The 7th Infantry watched them start up the side of the hill, then stood up with a shout and began their charge. They were followed quickly by the 5th Infantry. The Mexicans fled as the Texans and regular army troops swept into and around the fort. An officer in the 7th said that the rangers rushed the fort so quickly that none of them even stopped long enough to fire their weapons. The Mexicans abandoned a brass 9-pounder cannon and retreated to the larger adjacent fort, El Soldado. El Soldado's stone walls surrounded the hilltop, which was covered with tents. Thus reinforced, El Soldado, with a second cannon, began firing on the 5th and 7th regiments and the rangers as they gathered in the first fort.[91]

Their bloodlust aroused, the American soldiers began cheering and shouting, "Forward! Forward!" Impulsively, they surged across the open ground toward El Soldado. One officer in the 7th Regiment noted, "The bullets flying around us as thick as hail ... only accelerated [our] advance." The Mexican soldiers realized they were about to be overrun again and abandoned the second fort. They raced down the slope of Federación Ridge, waded across the Santa Catarina River, and struggled up Independencia toward Bishop's Palace. The U.S. soldiers and Texans poured musket fire onto the Mexicans and even turned the captured artillery against them. The Mexican retreat became a rout, as they fled up the hillside and into the palace.[92]

Captain Holmes was conspicuous among the 7th Infantry's company officers during the fight. He kept his men together and urged them to keep firing and moving forward as they clawed their way toward the Mexican earthworks. He was one of the first regular army officers to reach the summit as battle flags of the 5th and 7th regiments

41

were planted. Taylor's soldiers in the diversionary attack on the northeast side of town knew their comrades were winning. They could see U.S. flags raised on the hilltops.[93] The attack was witnessed by Jefferson Davis, who had resigned as a U.S. congressman to take command of the Mississippi volunteers. He stated later that Captain Holmes displayed great personal courage and leadership during the Monterrey fighting.

The 5th Infantry, the Texans, and the artillery battalion were withdrawn from Federación ridge. The 7th Infantry held El Soldado and watched the Saltillo road for Mexican reinforcements. The Mexicans still held Independencia Ridge and Bishop's Palace. Their gunners fired artillery shells onto Federación, keeping most of the 7th under cover for the rest of the day. Darkness brought a halt to the fighting, and a torrential rain began to fall. Fortunately, fifteen large tents were captured during the fight. Holmes and the men of the 7th had shelter for the night.[94]

Earlier in the day, Taylor's attack northeast of town, planned only as a diversion in support of General Worth's main attack, had gotten out of control. A last-minute change in commanders caused regiments of General Twiggs's division to charge into a crossfire between the Citadel and La Teneria, two strongly defended Mexican fortifications. The Baltimore Battalion of Volunteers broke and fled. The 3rd U.S. Infantry was taking heavy casualties. As the sound of gunfire increased, Taylor realized that his troops had been more deeply committed than he intended. Feeling that he had no choice but to support the battle, Taylor ordered more troops forward. Jefferson Davis's Mississippians and the Tennessee volunteers went into the attack "in gallant style."[95] The Mexican soldiers were slowly worn down by Taylor's persistent attacks and began to retreat. The Americans continued fighting their way through Monterrey's northeastern area. They captured two forts before dark. Taylor lost almost four hundred men, but his army was poised to continue both attacks the next day.[96]

General Worth stirred his troops at 3:00 A.M. for the dawn attack on Independencia Ridge. Like Federación, Independencia had two forts. One was a small artillery emplacement at the top of the ridge. The other was Bishop's Palace, well below the ridge line. Construction on the palace had been halted some time previously, and the building had no roof. Nonetheless, the Mexican army considered the building to be the key defensive position west of the city and were prepared to defend it. The cold rain continued as Worth arranged his troops at the base of the hill.[97] Captain Holmes's company and two other companies were sent from fort El Soldado to the base of Independencia. They were to watch for counterattacks and create a diversion when the main attack began.

The artillery battalion, Texas Rangers, 8th Infantry, and 5th Infantry started up the steep, slippery hillside in total darkness. Their objective was Fort Libertad at the summit. At dawn, about halfway up the ridge, a Mexican sentry spotted American soldiers climbing hand over hand in the rocks near his post. He fired a musket ball into Texas Ranger Captain Richard Gillespie, killing him almost instantly.[98] Firing erupted on both sides. The Mexican soldiers had the advantage as they fired downhill into the advancing U.S. infantrymen. They could then take cover as they reloaded. As a fog-enshrouded dawn broke, American soldiers crawled among the rocks, firing their muskets as they pressed up the hill.

Worth's attack on Independencia could be seen by the veterans of the previous day's fight north of the city. Through the mist, they could discern the crisp muzzle blasts of Mexican volleys fired down hill and the ragged fire of American troops climbing among the rocks. As the U.S. soldiers neared the summit, smoke from the battle mingled with the morning mist and produced a volcano-like effect at the top of the mountain. Smoke obscured the summit as the firing intensified, then cleared during hand-to-hand combat. The Mexicans ceased firing and abandoned their earthworks as the U.S. soldiers stormed the position at bayonet point.[99] As the smoke and fog cleared, U.S. Army flags could be seen waving on Independencia. The cheering by thousands of American troops could be heard by every Mexican in Monterrey.[100]

The Mexican soldiers retreated along the side of the ridge and downhill toward Bishop's Palace. In the palace, four more artillery pieces and additional troops were preparing for the American attack. The thick walls of the building, which still stood after years of neglect, made a perfect fortress. During the lull in the fighting, U.S. soldiers dismantled a 12-pounder howitzer and pulled it up the hill and into the captured Mexican works above the palace. Once reassembled, the gun began lobbing shells at the palace, several of which landed inside the walls and exploded. Mexican officers realized that if they had any chance of holding the position, the howitzer would have to be silenced. Mexican cavalry, which had been sent to reinforce the palace, gathered nearby.[101]

American officers expected a counterattack. Several companies of U.S. regulars were sent part way down the ridge and took cover in a ravine above the palace. The rangers, supported by additional infantry, were sent around the top of the hill and positioned themselves to attack when the command was given. The rest of the American force was removed from the earthworks and positioned on the far side of the ridge to shield them from the palace's cannons.[102]

Realizing the Americans were scattered along the ridge, the Mexican cavalry made a gallant uphill charge in an effort to capture the howitzer and retake the works. As they rushed forward, the horsemen came within close range of the American regulars hidden in the ravine. The soldiers rose from their position and fired deadly volleys, slaughtering Mexican cavalrymen and their horses alike. As the survivors retreated, the Americans, including the three companies of the 7th Regiment, quickly began a downhill attack. They pursued the fleeing Mexican cavalry so closely that gunners inside the palace could not fire without killing their own men. The palace defenders ran from the building and down to the road leading into Monterrey. Again, the U.S. troops quickly turned captured artillery onto its previous owners and shelled them as they fled into the city.[103]

The day's fight ended. General Taylor consolidated his position along the northeastern approaches to central Monterrey. General Worth did the same west of town. General Ampudia had lost some of his best defenses. On the city's west side, Independencia, Federación, and Bishop's Palace were gone. Ampudia's defensive works on the north and east, including the Citadel, had been captured or outflanked and had to be abandoned. He withdrew his forces toward the center of town, intending to make Taylor's final attack a bloody house-to-house fight. Mexican soldiers occupied buildings around a large church and the city's grand plaza. They cut holes in walls, fortified flat rooftops with sandbags, and positioned their artillery to fire down the streets. Ampudia still had plenty of soldiers and ammunition.

The 7th Infantry spent the night in the captured forts on Federatión Ridge. The next morning, the regiment returned to the Saltillo road, where General Worth was gathering his division for the final attack on the city.[104] By early afternoon, the 7th and 8th regiments and the artillery battalion had been re-supplied with ammunition and were ready to move. Worth spread part of his division in a wide skirmish line and ordered them forward. They swept through the residential areas and advanced "over hedges, fences, and walls, through beautiful gardens filled with the richest tropical fruit." Behind the skirmishers came the artillery units moving along the roads and supported by additional infantry. The division advanced for about a mile before coming under fire.[105]

Much the same was happening on the other side of Monterrey. The 1st and 3rd divisions advanced several blocks toward the grand plaza and came under deadly fire. They had to fight their way from building to building. They killed or captured the defenders as they went, but it was a costly process. Each structure, when captured, became the gathering place for an attack on the building next door. When the soldiers charged out of one house toward another, they were fired on by Mexican artillery on the streets and infantry on nearby rooftops.[106]

As Worth's soldiers advanced through town, they perfected their own style of urban warfare. Some soldiers of the 7th Infantry scaled the outer walls of buildings with makeshift ladders and fought hand to hand on the rooftops. Others quickly learned that once a building was taken, they could dig holes through the adjoining walls. They then tossed small artillery shells with lit fuses into the next building. The Mexicans either fled before the shell exploded or suffered the consequences.[107] The courageous Mexican soldiers withdrew from one position to another. They contested every foot of ground. Near the center of the city, they caught Lieutenant Franklin Gardner of the 7th Infantry and men of his company in a crossfire. Nearly every man was wounded. By the end of the day, Holmes had pushed his men so far ahead of other attacking troops that his company "was forced to fall back" during the night.[108] Nonetheless, Mexican soldiers and their officers realized that they were being steadily compressed toward the center of town.[109]

Late in the day, Taylor brought up his heavy artillery as darkness ended the infantry fight. Soon after, American gunners began dropping 24-pounder howitzer and large mortar shells into the center of town. The burning shell fuses made high arcs in the night sky. They exploded with a blinding flash above the heads of the helpless Mexicans and showered them with deadly shrapnel. The bombardment continued through the night. By morning, September 24, General Ampudia was ready to end the fighting.[110]

General Taylor initially demanded an unconditional surrender, but Ampudia refused. After hours of further negotiations, the frustrated Taylor made an offer that Ampudia found acceptable. The Mexican soldiers would be allowed to evacuate Monterrey with their weapons, including six artillery pieces, march unmolested to Saltillo, and enjoy an eight-week cease-fire between the two armies. Ampudia took the deal.[111]

The Mexican army marched out of Monterrey during the next several days. Taylor had agreed to maintain only a token force in the city and have most of his army remain camped on the outskirts of town. Some of the volunteer troops, notably those from Texas, stayed in the city. They looted homes and stores, assaulted Mexican civilians, and murdered Mexican soldiers who had remained in town. These atrocities spread to the surrounding countryside as well. General Taylor took only half-hearted measures to control the situation. Finally, the Texans, feeling that they had caused enough mayhem, applied for permission to leave the army and return home. Taylor quickly approved their request.[112]

Captain Holmes and other regular army officers were relieved to see the Texans leave. Drunkenness, brawling, thievery, and lack of military discipline by volunteers had been common throughout the campaign. Their actions undercut the regular army's desire to pacify Mexican civilians rather than alienate them. The conduct of many volunteer units was a continuing source of friction between their officers and those in the regular army. One of Captain Holmes's fellow company commanders, John C. Henshaw, was particularly outraged. He described the Texans as "banditti" and observed that "this band of villains ... would have disgraced the name of pirates."[113]

Taylor's army settled into a relaxed occupation of Monterrey. The 7th Regiment moved into two large private residences in town. Although Captain Holmes fell ill in September, he quickly recuperated in his comfortable quarters. He and his men feasted on the abundance of fruit purchased from townspeople. He may have accompanied his men when they went down to the river to watch naked Mexican women bathe.[114]

For the next several weeks, most of Taylor's army was at rest. The soldiers received letters and newspapers from home and were able to keep up with negotiations between Mexico and the United States. They hoped Taylor's string of victories would force the Mexican government to sue for peace. When the talks bogged down, the United States allowed General Santa Anna to return to Mexico from his exile in Cuba. Santa Anna promised President Polk that he would seize control of the government and end the war by selling the disputed territories to the U.S. for thirty million dollars. Once settled in Mexico, he double-crossed Polk and began rallying the Mexican population against the U.S. Army. Mexicans were suspicious of Santa Anna but knew he would fight for their country.[115]

By the fall, it was becoming clear to President Polk that Santa Anna was the problem and not the solution. Taylor's victories in northern Mexico had not forced the Mexican government into negotiations and were not likely to do so. At the end of October, the president, Secretary of War Marcy, and Gen. Winfield Scott (the ranking general in the army) agreed that a new strategy with Mexico City as its goal should be initiated. In order to keep part of the Mexican army tied down in northern Mexico, the president ordered Taylor to notify General Ampudia that the United States was ending the cease-fire agreement in that region. The main theater of operations was shifted. General Scott would invade Mexico from the coast.[116]

Scott submitted a three-stage plan. The campaign would begin with an amphibious landing on the Gulf of Mexico at the port of Veracruz, followed by a land campaign across central Mexico and the capture of the Mexican capital. He suggested that the initial invasion should consist of ten thousand troops. Once a base was established at Veracruz, the army was to be strengthened to twenty thousand men for the overland campaign.[117] As the plan's chief architect and the most respected general in the army, Scott, instead of Taylor, was President Polk's choice to lead the invasion. General Taylor was a Whig and a potential opposition candidate for the presidency. Taylor's popularity, however, had suffered as a result of his overly generous armistice with the Mexican army after the capture of Monterrey. Polk did not want Taylor's reputation to be restored with a military victory. On November 19, General Scott accepted the president's appointment as commander of the not-yet-assembled army that would capture Mexico City.[118]

At General Scott's disposal were the regular army regiments, half of which were currently serving under General Taylor in northern Mexico, and thousands of more recently organized volunteer militiamen. Since northern Mexico had been the focus of the war, most of the militia regiments were either already with Taylor or on their way to his field of operations. Scott issued orders that transferred four thousand regular army troops, including the 7th Infantry, and more than thirty-two hundred volunteers to his command. These troops were to proceed to one of Scott's two rear staging areas: Brazos, on the coast near the Rio Grande, and Tampico, farther to the south. They were then to sail to Lobos Island, approximately eight miles off the coast, where four weeks would be consumed in assembling the invasion force and fleet. When prepared, the army would sail one hundred seventy-five miles south to Veracruz for the amphibious landing.[119]

On December 13, 1846, the 1st, 3rd, and 7th Infantry regiments marched out of Monterrey and headed southeast toward Linares, approximately one hundred miles away. They were accompanied by Braxton Bragg's light artillery and volunteer regiments from Tennessee, Georgia, and Mississippi. The force got as far as the town of Monte Morales, sixty-five miles, when the regular regiments were force marched back to Monterrey amid fears that General Santa Anna was planning to attack part of Taylor's army near Saltillo.[120] Aware of Scott's plan to land an army at Veracruz, Santa Anna had indeed marched into northern Mexico with an army of twenty-five thousand men. He planned to unite with Ampudia's forces at Saltillo, defeat Taylor, then turn and fight Scott between Mexico City and the coast. As Santa Anna moved north, bad weather and rough terrain slowed his army and depleted its strength by a third.

When it became apparent that Santa Anna's campaign was of no immediate threat, the regulars were recalled from their march to reinforce Taylor. They arrived in Monterrey only to find that "it was all a flash in the pan and we had had a hard march for nothing."[121] The regulars retraced their steps to Monte Morales, then went on to Linares, reaching that city on December 28. Marching another one hundred twenty miles, they arrived at Victoria on January 4, 1847. After a ten-day rest, the division marched another one hundred miles, arriving at Tampico on January 23. Once the soldiers established camps outside Tampico, their officers allowed them little time to recover from their journey. The regiments commenced daily "drilling in Battalion and Evolutions of the Line."[122] In February, Captain Holmes was assigned to temporary duty with Brigade Artillery.

In northern Mexico, the armies of Santa Anna and Taylor finally fought at Buena Vista on February 23. The Mexicans lost nearly two thousand soldiers, compared to Taylor's loss of less than one-third that number. The first part of Santa Anna's planned double victory had failed. As a result of the defeats at Monterrey and Buena Vista, both Santa Anna and Ampudia lost the faith of the soldiers they commanded. Desertion was rampant as the battered army marched away from Taylor and toward the second part of the campaign. Santa Anna left Ampudia to manage the march toward Veracruz and went to San Luis to spread propaganda about his "victory" at Buena Vista.[123]

The Buena Vista campaign weakened the Mexican army and gave Scott enough time to consolidate his invasion force for the attack on Veracruz. The battle of Buena Vista also cemented friendship and trust between Jefferson Davis and Braxton Bragg. Colonel Davis's Mississippians blunted a Mexican infantry attack that threatened Bragg's artillery battery. Bragg, in turn, impressed Davis with his skill and daring. Their relationship would have a profound effect on Holmes in a future war.[124]

After spending several weeks in camp at Tampico, General Scott's soldiers boarded transport ships and began their sea journey. They sailed to join the rest of the army at Lobos Island and then on to Veracruz, a total of thirteen days at sea. By then, Scott had divided his command into three divisions. The First Division contained several regular army regiments and was commanded by General Worth. Worth had lost the services of the 7th Infantry. They had been transferred to the Second Division, commanded by Gen. David Twiggs. The Third Division contained most of the volunteer regiments and was led by Gen. Robert Patterson. A fleet of sixty freight schooners transported the American army. While at sea, the schooners were safe from attack. Mexico had no navy.[125] The invasion was set to begin on March 9, 1847.

When the fleet arrived in the vicinity of Veracruz, General Scott loaded his most trusted engineer officers onto a small steamer. They examined the shoreline and decided where best to land the army. The boat contained several officers who would become famous in an as-yet unforeseen war: Robert E. Lee, George Gordon Meade, Joseph E. Johnston, and P. G. T. Beauregard.[126] After the reconnaissance, Scott and Commodore David Conner chose Collado Beach, three miles south of Veracruz, as the beachhead. Collado Beach was well beyond artillery range of the city's main defense, the island fortress of San Juan de Ulúa. While the fleet lay offshore, the first attack wave of twenty-five hundred soldiers climbed down the sides of their ships and into large surfboats. Scott chose General Worth's division as the first troops to go ashore.

The landings began at 5:00 P.M. on March 9. When Worth's division was on board and the surfboats were properly arranged, the tow lines were cut. Sailors and soldiers rowed hard toward the beach four hundred fifty yards away. There were sixty-seven landing boats, in three different sizes, each carrying forty-five to eighty men. As the boats headed for the beach, steamships armed with heavy artillery opened fire. Shells screamed over the heads of the landing force and crashed into the sand dunes one hundred fifty yards beyond the water's edge. Mexican cavalry had been observed along the shore earlier in the day.[127] Scott wanted to get his beachhead established without having to fight on the shore, where his troops would be most vulnerable.[128]

As the flat-bottomed surfboats ran up onto the beach, Worth's soldiers climbed out and waded ashore. Captains quickly collected their companies and moved them toward the sand dunes. Company A of the Army Corps of Engineers, commanded by lieutenants George McClellan and Gustavus W. Smith, led the way. They scouted the area off the beach to locate roads and good defensive ground, should it be needed. Edmund Kirby Smith accompanied Worth's division.[129]

The infantry colonels quickly collected their regiments in the sand dunes and raised their colors. At seeing the first U.S. Army flags rise, Captain Holmes joined in the cheering of thousands of soldiers still on board the transport vessels. The sailors rowed their boats back to the transports to pick up the next division. The volunteer troops landed next, followed by Twiggs's division, including the 7th Infantry. Scott's entire army, eleven thousand men, was safely ashore by 10:00 P.M.[130]

Veracruz was a beautiful city and well fortified. In addition to the protection provided by the fortress of San Juan de Ulúa, nine smaller forts surrounded the city. The forts were connected by a network of defensive walls. The city had two hundred cannons, four thousand soldiers, and sufficient ammunition to withstand a lengthy siege.[131]

During the next several days, General Scott surrounded Veracruz with seven miles of earthworks, artillery positions, and infantry. General Twiggs's division held the area north of Veracruz. Scott planned to lay siege and compel the town to surrender before the beginning of the annual yellow fever season in late spring. If the army stayed too long near the coast, the disease would sweep through the ranks and end the campaign. General Juan Esteban Morales had approximately thirty-three hundred soldiers to defend Veracruz. He hoped either Santa Anna's army or yellow fever would soon arrive.

Nine days after the landing, most of the American soldiers still had no tents and infrequent hot meals. Bad weather and rough seas had prevented the landing of supplies.[132] Between rainstorms, Holmes and his soldiers suffered from blowing sand that sifted into everything. His men stood long hours of picket duty, night and day, to intercept communications to and from the beleaguered city. General Morales's frequent attempts to notify Santa Anna of his situation met with failure. One of Holmes's fellow officers reported, "They have made several attempts within the last few days to communicate the situation to friends outside, but we have intercepted all their letters."[133]

While the infantry kept the city isolated, heavy artillery units were brought ashore. Under the direction of Robert E. Lee, gun emplacements were constructed using soldiers, sailors, and marines as laborers. Once the bombardment commenced, everyone realized that Veracruz could not hold out long. From their camps and picket positions, American infantrymen watched and listened as the gunners worked day after day to destroy the beautiful city. The discharge of artillery pieces and the sound of exploding shells as they landed within the city walls was described as "crashing roofs; burning houses; flying pavements, doors, windows and furniture blocking the streets; a pandemonium of confused and frightful sounds; domes and steeples threatening to fall; the earth quaking; crowds of screaming women; terrible wounds and sudden deaths."[134]

The city's population and garrison were suffering two hundred deaths each day. After four days of shelling, General Morales ordered one of his subordinate officers to surrender the town. Scott's artillery had fired sixty-seven hundred shells into the city. Return fire from Mexican batteries caused nineteen American deaths and wounded approximately sixty.[135] On March 28, the city surrendered. Completely isolated, the island fortress of San Juan de Ulúa was evacuated by its garrison as well.

General Scott had no intention of making enemies of Veracruz civilians during the occupation. Very publically, he and his staff attended Mass, where Scott lit a candle at the altar. Work parties of soldiers helped clear the streets of rubble produced by the bombardment. Under the watchful eyes of their officers, soldiers went sightseeing in town and bought food and souvenirs from street vendors. Unlike Taylor's volunteers at Monterrey, American soldiers were quickly punished for crimes against Mexicans. At least one soldier was executed for raping a Mexican woman.[136]

The army had won a decisive victory, with few casualties, in record time, but Scott needed to get his soldiers moving. Cases of yellow fever were starting to show up in reports from his medical officers. There was no time to wait for the navy to bring enough wagons and food to Veracruz for the march on Mexico City. Commissary officers scoured the city and surrounding countryside. They purchased (rather than seizing) all the food, wagons, and draft animals they could find. Public notices, printed in Spanish by the American army, abolished all Mexican sales taxes on goods sold to Scott's army.[137]

The supply and transportation problems forced Scott to send his army westward in a piecemeal fashion. Twiggs's division, led by the 7th Infantry, left Veracruz on April 8. Captain Holmes would not take part in Scott's final campaign against Mexico City. In April, he was ordered to begin a six-month tour of duty with the army recruiting service. He left Mexico, met Laura and the children, and traveled to New York City. He worked at the army's recruiting center on Governors Island. His brevet promotion to major for gallantry at Monterrey had been recommended by Secretary of War W. L. Marcy and sent to the U. S. Senate for approval in March. The brevet was granted, but not without controversy. Holmes's name was not included on General Taylor's initial list of officers who had distinguished themselves during the campaign. The matter was brought to the attention of President Polk. The president initiated further inquiries, which resulted in the submission of "additional evidence."[138]

Soon after Holmes's departure, Scott's army started toward Cerro Gordo, arriving there on April 15, 1847. General Santa Anna's army was entrenched along the hills and ridges east of town. On April 18, General Scott sent his volunteer troops, under the command of Tennessee's Gen. Gideon Pillow, against the Mexican army's right flank. Scott attacked the Mexican center and left with his regulars. The 2nd U.S. Infantry, the U.S. Mounted Rifle Regiment, the 7th Infantry, and the 3rd Infantry converged on El Telegrapho Hill.[139] After vicious hand-to-hand fighting, the flag of the 7th Regiment was planted atop the Mexican earthworks. General Scott later wrote, "The highest praise is due to Colonel Plympton, 7th Infantry, and the gallant officers and men of the regiment for their brilliant service."[140]

The 7th Infantry and the rest of its brigade attacked and stormed Mexican defenses at Contreras on August 19. A large number of Mexican soldiers and their equipment was captured. The 7th regiment was then detached from its brigade and participated in the attack on Churubusco the next day. On September 12, a detachment of officers and enlisted men from the regiment joined other troops for an attack on Chapultepec. The force, under the command of Captain Paul, 7th Infantry, overran the Mexican position and captured five artillery pieces, along with four hundred fifty prisoners. On September 15, the 7th Infantry and other units marched into Mexico City. The regiment occupied the town until after the peace treaty with Mexico was ratified.[141] In December, Holmes rejoined his company at Mexico City, after settling Laura (who was pregnant with their fourth child) in North Carolina, at the home of Laura's mother, Mrs. Elizabeth Wetmore. In early 1848, Laura informed her husband that their second son, Gabriel, had been born on January 25.

As a brevet major, Holmes served as the 7th Infantry's field officer (acting commander) from January through May, while the regiment occupied the Mexican capital. In the late spring, the 7th Infantry was ordered to return to the United States for duty in Missouri. Most of the regiment left Mexico aboard the ships *Milaoden* and *Suffolk* and landed at New Orleans on July 18, 1848. When his regiment left Mexico, Major Holmes was given thirty days' furlough. He traveled to North Carolina and accompanied Laura and the children to Jefferson Barracks, Missouri.[142] Laura brought a family slave, Sarah, to help her with the children and cooking.[143]

4

The Frontier, Governors Island
and Fort Sumter

The 7th Infantry, with Holmes in command, remained at Jefferson Barracks for most of the next year. (He was listed as "sick, present" in June.) Troubles flared up again in Florida, and the regiment returned for duty there in September 1849. The regiment's companies were scattered at various outposts in the Tampa Bay area. Although Laura was pregnant, Holmes took her and the children along for part of this tour of duty. Tampa Bay was the regimental headquarters and quite safe. Several of the regiment's companies usually stayed there while others were stationed at the more remote forts. The family spent time swimming and gathering oranges, lemons, and wild figs.[1] Laura and the children returned to Jefferson Barracks before spring 1850. In March, Holmes escorted a small band of Seminoles from Fort Arbuckle, Florida, to New Orleans on the first leg of their journey to Indian Territory.[2] He went back to Florida during the first week of April and missed the birth of his third son, Wetmore, on March 2. He and his company returned to Jefferson Barracks in June, and by July most of the regiment was reunited at that post.[3]

The 7th did not have much time to enjoy Jefferson Barracks. The regiment was ordered to Fort Leavenworth, Indian Territory, in August. They were to prepare for frontier duty in New Mexico Territory. Companies C, D, F and H were trained and equipped for cavalry service and started for New Mexico Territory in mid–September. The column traveled until October 1, when the expedition was canceled and the regiment was ordered back to Jefferson Barracks. The 7th stayed at Jefferson Barracks until being reassigned to Indian Territory in the spring of 1851. They arrived at Fort Washita at the end of May. Holmes was the post commander from June 1851 through early 1854. The mounted companies of the 7th stayed at Washita, but the infantry companies returned to Jefferson Barracks.[4]

Army life at Fort Washita was pleasant and uneventful. The soldiers and their families were able to get wild grapes, strawberries, pecans, grouse, and wild turkeys from local tribes that did a brisk barter business with the fort.[5] Laura Lydia Holmes, the couple's sixth child, was born at the fort on Nov. 18, 1852. The family called her "Little Lottie." Major Holmes did a brief tour of duty as commander at Fort Smith, Arkansas, from August to October 1853.[6] Most of the 7th Infantry was transferred to Fort Arbuckle, Indian Territory, in June 1854. Holmes, his family, and Company C had moved to that location several months earlier. Hardy Lucian Holmes was born at

Fort Arbuckle on January 15, 1855. The family remained there until March of that year.

After almost nine years as a brevet major, Holmes was formally promoted to that rank on March 3, 1855, and transferred to the 8th Infantry. The companies of his new regiment were scattered at various camps and forts in Texas. The 8th had been on frontier duty since the end of the war with Mexico. While in Mexico, the 7th and 8th Infantry regiments served together in Taylor's northern Mexico campaign and during Scott's campaign from Veracruz to Mexico City. The 8th had also fought the Seminoles during the same years the 7th was in Florida. Holmes knew several officers in his new regiment and felt a special kinship with men who had fought on so many of the same far-flung battlefields.

Within months of his new assignment, Holmes was ordered back to Fort Washita to sit on a court-martial of Major John C. Henshaw. While serving together in the 7th Infantry, Henshaw and Holmes had not been close. Holmes was a conventional army officer. Henshaw was something of a misfit and was court-martialed four times during his career. On this occasion, he was charged with disobedience of orders, contempt and disrespect to the commanding officer, and conduct unbecoming an officer and a gentleman. He was also politically outspoken and disagreed with Holmes's attitudes concerning slavery and state's rights. At his trial, Henshaw objected to Holmes serving as one of the judges, but his request to have Holmes removed was denied.[7]

In 1856, Holmes traveled, working with the army's recruiting service and escorting recruits to Texas. He was assigned to Fort Bliss that year, but traveled to Fort Stanton, New Mexico Territory in 1856 and 1857. Tragedy struck the family early in 1857. Laura Holmes's namesake, daughter Laura Lydia ("Little Lottie"), died on January 29 at five years of age. Holmes was transferred back to Fort Bliss in 1858. The family remained there until the summer of 1859.

As towns grew up around the forts, they became "charming," close-knit little communities on the prairie. Like Holmes, many officers and some enlisted men kept their families with them in the West. Servants lived near the forts, did the family cooking, and took care of the children. Dinners, dances, band concerts, picnics, church activities, and business with local merchants all gave the posts a small-town atmosphere. Rigid military life took on a more social and relaxed tone in peacetime. Even the daily lowering of the large garrison flag at sunset lost some of its military formality. Army wives gathered their children in the late afternoons and watched their husbands stand in formation during the ceremony. Often, while the post musicians played "retreat," the children played at the base of the flagpole. They had to be shooed away so the color guards could fold the flag.[8]

During the early summer of 1859, Holmes received word from the war department that he would be transferred to Governors Island in New York Harbor. He had been chosen to become the army's chief recruiting officer. He was ordered to assume his new command on July 1, 1859.

The previous several years on the frontier had been happy times for the family.

Except for the deaths of two children and occasional assignments away from his home post, army life in the West had been peaceful and comfortable. But Holmes was fifty-five years old. Thirty-four years of army life had taken its toll on him. He and Laura were ready for a change. The move back east was full of promise. He could look forward to spending his last army years with his family at a permanent post. Governors Island gave the children stability and better schooling. New York City was only a short boat ride away. Holmes and Laura could begin planning for his eventual retirement and their return to North Carolina.

Holmes assumed command at Governors Island on July 2. The post commander's quarters were spacious, large enough for Holmes, Laura, and the five children. The children ranged in age from the oldest, eighteen-year-old Elizabeth, to the youngest, five-year-old Hardy. The middle children were Theo Jr., age fifteen, Gabriel, twelve, and ten-year-old Wetmore. The family hired a servant, an Irish immigrant named Margaret. Soon enough, Laura would need additional help with the household. Around the time the family was settled in their new home, Laura announced that she was expecting another child to be born in March.

Theo had shown interest in a military career and an aptitude for engineering. The family, having mixed feelings about his choice, arranged for his admission to the University of North Carolina. Still, the boy persisted and asked his father to apply for an appointment to West Point. Major Holmes filed the application in January 1860. He wrote to the new secretary of war, John Floyd, and recounted his own military service on the frontier. (Secretary of War Jefferson Davis had left the cabinet in 1857, with the end of the Pierce administration.) Holmes reminded Floyd that he had been commended by General Taylor for his service and had received a brevet during the Mexico campaign. He apologized to Floyd for speaking of his own merits in seeking the appointment, but stated that he did so only in "the hope of benefitting my promising boy."[9]

Holmes sent a copy of his request to the U.S. Army's chief engineer, Col. R. E. De Russy. He also enlisted the aid of Senator Jefferson Davis. Davis recounted, for De Russy, Major Holmes's seniority and recommended that the application for young Theo be given the "favorable consideration of the Secretary of War." It took nearly a year of letter writing and political pressure to secure Theo's appointment to West Point. Theo's age at the time of the application became a problem. Holmes advised De Russy that by the time Theo would report to West Point (presumably in the summer of 1861) "he will be sixteen years and six months old." He also informed De Russy that Theo possessed "all the physical requirements of a Cadet and is now, I think, prepared to enter the Sophomore class in the University of North Carolina."[10]

By December 1860, when the appointment was assured, Holmes had gathered additional endorsements from North Carolina congressman Warren Winslow and the highest-ranking officer in the army, Major General Winfield Scott.[11] Holmes was gratified at the support he and Theo had received, but in the meantime, the family had suffered an overwhelming loss. The Holmes's eighth child, a girl, was born on March 4, 1860. Three days later, Laura died. Holmes was devastated. Laura was the love and guiding influence of his life and had "Made Her Husband a Christian."[12] The grief-stricken old soldier buried his wife in the Fort Columbus cemetery on Governors Island. He named the baby Laura.

For months, Holmes struggled to control his grief and depression. He hired a nurse for the baby. By early 1861, his health had failed. He was unable to care properly for the children, even with the help of his oldest child, Elizabeth, and the servants. In February, he wrote to his sister-in-law, Lydia Wetmore, and confessed, "I am greatly changed.... My desolation has come on me too late in life for Nature to admit of anything like recuperation." He was constantly troubled by dreams "of the past.... I am still very weak and suffering with a cough and pain in the chest."[13]

Holmes sent his children to live with relatives. Theo went to North Carolina, where he enrolled at the university. His appointment to West Point had fallen victim to the impending war. South Carolina had seceded on December 20, 1860. In the letter to his sister-in-law, Holmes said of his youngest child, "My beautiful lovely little Laura will probably never know a father's love, for I have given her to my good sister."[14] Laura's death aged Holmes and broke his spirit. As he dealt with depression, illness, and family upheaval, his country hurtled toward disunion and war. Between South Carolina's December secession and mid–February, six additional Southern states seceded. As U.S. troops evacuated or were evicted from military installations throughout the South, Fort Sumter in Charleston harbor became the focus of the crisis.

If Fort Sumter was to remain in Union hands, the garrison of eighty-five men under the command of Major Robert Anderson had to be re-supplied. South Carolina military officials in Charleston had cut most of the normal channels of supply and communication to the fort.[15] In order to withstand an attack, more soldiers, weapons, and artillery ammunition would have to be sent to Anderson. Public perception in the North was that the fort's garrison was suffering. The Buchanan administration wanted to find a way to get food and other necessary supplies to the fort without appearing to be preparing for an invasion of South Carolina. General-in-Chief Winfield Scott asked President Buchanan to send navy vessels to Fort Sumter "as secretly as possible ... with two hundred and fifty recruits ... together with some extra muskets or rifles, ammunition, and subsidence stores."[16] Scott's plan was calculated to reinforce the fort, relieve the food shortage, but be insufficiently provocative to start a war.

On January 5, 1861, Holmes received an order from Assistant Adjutant General Thomas to put "two hundred of the best instructed men at Fort Columbus" on board the steamship *Star of the West* "to re-enforce the garrison at Fort Sumter, South Carolina." Holmes was told to issue each man "one hundred rounds of ammunition ... furnish one hundred stand of spare arms" and provide the force with enough food for three months.[17] At the same time, there was a civilian effort underway to help the fort.

Frustrated by government's slow response, Mr. Washington A. Bartlett of New York organized local merchants to donate supplies and have them shipped to the fort. The plan was well developed before *Star of the West* sailed. Bartlett insisted, "The private enterprise was kept secret, — and well kept, (which was more than the government could do).” When *Star of the West* departed, the private effort was halted. After the expedition failed, Bartlett wrote, “It is my opinion now, that if the Government had not taken the matter out of our hands, no one would have known of it until it was executed.”[18]

Star of the West sailed from New York and arrived off Charleston Harbor at midnight on Tuesday, January 8. The army commander on board, Lt. Charles Woods, reported that the ship groped around “in the dark until nearly day” before the light at Fort Sumter “told us where we were.” The ship was spotted almost immediately by a Southern vessel, which fired off rockets alerting the harbor’s defenses. Lieutenant Woods ordered United States flags aboard the *Star* to be raised as she entered the harbor. Confederate shore batteries opened fire. Southern ships appeared and began maneuvering to trap the expedition. After *Star of the West* took one hit and several near misses, Woods decided to abandon the mission rather than suffer an outright military fiasco. *Star of the West* returned to New York Harbor on January 12.[19]

The *Star of the West* expedition was never a secret. South Carolinians were convinced that the fort would be reinforced and used as a base for an invasion of the state. By the time the ship set sail, rumors were flying in Washington, New York, and Charleston. After the mission failed, newspapers reported on how little secrecy was involved. Harper’s magazine stated, “The attempted deceit entirely failed. The Charleston people were fully informed as to the project by some of their innumerable spies, who swarmed over the country.”[20] The *Daily Advocate* of Baton Rouge, Louisiana, noted, “A constant watch has been kept for the last two days in expectation of the arrival of the steamship Star of the West, with reinforcements, fuel and provisions for Fort Sumpter.”[21] The *Daily Dispatch* in Richmond reported on January 12 that Charleston “had been notified fourteen hours in advance of the expected arrival of the steamer.”[22] In his official report, Lieutenant Woods stated, “From the preparations that had been made for us I have every reason to believe that the Charlestonians were perfectly aware of our coming.”[23]

The incident provoked a national crisis. Headlines in the *Daily Advocate* shouted, “THE WAR HAS COMMENCED!”[24] Southern states held secession conventions and referendums. The Confederate States of America was formed in February. That same month, North Carolinians voted against holding a convention to consider seceding from the Union. The referendum was defeated by a clear majority.[25] North Carolina’s small-farm economy was not fertile ground for conflict on the issues over which the North and South collided. Tariffs, slavery, and the legality of secession did not inflame a majority of the state’s population. North Carolina’s slave-holding plantation owners, more directly connected with those issues, favored secession, but did not have the same strong political influence they enjoyed in South Carolina and the Deep South. The possibility of war still loomed and Fort Sumter was still occupied by the United States, but that situation was regarded by most North Carolinians as a problem for South Carolina and the Confederacy. Most North Carolinians, while agreeing with secessionists on most issues, saw no reason to secede, nor to fight a war in defense of another state’s right to do so. Local secession-minded communities, however, were acting on their own.

During the *Star of the West*'s voyage, North Carolina citizen militias began seizing U.S. government property.[26] Forts Johnston and Caswell on the coast were taken on January 9 and 10, respectively. Similar seizures occurred throughout the South as additional states seceded. Anxiety in the North grew with each incident. By January 23, Holmes's garrison on Governors Island had been increased to seven hundred thirty men. On February 16, he was ordered to "prepare three Companies of United States soldiers" for duty in Florida.[27] President Buchanan delayed taking any definitive action, preferring to hand the problem over to Lincoln at his inauguration on March 4.

The day Abraham Lincoln took his oath of office, a messenger was sent to Major Holmes at Fort Columbus by "public authorities" in New York City. Holmes was told that "certain parties in the city threatened to take possession of the public property in this harbor." The next day, he notified Col. Samuel Cooper, adjutant and inspector of the U.S. Army, about the report. Holmes sent troops to Fort Wood on Bedloe's Island as a precautionary measure. When notifying Cooper, Holmes gave little credence to the rumors. He saw no reason to comment on the likely political motivations of such an act. Holmes remarked to Cooper only, "We are in times when men are governed by passion rather than reason." Cooper was from New Jersey and had graduated from West Point in 1815. He was a friend of Jefferson Davis and a Southern sympathizer.[28] Three days later, Cooper resigned and ended his forty-six-year career in the U.S. Army.

On March 11, T. B. Wetmore, Holmes's brother-in-law, wrote to Confederate president Jefferson Davis. He recommended (without Holmes's knowledge, according to Mr. Wetmore) that Holmes should be offered command of a Confederate regiment. Wetmore knew that as a U.S. Army officer from a state that was still in the Union, Holmes could not personally lobby for a commission in the Confederate army. He said that Holmes felt his first allegiance was to his native state and was frustrated that North Carolina had not seceded. Wetmore believed that Holmes would gladly transfer to Confederate service if he was offered a military command. (Such letters on the behalf of appointment seekers were common in the 19th century. Politicians and others of the period routinely offered themselves for office and campaigned through third parties. It is likely that Holmes, without requesting the letter, made comments to Wetmore implying that such an appointment would be accepted. Thus, Wetmore and Holmes could say that Holmes had no specific knowledge of the letter.)

Informed that Fort Sumter would run out of food in mid–April, President Lincoln ordered another relief expedition on April 4. Again, preparations were made in New York Harbor. Troops for the mission were assembled at Fort Columbus. Like everyone involved, Holmes knew of the plan. President Lincoln notified South Carolina's Governor Pickens that the expedition would resupply the fort's garrison with food. Lincoln's message was delivered to Pickens on the evening of April 8.[29] Earlier that same day, the *New York Times* announced the "resignation of Major Holmes." The accompanying article reported that rumors of Holmes's impending exit had been common for several days. Holmes was quoted as having said that he would not accompany U.S. soldiers when they "go South to fight." The article stated that Holmes "hails from North Carolina" and implied that he had spread "extensive disaffection among the troops" at Governors Island.[30]

Holmes had realized that President Lincoln meant to reinforce Fort Sumter and precipitate a crisis. The president's "relief" fleet consisted of a revenue cutter, a troop transport, three tugboats, and three gunboats.[31] Holmes also knew the Confederacy would not allow the fort to be strengthened. War was inevitable. Holmes left Governors Island on April 9.[32]

The next day, at Washington, D.C., Holmes boarded a steamboat bound for the landing at Aquia, Virginia. During the trip down the Potomac River, he struck up conversations with fellow passengers. There were no "Republicans" on board and most of the travelers shared "secession proclivities." They spoke openly about politics and the possibility of war. Holmes told them that he had refused to accompany the relief expeditions to Fort Sumter and of his resignation from the army. In replying to questions about prominent Southern military men, Holmes said that President Davis had made excellent choices in appointing the Confederacy's first group of generals, including Braxton Bragg and P. G. T. Beauregard.[33] Holmes knew both men. They would be prominent in the coming war and in Holmes's career as a Confederate officer.

On a more ominous note, Holmes warned that if war started, it would be "a desperate, if not a prolonged struggle." Fellow passenger John B. Jones was impressed with Holmes. He wrote in his diary that Holmes "is a little deaf, but has an intellectual face ... and the prudence so necessary for success in a large field of operations."[34]

The desperate if not prolonged struggle Holmes spoke of to his fellow steamboat passengers started while he was en route to North Carolina. The Union fleet arrived off Fort Sumter before midnight, April 11. Five hours later, Charleston harbor shore batteries began shelling the fort. During the thirty-four-hour bombardment, Holmes arrived at the train station in Goldsboro, North Carolina. There, he received a telegram from relatives at Wilmington. The message stated, "You must come to Wilmington tonight ... your friends are going to give you a reception.... Fort Sumpter is on fire[,] cannonading going on fiercely."[35]

On April 15, President Lincoln required states still in the Union to provide soldiers to put down the "rebellion." North Carolina's quota was two regiments of infantry, fifteen hundred men. In his response, Governor Ellis told the U.S. secretary of war, "You can get no troops from North Carolina."[36] Ellis knew his citizens would choose to secede rather than participate in a military campaign against the Confederacy. Whether they seceded or not, North Carolinians were at war. Ellis called for a state convention to be held at Raleigh in May. Volunteer companies began organizing throughout the state. President Lincoln's call for troops had the same effect all over the South. Virginia seceded on April 17. Robert E. Lee resigned from the U.S. Army three days later. President Lincoln declared a blockade of most Southern ports on April 19. Arkansas and Tennessee seceded on May 6 and 7.

Holmes stayed at Wilmington until April 19, then left for Fayetteville. There, he met with the chairman of North Carolina's Department of Military and Naval Affairs, Warren Winslow. On instructions from Winslow, he traveled to the Confederacy's capital city, Montgomery, Alabama, to meet with Jefferson Davis.[37] President Davis appointed him a colonel in the Provisional Army of the Confederate States of America. Holmes was then ordered by Samuel Cooper, the Confederate army's new adjutant and inspector general, to report to Raleigh, North Carolina. Holmes left Montgomery on April 22. Requests for his services on the North Carolina coast had been arriving at Governor Ellis's office since mid–April. On the 26th, Ellis appointed him brigadier general in the "Volunteer Forces" and put him in command of the state's coastal defenses.[38]

Although the state had not seceded, many North Carolinians had been preparing for war since the *Star of the West* expedition in January. On April 15, Fort Macon, near Beaufort, was seized by the state militia. The United States arsenal at Fayetteville was taken on April 27. By then, President Lincoln had added North Carolina to the states covered by the Union blockade.[39] North Carolina's General Assembly authorized $200,000 for the manufacture of weapons, empowered the governor to appoint a commissioner to the Confederate States, and authorized the recruitment of ten thousand "state troops" and twenty thousand volunteers. A provision was approved to accept at equal rank (at least) any officers resigning from the United States military.[40] Holmes established his headquarters at Wilmington. He, General W. H. C. Whiting, and Governor Ellis began planning for the defense of North Carolina's coast and inland waterways.[41]

During May, Holmes conducted an inspection tour of the North Carolina coast. He recommended that forts Caswell and Macon should be strengthened and supplies and reinforcements sent to New Bern, Wilmington, and either Morehead City or Caroline City. He observed that New Bern and Wilmington were of great importance. Both cities were ports with railroad links to Goldsboro. Should either city be occupied by Union forces, commerce with Europe would be lost and the Union army would have a direct invasion route to the interior of the state. Holmes recommended that a more experienced officer should be sent to command Fort Caswell, below Wilmington. While at Wilmington, he approved construction plans submitted by Maj. Charles Bolles. Bolles was building heavy artillery fortifications that would later become part of Fort Fisher.[42] Holmes left Wilmington on May 13 to evaluate New Bern and earthworks under construction south of the city.[43]

North Carolina's secession convention was convened in Raleigh and met for several days. On May 20, the delegates voted unanimously to dissolve "the Union now subsisting between the State of North-Carolina and the other States, under the title of the United States of America." North Carolina joined the Confederacy the same day.[44] While Holmes was at New Bern, a question about enlisting African American volunteers arrived at his headquarters. From Fayetteville, Lt. W. B. Ochiltree asked for a decision on the issue. Holmes's adjutant answered by advising the lieutenant, "You must confine yourself to the regulations and enlist only white men."[45]

Holmes sent reports to Governor Ellis from New Bern and Ocracoke on May 16 and 24. Construction on coastal defenses was lagging behind Holmes's schedule due to a shortage of laborers. He had been promised the arrival of "500 negroes to the works at Ocracoke and Hatteras early this week," but none had arrived. There were only twenty-five workers at the forts below New Bern. They were there only because a local colonel "put his own note in the bank to procure the money to support them." In the wake of the May 20 vote for secession, public enthusiasm for the war increased. Additional volunteer companies were forming in every town. Holmes asked the governor to "authorize me to call into service the volunteer com[panies] in New Bern and Washington [North Carolina]." He wanted to use them as laborers before they left to learn the business of soldiering at the camps of instruction.[46]

Holmes's May 24 report stated that four infantry companies had arrived at Ocracoke and Hatteras. Only one of the companies had weapons, and those were obsolete muskets. There was still no artillery at the unfinished earthworks. Holmes also revised one of his earlier recommendations about the use of a "flotilla of armed vessels in defense" of New Bern. He advised the governor that such a collection of ships would be useful in preventing Union "boat expeditions" but of no use if the proposed fortifications around New Bern fell to a land attack.[47]

Several days later, the adjutant general of North Carolina, John F. Hoke, divided the coastal defenses into northern and southern regions. Holmes was placed in command of the southern region, but was not able to accept the assignment. President Davis wanted him in Virginia. In early June, Davis promoted Holmes to brigadier general in the Provisional Army of the Confederate States and ordered him to Fredericksburg. He replaced Col. Daniel Ruggles and assumed "command of the troops in that vicinity."[48] Holmes had been in North Carolina for only one month, but he had done a credible job of beginning to prepare the coast for an invasion.

Prior to Holmes's arrival in Virginia, Colonel Ruggles had been given the task of defending the landing at the mouth of Aquia Creek on the Potomac River and the rail connection running from the landing through Fredericksburg and on to Richmond. General Robert E. Lee, military advisor to Jefferson Davis, believed the rail connections made Aquia Creek a likely place for a Union invasion of Virginia. Ruggles was also ordered to interrupt Union commerce along that portion of the Potomac River. Well-placed shore batteries in the area could discourage attacks, cause economic hardship in Washington, and result in political pressure on the Lincoln administration. By May 8, Confederate artillery was in place near the mouth of the creek.[49]

The shooting started at Aquia Creek before Holmes arrived. Union gunboats and Confederate shore batteries bombarded each other between May 29 and June 1. Confederate gunners scored hits on several Union vessels, but the wharf, railroad, and buildings at the landing were damaged. Fearing a large invasion when Union soldiers made a small amphibious landing, Ruggles sent several hundred men from Fredericksburg to Aquia Creek.[50] Holmes arrived at Fredericksburg four days later. He assumed command of a brigade consisting of the 1st Arkansas Infantry, the 2nd Tennessee

Infantry, and Walker's artillery. He soon moved his headquarters to Brooke's Station, five miles from the Aquia Creek landing. Ruggles, until his promotion and transfer in July, would remain in the area as one of Holmes's subordinate officers.

During his first month as a brigade commander, Holmes wrote instructions governing the conduct of his troops. He began General Order No. 2 with a warning about the gravity of the Confederacy's situation and the responsibilities borne by officers and enlisted men alike. The coming struggle, he said, was "not a war of boundaries, of glory or of military ambition, but of national and social existence." He specifically reminded his troops of the societal upheaval that most Southerners feared should the war be lost: "Everything dear to us is at stake.... On the morning of battle, think not of yourselves or your property, think of your aged parents, your wives, your children [being made] the slaves of slaves ... beneath the insults of a negro or yankee military governor." Regarding the treatment of enemy soldiers, Holmes told his men to "spare the prisoner and treat their sick and wounded as gently as your own."[51]

In great detail, Holmes's order gave instructions regarding the duties of his medical officers, quartermaster, commissary, guards, encampments, drill, camp equipment, and the amount of baggage allowed when the brigade was on the march. Every officer in the brigade was "expected to know and follow the Army Regulations and to instruct his men in them." He reminded his men to keep physically fit. "The duty of a soldier tests ... his moral and physical powers to the utmost."[52]

Holmes made clear his instructions regarding enlisted men fleeing from battle and officers who considered surrendering part of the brigade without orders from him. "During a battle no person shall leave the ranks under any pretext whatever without permission of the captain of his company. Anyone violating this regulation shall be put to death immediately by the file closers [company sergeants and lieutenants].... No order commanding any portion of the Brigade to lay down its arms shall be obeyed. Should any officer give such an order, the next in command shall immediately arrest him, killing him if necessary."[53]

Holmes intended that everyone under his command should hear and understand General Order No. 2. He ordered it to be read to the brigade at three successive formations and on the first day of every month thereafter. Richmond newspapers took notice of Holmes and liked what they saw. According to the *Daily Dispatch*, "General Holmes is undoubtedly a man of considerable military qualifications ... of firmness and decision without being morose or overbearing ... and has the entire confidence of his men."[54]

After touring his area and giving some thought to the likely intentions of the Union army, Holmes decided that his district would not be the first point of an attack in a campaign against Richmond. On June 15, he wrote to Adjutant and Inspector General Cooper and advised him that the railroad junction at Manassas was a more likely target than Aquia Creek. He offered to leave five hundred men at Aquia Creek and march with the rest of his brigade toward Manassas "or some other point where they can be made available, to resist the first great onslaught of the enemy." At General Cooper's direction, General Lee ordered Holmes to keep his brigade at Brooke's Station and Aquia Creek, but said, "It is, however, desired that you keep your command in condition to move at any point when required."[55]

A small Union raiding party landed at Mathias Point on June 25 and burned a private residence. Holmes advised Lee of the incident and theorized that the object of the raid had been to determine if earthworks for Confederate heavy artillery batteries were being constructed in the area. Mathias Point and Evansport had been considered as good locations for batteries that could impede Union river traffic to and from Washington. Holmes recommended to Lee that Evansport was the better location for that purpose. Roads from Fredericksburg and Manassas, converging at Evansport, offered quick reinforcement should the area be the object of a large amphibious landing. Holmes told Lee, "If you can send me two 32-pounders (rifled), or two 8-inch Columbiads, I believe I could stop the navigation on the river." Wherever the heavy guns were placed, both positions needed strengthening against attack. Under cover of a naval bombardment, another small Union force landed at Mathias Point on the 27th. One of Colonel Ruggles's majors, R. M. Mayo, and his men drove the attackers back aboard their boats.[56]

Holmes's Arkansas and Tennessee troops were stricken with measles and dysentery in June. His soldiers, like most Southerners, had lived on isolated farms all their lives and were especially susceptible to disease when crowded in camps. The epidemic sickened so many of his men that Holmes made arrangements for an additional hospital in Fredericksburg. He appointed a naval surgeon as his medical director.[57] General Lee approved the hospital expenditures within a day.[58] Lee and Holmes had spent years in the army watching soldiers die from lack of proper medical attention. Holmes was determined to keep his command in good health.

During June and July, Holmes, Lee, and General Beauregard communicated frequently about the best way to defend the Potomac River and northern Virginia. Recommendations for earthworks, artillery positions, and troop placements were passed back and forth. The three generals often disagreed on how best to deploy the area's meager troops and artillery. At one point, Holmes (reversing his previous offer to Lee) strenuously objected to a recommendation from Beauregard that Holmes's command should be divided.[59] Holmes wrangled with Lee for weeks over the placement of river defenses. Lee was polite but firm and Holmes did as he was ordered. The Confederacy intended to fight a defensive war. Holmes applied that strategy at the local level. He became obstinate when suggestions were made, without sufficient reason, to send part of his force away from his assigned area. In the absence of an emergency, he saw no reason to strengthen another general's command at the expense of his own. His stubbornness on this issue would be a trait wherever he commanded troops and would result in a great deal of criticism.

In an effort to have local insight and political pressure available, Holmes appointed a prominent Fredericksburg resident as a volunteer aide-de-camp. James Horace Lacy, "a gentleman of wealth in this city," was to act as Holmes's contact with General Beauregard "on any matters that may require concert of action between us."[60] Lacy could also pass along to Beauregard the concerns of Fredericksburg's influential citizens.

On July 6, General Holmes's efforts on behalf of his nephew, John Wetmore Hinsdale, resulted in the eighteen-year-old's commission as a 2nd lieutenant. Holmes had used his influence with Governor Ellis to secure the appointment and have Hinsdale assigned to his staff at Brooke's Station as an aide-de-camp. Holmes saw great promise in young Hinsdale and would keep him close, guiding his career, for the entire war.[61]

While Holmes was fortifying Aquia Creek, Union general Irvin McDowell was building an army at Alexandria, Virginia. Regular army, militia, and volunteer regiments were streaming into the Washington area. At a June 29 Federal cabinet meeting attended by other top Union generals, McDowell did as Holmes predicted. He proposed moving his army toward Richmond by way of Centerville and Manassas Junction. General Winfield Scott favored a campaign down the Mississippi River, but public pressure for a move directly against the Confederate capital resulted in the adoption of McDowell's plan.[62]

Horace Greeley's *New York Tribune* had been demanding military action since Fort Sumter's surrender. At the end of May, a *Tribune* reporter coined the phrase, "On to Richmond!" By mid–July, public pressure to start the campaign had become politically unbearable for President Lincoln's administration.[63] A reconnaissance mission to ascertain Confederate positions and strength fanned out from Alexandria. Within days, McDowell's army left camp and headed toward Centerville and Manassas.[64] The Union army was marching toward General Beauregard's twenty-two thousand men. Beauregard was expecting additional troops under the command of Joseph E. Johnston to move from the Shenandoah Valley and join him before the battle was fought.

Colonel John Wetmore Hinsdale, 1843–1921. General Holmes mentored Hinsdale throughout his military career and beyond. After the war, Hinsdale became a successful lawyer and businessman in North Carolina (courtesy Duke University, David M. Rubenstein Rare Book and Manuscript Library).

Confederate spies in Washington and newspaper reports on McDowell's plan let General Beauregard know of the campaign before it got underway. Neither McDowell nor any of his subordinate generals had led an army of this size, thirty-seven thousand men. Lack of organization, long wagon trains laden with unnecessary baggage, the straggling of undisciplined volunteers, and confusion slowed his army's pace. His troops managed to move only six miles on the first day.[65]

On July 17, McDowell's lead division skirmished with Confederate pickets, who quickly retreated. The next day, General Beauregard notified President Davis that his army "had fallen back on the line of Bull Run." Beauregard's position was eight miles long and drawn up along the west side of the creek. Another fight occurred at Blackburn's Ford, where a Union attack was repulsed. Beauregard called on Richmond to send reinforcements.[66]

Manassas, North Carolina's Coast and Virginia's Peninsula

At Brooke's Station, thirty miles from Manassas, General Holmes received orders from Adjutant and Inspector General Cooper on July 18: "General Beauregard is attacked. Move with three regiments and a light battery to support him."[1] Holmes ordered Virginia militia units attached to his command to guard Aquia Creek. He gathered his troops and began a forced march toward Manassas Junction. His brigade consisted of Col. James Fagan's 1st Arkansas Volunteers, the 2nd Tennessee Regiment, and six artillery pieces. They arrived at Union Mills on Bull Run Creek on the 20th, "perfectly broken down after a very fatiguing march."[2] The brigades of Holmes and Gen. Richard Ewell were designated as reserves and ordered to remain behind the right flank of the army. General Joseph Johnston's troops arrived later that day swelling the Confederate army to thirty-five thousand men.[3]

Beauregard's battle orders called for a dawn strike against the Union left flank on July 21. Holmes and Ewell were to support the initial attack, but that plan had to be abandoned. Before the attack could get underway, part of McDowell's army crossed Bull Run and struck the other end of the Confederate line. During the first part of the day's fighting, Beauregard was forced to turn his battle line almost ninety degrees. By noon, Holmes could tell that the battle had developed northwest of his position. As deaf as he was, he could hear that "the firing on our left became very heavy." For approximately two hours, he and Ewell waited for orders to move. Finally, both generals received word to "hasten forward as soon as possible."[4]

Holmes hurried his troops along a country road toward Warrenton Turnpike, crossed Flat Run Creek, and arrived at the army's field headquarters near the Lewis house. His soldiers made the eight-mile march "in good time" but arrived at the end of the battle. McDowell's army was in retreat toward Centerville. A bottleneck of Union infantry, artillery, and wagons at Cub Run bridge was beginning to transmit panic among the troops, but Holmes and Ewell had arrived too late on the field to pursue the opportunity. Holmes's "brigade was halted ... by order of General Johnston and did not participate in the fight."[5]

As the firing subsided, Confederate ambulances and wagons moved onto the field in front of Holmes's brigade. The teamsters were startled by several loud explosions of "shells in the boxes of a burnt artillery carriage which suggested the return of the enemy." The teamsters whipped their teams around and fled to the rear, past Holmes's troops, shouting that they were under attack. Holmes's brigade was "unmoved by the general panic which had seized upon the teamsters and instead of imitating their retreat, clamored for a forward movement" against the imaginary attack.[6] As the Union army's retreat turned into a rout, Holmes sent his artillery and Major John Scott's "Black Horse Cavalry" forward to join the pursuit. Holmes reported that the "fire of the [artillery] was exceedingly accurate, and did much execution." Scott's cavalrymen took a number of prisoners and captured equipment abandoned by the Union army.[7]

After the battle, generals Holmes and Ewell were criticized for not having arrived earlier on the Confederate left. An attack by two fresh Confederate brigades as the Union army retreated might have resulted in a more complete victory. Later inquiries revealed that an unidentified messenger had been given orders that, if delivered on time, would have brought both brigades to the Confederate left flank hours earlier. The messenger had left headquarters and disappeared. Neither Ewell nor Holmes received the order until later in the day.[8]

Holmes's brigade returned to its assignment of watching for Union gunboats and amphibious attacks along the Potomac and Rappahannock rivers. Artillery abandoned by the Union army at Manassas gave Holmes some of the heavy ordnance he needed. He selected five captured cannons, including a 30-pounder, to arm his river defenses. At the end of August, he began building earthworks at Evansport.[9] The work was made difficult by constant rain and duels with Union artillery that occurred "every two or three days." Holmes reviewed the 35th North Carolina regiment on August 20. One of the regiment's youngest officers, Lt. Walter Clark, wrote to his mother after seeing Holmes, "Gen-Holmes from N.C. (Pa's old acquaintance) is Commander of this Department, he reviewed our Regiment today; He is not an Adonis in beauty by any means." At the time, Holmes's brigade was the size of a division, more than eight thousand men. By the end of September, he commanded 9,407 soldiers.[10]

The Confederate government knew that another campaign against Richmond would be attempted. To provide a systematic defense of the capital, the army in northern Virginia needed well-defined areas of responsibility and clear chains of command. Holmes's original orders had given him authority over troops in the "vicinity of Fredericksburg." After Manassas, his area was designated the Department of Fredericksburg. As Confederate defensive strategy evolved in late summer and early fall, President Davis and Adjutant and Inspector General Cooper reorganized the forces in northern Virginia.

On October 7, Holmes was promoted to major general, the appropriate rank for a division commander. Joseph E. Johnston, a full general, was made commander of the Department of Northern Virginia on October 22. The department was then divided into three districts, each commanded by a major general. Major General T. J. "Stonewall" Jackson commanded the Shenandoah District, Major General Beauregard was assigned to the Potomac District, and Holmes's area was designated the Aquia District.[11]

The Aquia District embraced the Northern Neck area on the southwest side of the

Potomac River and the counties on either side of the Rappahannock River, from Chesapeake Bay to Fredericksburg.[12] Holmes's division consisted of ten regiments from North Carolina, Tennessee, Arkansas, and Virginia, and several Virginia Militia units. The troops were scattered between the Rappahannock, Aquia Creek, Brooke's Station, and Evansport. A brigade of four regiments at Evansport was commanded by General Isaac Trimble. Holmes's other regiments were commanded by colonels who reported directly to him. This arrangement forced Holmes to spend most of his time at Brooke's Station so communications from the colonels could reach him and be answered in a timely manner. If he was to move freely throughout the district, he needed to reorganize his chain of command.

In late October, Holmes requested permission to group his unattached regiments in two brigades. He recommended Col. John G. Walker's promotion to brigadier general and assignment to command Gen. Isaac Trimble's brigade at Evansport. Trimble was a talented and respected engineer officer, but Holmes pointed out that he was "entirely unacquainted with the management and maneuvering of troops." He wanted to transfer Trimble to the newly designated 1st Brigade, where his deficiencies would have less impact. (Trimble was an 1822 graduate of West Point but had resigned from the army in 1832.) Walker would command the 2nd Brigade. Holmes also recommended Col. George E. Pickett for promotion and command of the Virginia troops, the 3rd Brigade, stationed along the Rappahannock River.[13]

In an October letter to his cousin, John H. Overton, Holmes discussed the defensive "line of the Potomac." Holmes believed that if the South was going to win the war in Virginia, it needed to be done quickly. He told Overton, "The enemy is too strong both in numbers and position for us to attack on the Potomac." The Union army seemed to be biding its time in Virginia. Holmes observed, "As he delays the disparity will increase as most of our men are enlisted for one year while all of his are for the war."[14] Holmes recognized that the Confederate army's reliance on short-term enlistments would soon become a disadvantage. After First Manassas, the autumn of 1861 saw a sharp decrease in the number of Southerners volunteering for the army. The Confederate congress was beginning to grapple with the problem by offering a variety of enlistment incentives but was meeting with limited success. Veteran officers such as Holmes knew that if the war did not end quickly, the Confederacy would need to consider alternatives to an all-volunteer army.

On October 28, Holmes received a report from an informant, "Doctor Van Camp just from Washington," that sixty-five thousand Union soldiers would "land below Mathais Point tonight and that sixteen regiments are opposite Evansport." Van Camp told Holmes that the Union force would "march on Fredericksburg and Richmond."[15] No attack was made, but similar rumors were commonplace. Richmond and Washington were infested with spies like Van Camp. Neither capital could keep a secret. Newspapers in both cities frequently published reports of troop movements and rumors of planned campaigns. Commanders in each army gathered as many newspapers from enemy territory as possible. Holmes coordinated secret shipments of Northern newspapers to Richmond through the Aquia District.[16] Separating rumor from reliable information became increasingly difficult.

Frequently, Union gunboats steamed upriver from the Chesapeake Bay. They gathered information on defenses and shelled Confederate positions. On December 9, soldiers of Holmes's division exchanged gunfire with Union field artillery and gunboats.[17] On at least one occasion, Holmes made arrangements to have boats, loaded with stone, sunk in the Rappahannock River to discourage these attacks.[18]

Holmes also contended with a new method of intelligence gathering employed by the Union army. Observation balloons were watching his defenses at Aquia Creek and on the Rappahannock River. Observations made from an altitude of fourteen hundred feet enabled "aeronauts" to make accurate reports to Union commanders and, frequently, newspaper reporters.[19] Holmes could read about his own troop movements in the Northern newspapers that were smuggled to him. In reporting on an ascension of the observation balloon *Constitution*, a newspaper correspondent wrote, "rebel forces, under General HOLMES, are quartered up at Dumfries Creek, toward Manassas." The reporter went on to editorialize that Holmes's "troops recognize no principle as the basis for their antagonism, but apparently fight from an innate love of bloodshed."[20]

Southern soldiers, not at all familiar with ballooning, often misjudged the altitude, distance, and size of the balloons they saw. On one occasion, a North Carolina soldier wrote home that he had seen the "yankeys Balloon up last monday ... it was hy again as a tree." He estimated the distance to be eight or nine miles from where he was and that the balloon looked to be "a bout as big as a blanket spread out."[21] Confederate artillery frequently fired on the balloons, with little effect.[22] Holmes could do little about the balloons other than camouflage his batteries and move his troops at night.

In December, General Holmes became concerned with the morale of civilians on Northern Neck. Many of the men from this area had joined the army. The rest were in the militia and were augmenting Holmes's division with duty in his district. He advised General Cooper that the disruption of trade and prolonged absence of the community's men were causing "heavy stress on the women and children." He recommended that the militia companies should be disbanded and sent home. He offered to substitute one of his regiments stationed at Evansport for a regiment that had been raised in Northern Neck. The Northern Neck soldiers could then return to their community and do service there. He advised Cooper that the presence of the hometown regiment "would not fail to have a powerful moral[e] effect on the people and ... give them the protection of property they are so clamorous for."[23]

The year was drawing to a close and with it the likelihood of another campaign before spring. Most of Holmes's division went into winter quarters around Brooke's Station. The regiments rotated duty at outposts along the rivers. His command was described by a Richmond newspaper as being a "well organized and efficient division" containing "brigades which are in a fine statement [of] health."[24]

Holmes corresponded with the president of the University of North Carolina in January 1862. Mr. David Swain wanted to establish a "Military Attachment to the University" composed of students. Holmes advised him that the war was likely to last for "many years" and that there would be time enough for the students to serve their country after they graduated. He pointed out, "Immature youths are new encumbrances to the Service, filling the Hospitals, or excused from the more arduous duties of a Soldier in consequence of physical inability." He told Swain that the students, rather than being trained as soldiers, should be developed to their full potential as future leaders of the Confederacy.[25]

Holmes was dealing with a similar situation on a more personal level. His oldest son, seventeen-year-old Theo, was a student at the university. Theo was pressuring his father and Swain to be allowed to leave the university and join the army. In the same letter, Holmes thanked Swain for taking a personal interest in the boy and advised him, "I had great difficulty in dissuading him from entering the Army.... He has returned to you and promises to apply himself."[26] Holmes also "bribed" his son with a gold pocket watch. The agreement with Theo would last only a few months. Holmes was already keeping his nephew, John Hinsdale, out of combat with a staff position. He would soon need to make the same arrangements for Theo.

As the district's commander, Holmes had some responsibility for the security of the civilian population. The war was making Fredericksburg an "army town" complete with the problems generated by thousands of soldiers stationed nearby. The Aquia District and immediate vicinity contained more than thirteen thousand soldiers. Stragglers, deserters, prostitution, and barroom brawls made Fredericksburg a dangerous place and overwhelmed local law enforcement. In December, the mayor complained to Holmes about the "disorders" created by soldiers. Holmes issued orders on the 24th of that month forbidding his men from entering Fredericksburg unless authorized by their brigade commanders.[27]

In early January, Holmes created a military police force to patrol Fredericksburg. He appointed Lt. William J. Coleman of the 30th Virginia Regiment as the provost marshal. Coleman's soldiers were instructed to arrest "all soldiers found drunk or disturbing the peace." The sale of alcohol for non-medicinal purposes had already been forbidden by President Davis, but Holmes issued his own orders and closed all of Fredericksburg's bars. Coleman and his men routinely seized quantities of alcohol possessed by those whose "inclination and taste might induce them to violate ... the President's proclamation." In reporting on the creation of Coleman's provosts, the Richmond *Daily Dispatch* warned, "All soldiers found drunk or disrupting the peace are to be arrested and summarily disposed of."[28]

In addition to arresting soldiers for violations of civilian and military law, the provost guards were authorized to arrest civilians for purely political crimes: "suspicion of disloyalty" and "refusing to take the oath of allegiance." On one occasion, thirteen Fredericksburg citizens were arrested "by order of Maj.-Gen Holmes" for refusing to accept Confederate money and "belonging to a club of Unionists." A typical day's work for the provosts in March netted seven civilians and five soldiers.[29]

Confederate generals and politicians knew the spring of 1862 would bring another attempt to capture Richmond. Most Confederate volunteers had enlisted for a period of one year during the spring and summer of 1861. Their enlistments were due to end about the time Richmond would again be in danger. The volunteers wanted to get home in time for spring planting. They believed that the thousands of Southerners who had not yet volunteered should join the army and replace them. The Confederacy's efforts to spur enlistments and re-enlistments had not been sufficiently productive. Confederate generals did their best to convince soldiers to remain in the army.

On January 11, 1862, Holmes issued a statement to his division: "The Major General commanding this district urges upon the Troops the importance of promptly re-enlisting for three years or the war." He told his soldiers, "The present indications do not justify the belief that our struggle is near its end." He reminded his command that the enemy "craftily and surely bides the time when the present term of enlistment of our Troops expires, as the propitious moment for his advance." A Southern defeat, he said, would allow the Union to "triumphantly execute upon our undefended country the behests of the despotic advocates of Emancipation, who have inspired this horrid war. Our existence as a Nation, the very defense of our homes and the honor of our women forbids us to be laggards now."[30] On January 28, one of Holmes's regiments, the 1st Arkansas Infantry, re-enlisted en masse. The Richmond *Daily Dispatch* reported that the regiment was "the bravest of the brave, and the most gallant of the gallant, after many months of hard service. They are attached to Gen. Holmes's Brigade, on the Potomac."[31]

While Holmes worked to keep his soldiers in the army, he argued with his son about leaving school. In mid–February, the general received a letter from Theo. The young man had been suspiciously quiet for several weeks. Theo's letter began with an apology for not having written sooner but quickly reopened the issue of military service. He referred to North Carolina newspaper editorials critical of men "who have not gone in defense of their country."[32] In a roundabout manner, Theo reminded his father that he would turn eighteen the next December. At that age, he would be required to join the state militia or could volunteer for the army. The governor of North Carolina was already drafting men out of the state militia and sending them off to war.[33]

Several of Theo's classmates had dropped out of college and joined the army. Those left behind, including him, were not applying themselves: "there is no studying done here at all." Theo told his father he would like "to have a cadetship, but if you do not want me to have it I wish to go as a private." Theo ended his letter with the impassioned plea of a teenager: "Pa, my country needs me and everyone else she can get.... Even if it kills me, as you think it might, I would rather die in the service of my country than to stay at home and be looked on and avoided as a coward. Please sir, write immediately. Your loving son T. H. Holmes."[34]

General Holmes was trapped by his son's thinly veiled ultimatum. One way or another, Theo would be in the war within ten months. The general could either exercise some control over the situation or not. He contacted a friend in Richmond, Congressman Owen R. Kenan. Kenan wrote to President Davis on April 7 and recommended that Theo be appointed a "cadet in the Confederate Army." The request would spend several weeks in the Confederate bureaucracy. In the meantime, on April 9, Holmes appointed Theo as a civilian volunteer aide-de-camp and brought him to Brooke's Station.[35]

The winter months gave Holmes an opportunity to get his division in better shape. He arranged for Captain John Burton's permanent assignment as the division's quartermaster. Holmes had "detailed" Burton to division staff some months previously but was about to lose him. His regiment, the 1st Arkansas Infantry, was being transferred to Mississippi. Holmes saw potential in Burton and did not want him transferred away. When approved, Burton's assignment to Holmes's staff resulted in a promotion to major.[36] In March, when General Johnston conducted a review and inspection of the division, Holmes's efforts to improve his command were obvious. Johnston pronounced one of Holmes's regiments, the 35th Georgia Infantry, the best uniformed and drilled unit in the review.[37] Holmes also kept up with what was going on in North Carolina. He believed the Confederate government's obsession with protecting Richmond was allowing the Union army a free hand in his home state.

Union army activity in northeastern North Carolina, which began in August 1861, was reaching a crisis in March 1862. After the battle of Manassas, both the United States and the Confederacy had begun to realize that the war would not be won quickly. In the South, a defensive posture dominated strategy. In the North, capturing Richmond still overshadowed military thinking, but maintaining pressure on northern Virginia while opening a second front in eastern North Carolina offered a variety of advantages to Union strategists. The capture of North Carolina's coast would allow the Union army to attack Richmond from the north or south. Closing the seaports of Hatteras, New Bern, and Wilmington would restrict the Upper South's ability to import war material from Europe. Establishing strong military bases at these ports would enable an invasion to strike at North Carolina's vital north-south railroads. These rail lines were keeping the Confederate army in Virginia supplied from the coast and the Deep South. Northern military planners knew the Confederacy had to maintain a sizable army between Richmond and Washington, but attacking coastal North Carolina would divide Confederate resources by keeping thousands of troops tied up defending North Carolina's ports and rail lines.

Union general Benjamin Butler saw these strategic opportunities in August 1861 while leading an expedition against the city of Hatteras on North Carolina's Outer Banks. His fleet of nine warships and two troop transports captured forts Clark and Hatteras at Hatteras Inlet. The fall of these two forts closed the port and forced the Confederates to abandon other fortifications in the area. Butler's original orders were to capture the forts, obstruct the inlet, and withdraw. He saw, however, that by using Hatteras Inlet as a gateway to Pamlico and Albemarle sounds, the Union could attack many of North Carolina's port cities. The state's rivers and railroads could then become avenues for attacks farther inland. Ignoring part of his original orders, Butler left an occupying force at Hatteras Inlet and took his plan back to Washington. By late 1861, the Union army and navy were planning a joint operation against Albemarle Sound.[38] In February 1862, General Burnside captured Roanoke Island with an amphibious landing of ten thousand men. The fall of Roanoke Island opened northeast North Carolina and southeast Virginia to Union military operations. During the month of March, the port cities of Beaufort, Caroline City, and Morehead City were captured.[39]

The fall of New Bern, also in March, proved to be a particularly severe blow. New Bern was a thriving city near Pamlico Sound at the confluence of the Neuse and Trent rivers. Goods of all descriptions moved up and down the Neuse as far as Goldsboro. More significantly, a railroad line connected New Bern with Goldsboro, Raleigh, and finally Weldon near the Virginia border. Most railroad traffic from North and South Carolina crossed the Roanoke River bridge at Weldon, then went to Petersburg and Richmond to supply the Confederate army in Virginia. If New Bern fell, North Carolina's ability to import and distribute war material would be significantly reduced. Holmes had warned his superiors of this danger while commanding the North Carolina coast. He had spent enough time working on New Bern's defenses to know the dangers posed by an amphibious attack. He was reminded of Veracruz. If a Union army came ashore and moved quickly, New Bern could fall.

The fall of Roanoke Island, due in large part to the Confederacy's failure to reinforce the garrison sufficiently, demonstrated to North Carolinians that they could expect little help from Richmond. The commander of the Department of North Carolina, Gen. Richard C. Gatlin, one of Holmes's fellow officers in the 7th U.S. Infantry, was worried about attacks on Wilmington and New Bern, but New Bern was the next most likely target. Gatlin ordered the Pamlico District commander, Gen. Lawrence O'Bryan Branch, to strengthen defenses south of New Bern and along the Neuse River. He sent Branch the few troops he could spare, approximately forty-five hundred men, and some artillery. Branch obstructed the river below New Bern and mounted cannons at small forts along the river. He constructed a line of earthworks six miles south of town, from Bullen's Branch creek to the Neuse River and ending at Fort Thompson, which mounted thirteen cannons.[40]

Troop ships carrying Gen. Ambrose Burnside's twelve thousand Union soldiers left their base at Roanoke Island on March 11. They were joined by thirteen gunboats and steamed up the Neuse River toward New Bern the next day. Burnside landed his force on the west bank of the Neuse, well below Bullen's Branch and the Neuse River earthworks, on March 13. The next day, his force, accompanied by light artillery, advanced toward General Branch's main earthworks. In response to the quickly changing situation, Branch concentrated his troops by pulling regiments away from several fortifications along the river and reinforcing his main line facing south. A "special battalion" of North Carolina State Militia, approximately three hundred men under the command of Colonel H. J. B. Clark, was organized at New Bern. They were placed in the center of the Confederate position near the railroad tracks and a brickyard.[41]

While constructing his defensive position and placing his regiments, Branch would have preferred a straight, unbroken line of breastworks and troops facing the Union advance. Between Fort Thompson, near the river, and the railroad tracks, Branch's North Carolina regiments presented a solid line consisting of the 7th, 27th, 35th, and 37th regiments, and several pieces of light artillery. In the center of the line, near the railroad and brickyard, was an artillery position with two 24-pounders and Colonel Clark's Special Militia Battalion.[42]

Unfortunately for the Confederates, when the 26th North Carolina Troops arrived on the Confederate right flank, they found that their position was neither on line with nor connected to the rest of the Confederate earthworks.[43] Several hundred yards of swamp was open between them and the artillery and militia. Branch posted the 33rd North Carolina Regiment on the railroad tracks four hundred yards to the rear of this weak spot. At the brickyard, the two 24-pounders had been delivered but were not mounted on their carriages. Until mounted, they were useless.[44]

On the morning of March 14, Union infantry advanced with two brigades, followed closely by General John G. Parke's brigade in reserve. General John G. Foster's brigade moved toward the strong Confederate left. General Jesse Lee Reno's brigade went against the 26th North Carolina Regiment on the Confederate right. Foster's attack stalled under heavy fire from the North Carolina infantry regiments and artillery. As the battle developed, it became apparent that the least trained and experienced soldiers, the militia, occupied the weakest part of the Confederate battle line.[45] Realizing that the Confederate left could not be taken by frontal assault, Foster satisfied himself with keeping the Confederates in front of him busy and replacing his first engaged regiments with fresh units from Parke's reserve. On the Union left, Reno's brigade was doing much better.[46]

Reno's troops first attacked the 26th North Carolina Regiment. The 26th held firm, but Union officers quickly noticed the unoccupied portion of the Confederate line. Reno ordered his men to that area and toward the brickyard where the militia was posted. Confederate artillerists were working feverishly to lift the heavy cannons onto their carriages. As soon as they saw Union soldiers advancing against their useless guns, they fled and left the militia completely exposed. Reno's soldiers occupied the gap between the 26th North Carolina and Clark's militiamen. They began firing on the militia from the front and right.[47]

At first, the militiamen held their position and fired several volleys. When they were outflanked, they began a disorganized retreat. Colonel Clark steadied his men briefly and even considered a counterattack. Most of the militiamen were armed with civilian rifles and shotguns, but some carried military muskets with bayonets. Clark gave the command that "caused bayonets to be fixed." Almost as soon as he gave the order, he realized that his men would be slaughtered if they attacked alone and unsupported. His battalion was now taking fire from the front, right, and rear, where Union sharpshooters had managed to get behind his right flank. He ordered a retreat, which quickly became a stampede under increasing Union fire. Clark managed to rally a few of his men approximately sixty yards to the rear, but they fled again when a rumor swept through their ranks that other North Carolina regiments were retreating as well.[48]

Before they left the fight, four of Clark's militiamen were killed and fifteen were wounded.[49]

General Branch mounted a successful counterattack by shifting the 37th and 7th North Carolina regiments toward the 35th Regiment, which was now exposed by the rout of the militia. The men of 35th, like the militia, found themselves taking fire from two directions. They retreated "in the utmost disorder."[50] The 33rd North Carolina Regiment was brought forward to support the exposed left of the 26th Regiment. The 26th was pouring a deadly fire into the Union soldiers who had initially broken through. The battle raged for three hours, but before noon, Union commanders had counterattacked and broken the Confederates at the brickyard. As the North Carolina regiments were pushed back, more Union troops poured into the breached Confederate line. Branch realized the fight was lost and ordered the retreat of his entire force.[51]

The Confederates fell back, crossed the Trent River bridge and set it on fire. General Branch hoped he could make another stand near New Bern, but Union gunboats had fought their way past the river obstructions and Fort Thompson and were approaching town. Branch knew that Union infantry would soon be ferried across the Trent River. He ordered all military supplies in the town to be burned and moved most of his army toward Tuscarora, eight miles away. The evacuation of New Bern was chaotic. Panic seized the Confederates as they fought to board the last train leaving the city. There was no coordinated effort to burn the military equipment left behind. A great deal of the army's weapons, munitions, and camp gear fell into Union hands.[52]

The inadequate and defective fortifications south of New Bern had worried General Holmes the previous May. As he had warned, the city fell to a land attack. His low opinion of untrained militia troops was sustained, but a regiment of North Carolina volunteers had fled along with the militia. The loss of New Bern forced the abandonment of territory all the way to Southwest Creek, east of Kinston, and would vex the Confederacy and Holmes for the remainder of the war.

Too late to save New Bern, the Confederacy finally realized the strategic implications of the situation in North Carolina. On March 23, 1862, General Holmes, along with Walker's and Wilcox's brigades, was transferred away from the Aquia District for duty in North Carolina, "temporarily with General Lee." From Richmond, Lee would supervise Holmes in North Carolina as he had in Virginia.[53] Additional orders were issued the next day. Holmes was appointed commander of the Department of North Carolina. Regiments assigned to his command were ordered to gather at Goldsboro. Orders from Lee directed Holmes to defend Goldsboro and Wilmington and to protect the state's railroads leading to Virginia.[54] The transfer of Holmes and his troops coincided with the Confederate army's pull-back from the Potomac River line. Holmes had received orders on March 8 to move back toward the Rappahannock River.[55] The repositioning of the army along the south bank of the Rappahanock River was designed to reduce the length of the defensive front and compact Confederate forces.

Including troops already assigned to the state, Holmes assumed command of approximately twenty-eight thousand men, twice the troop strength of the Aquia District.[56] He issued his first orders within days of arriving at Goldsboro. Most of General Order No. 7, issued on March 25, reflected the military philosophy expected of a veteran army officer, but the first few lines were a call to the civilian population as well. (General Orders from army commanders were routinely printed in newspapers.) He warned of the imminent advance of the enemy and added, "If we do not defeat him North Carolina will be under his worse than vandal despotism." He called on the people of North Carolina to give themselves up, "body and mind, to the sacred duty" of their state's defense.[57]

The rest of the order reminded his officers and enlisted men that Holmes was a professional officer, a product of West Point and the tradition of unquestioned obedience to superiors. Under Holmes, the chain of command would be strictly followed: "The strictest discipline must be preserved.... The commanders of companies, regiments and brigades are required to enforce the most exact obedience to all orders and regulations." He further ordered his subordinate officers to initiate a "most active system of drills.... Every commanding officer is held responsible that his command is ready to march at a moment's notice."[58] Typical of "state's rights" Southerners of the period, Holmes loved his home state. He was loyal to North Carolina, more so than to the Confederacy, even more so than to the United States Army in which he had served for so many years. But, before everything except his family and his religion, Theophilus Hunter Holmes was an "army" man.

General Holmes conducted several inspection tours during his first weeks in North Carolina. The loss of Roanoke Island and New Bern were near death-blows to the Confederacy's ability to defend the state's coast against General Burnside's increasingly aggressive army. While Holmes was glad to be back in North Carolina, he was not optimistic about his ability to be successful in the new assignment. There were not enough troops assigned to defend the state, much less retake New Bern and Roanoke Island. There were not enough weapons to arm the troops he had. On one occasion, Lee suggested that Holmes arm some of his soldiers with spear-like "pikes" instead of firearms.[59] The state's civilian population was demoralized. Holmes reported that "indifference to our cause" and despondency were emerging among civilians.[60] There was friction between the state and Confederate governments dating back to the loss of Roanoke Island. Furthermore, Holmes had arrived in the early spring. Lee would soon be pressuring him to send troops to Virginia in anticipation of the Union army's next attempt to capture Richmond.

Lacking sufficient Confederate troops for his task, Holmes looked to the state military force for help. On March 29, he authorized Gen. David Clark, of the North Carolina State Militia, to assume responsibility for defending the Roanoke River and commanding the militia regiments in Bertie, Martin, and Washington counties. He also authorized Clark to seize civilian wagons, draft animals, and boats for troop and supply movements. General Clark was no stranger to North Carolina's problems. Since late 1861, he had been traveling between northeastern North Carolina, Raleigh, and Norfolk, Virginia, in search of arms and ammunition.[61]

Early in his correspondence with Lee, Holmes revealed his misgivings and lack of self-confidence. On March 27, he told Lee, "I am oppressed with the responsibility upon me." He asked Lee to come to North Carolina and "straighten out this tangled yarn." If Lee could not come, Holmes suggested that General Gustavus Smith be sent and said, "I will assist him in every way possible, and will be pleased to serve under him."[62]

Amid his growing pessimism and self-doubt, Holmes did what he could. He began moving brigades and individual regiments to different locations. He wanted to maximize his ability to watch Union movements and transport soldiers to trouble spots more quickly. He strengthened Wilmington's defenses with additional troops and construction. He wanted to attack New Bern if proper preparations could be made, but Lee was more worried about Union attacks on Wilmington, Norfolk, and later, Fredericksburg. Lee also suggested that Holmes send more troops to defend the railroad bridge across the Roanoke River at Weldon, North Carolina.[63]

Militarily, the state's situation continued to deteriorate. The Union navy was transporting army units along the coast and attacking at will. By early April, detachments of Burnside's army had occupied Washington, North Carolina, and laid siege to Fort Macon. Holmes made arrangements to purchase privately owned weapons for his soldiers as "none can be had unless they are paid for at the time."[64] Southern volunteers were coming forward at this time by the thousands. They had, to a large extent, been coerced into the army by the impending passage of the Confederate conscription law, generous bounties offered to volunteers, and their choice of regiments. Camp diseases were sweeping through regiments assembling at camps around Raleigh. Civilian and military hospitals were full of sick soldiers. New regiments could not move until they were up to strength. There were just enough weapons to arm the guards at the Raleigh camps of instruction. The recruits had to be guarded to prevent them from deserting their disease-ridden quarters.[65]

In April, Holmes became involved with an effort to establish an additional military hospital at Raleigh. Doctor N. S. Crowell, the Confederacy's North Carolina medical director, and surgeon Thomas Hill, approached Holmes with a plan to assume control of Raleigh's St. Mary's School and convert its buildings to a hospital. Holmes initially supported the plan, but St. Mary's founder, Rector Albert Smedes, appealed the decision. Holmes and surgeon Hill developed an alternative plan to use an unfinished building at Peace Institute. Hill wrote, "General Holmes' orders were to hurry up matters and, if necessary, to impress every able-bodied man in Raleigh and put him to work and get the building ready."[66]

Holmes reported to Lee that he had an effective force of fourteen thousand men, but three of his regiments were "raw recruits." He estimated Burnside's effective strength at "about 20,000 with ten gunboats in the Neuse and Trent Rivers."[67] Holmes's first duty was to protect the railroads from attack by Burnside's main force at New Bern. He did not have enough troops to hold Burnside at New Bern and attempt to relieve Fort Macon, much less to react to amphibious attacks elsewhere. On April 15, Lee gave

Holmes permission to evacuate Fort Macon, but by that time, Macon was surrounded and the garrison could not escape.[68] If eastern North Carolina was to be saved, sooner or later New Bern would have to be recaptured. To that end, Holmes was having maps prepared of the approaches to the city. He offered them to Lee "as the last service I can render to the general you must send here to command." Holmes again asked to be relieved: "I know my deficiencies.... All my life has been passed in executing the orders of others; send therefore a superior to me, or else change me for another who is capable, or who has his own as well as your confidence.... I can execute, but I cannot originate."[69]

Holmes commanded five brigades consisting of twenty-two infantry regiments, two cavalry regiments, and eight artillery batteries. Four of the brigades were commanded by brigadier generals Robert Ransom, J. R. Anderson, Lawrence O'Bryan Branch, and John G. Walker. In the District of the Cape Fear, Brigadier General Samuel French had three infantry regiments and twenty companies of infantry, cavalry, and artillery. Most of the regiments were from North Carolina, but units from South Carolina, Georgia, Virginia, Arkansas, Mississippi, and Louisiana were under Holmes's command as well. His rosters showed 26,432 officers and enlisted men, of whom 8,485 were sick in camp or absent from their units.[70]

One of Burnside's brigades struck on April 19 at South Mills near Elizabeth City. The objective was to threaten Norfolk and destroy the Dismal Swamp Canal. The Union force was transported from New Bern to Elizabeth City by troop ships. They disembarked, marched approximately sixteen miles, were repulsed by a small local Confederate force, returned to their ships, and started back to New Bern. All of this was accomplished within twenty-four hours, allowing no time for a coordinated Confederate response.[71]

Weeks before the battle at South Mills, General George McClellan had started landing his army, one hundred thousand men strong, in Virginia. He began the Peninsular Campaign to capture Richmond on March 17. For the next three months, Confederate attention and resources would be directed toward saving the nation's capital. Holmes was in an impossible situation. He sent numerous requests to Lee between March 27 and April 30 for more soldiers, weapons, and transportation. During the same period, Lee began removing troops from North Carolina to defend Richmond.[72] The war and the Confederacy's manpower shortage were reaching a crisis point.

The Confederate congress began debating compulsory military service in early 1862. There was strong opposition to the plan. Many congressmen felt that if there was to be a draft, the states should pass laws individually.[73] National conscription was completely contrary to the concept of state's rights. But by March, with McClellan's huge army on the Virginia peninsula, the capture of Richmond was becoming a very real possibility. Enlistments for one hundred forty-eight Confederate regiments were due to expire beginning in May. The number of soldiers reenlisting was not expected to be enough to save Richmond. Men who had not enlisted during the first eight months of the war were not entering the army in sufficient numbers.[74]

While the immediate crisis was in Virginia, the South needed more soldiers everywhere. In southwestern Tennessee, the Confederate army suffered ten thousand casualties at Shiloh in April as the Union army maneuvered to gain control of the Mississippi River.[75] Congress faced a stark choice: pass a conscription law or lose the war. When the final vote was taken, conscription passed with a large majority. On April 16, President Davis signed the act into law. All twelve-month volunteers currently in the army were required to remain for an additional two years. Civilian men between the ages of eighteen and thirty-five were to be enrolled for three years. Unless exempted, they could expect to be sent to camps of instruction within weeks.[76]

The immediate effect of the conscript law was that the Confederacy would not lose the twelve-month volunteers. General Johnston's army would remain intact and in the field for the fight against McClellan. The conscription camps of instruction would not produce large numbers of conscripts until July, but publicity surrounding the conscription debate had a profound effect on volunteering. The inevitability of army service induced thousands of Southerners to enlist between March and June. They took advantage of generous enlistment bounties that would soon end.[77] In North Carolina, General Holmes could use new recruits to replace some of his veteran regiments that were being sent to Virginia. His troop strength would not increase, but perhaps he could hold Union forces at bay during McClellan's Peninsular Campaign.

The same day President Davis signed the conscription law, Holmes issued General Order No. 19 to his department. He told his soldiers they would have to stay in the army for two more years. He explained in detail how the law would be implemented with regard to furloughs and electing new officers. Mindful of their disappointment, he told his veterans, "At the very crisis of our struggle, with vast armies of the enemy threatening to overrun the valley of the Mississippi and pressing to the gates of the Capital, the Chief Magistrate and Congress of the Confederacy respond to the unanimous voice of the country and insist that her trained soldiers shall not forsake her until the battle is fought and independence is won."[78]

As the commander of Confederate troops in North Carolina, a personal friend of President Davis, and the son of a former governor, Holmes had political influence in the state. He believed that conscription, if enforced efficiently, could produce enough troops for the South to win the war. To ensure that North Carolina would be successful in the effort, Holmes considered how conscription should be managed and who should manage it. He decided that Peter Mallett, the son of another prominent Fayetteville family, was the man who should oversee conscription in North Carolina. He started recommending Mallett to politicians and high-ranking army officers as soon as the conscription law was passed.

General Lee continued to transfer Holmes's troops to Virginia. The 34th and 38th North Carolina regiments boarded trains for Richmond on April 23.[79] The next few weeks saw Lee constantly pressuring Holmes for more troops in Virginia and at Weldon. He requested that Holmes send to Fredericksburg "an engineer and an ordnance officer whose services can be spared." Holmes agreed to send an engineer major, but advised

Lee, "Colonel Deshler is the only ordnance officer I have and he cannot be spared, as he is also my chief of artillery."[80]

James Deshler was a West Point graduate, class of 1854. He had come to Holmes's staff after recovering from leg wounds received at the battle of Allegheny Mountain, Virginia. Holmes liked Deshler, respected his ability, and needed a good artillery officer. Deshler joined John Hinsdale and Theo on the general's staff in April. Theo did routine administrative work and acted as a courier. In May, he was sent to Fayetteville with ten thousand dollars to purchase "public animals" for the Department of North Carolina.[81]

North Carolina's troop strength had been reduced by twenty percent since Holmes took command. He supposed that General Burnside might advance from New Bern in conjunction with McClellan's Peninsular Campaign.[82] In April, he reported sixteen thousand men ready for duty, out of twenty-two thousand aggregate.[83] On April 25, Fort Macon surrendered after a month-long siege. The port of Beaufort was closed.

On the Virginia peninsula, McClellan's army was preparing to bombard Yorktown with siege guns. General Joseph Johnston stalled McClellan as long as he could, but finally evacuated the city on May 3. The battle of Williamsburg was fought on May 5, but overwhelming numbers forced the Confederates to withdraw. Johnston's army, approximately fifty-five thousand men, began its retreat toward Richmond. They were withdrawing in the face of a Union army nearly twice their size. On May 8, Holmes sent Gen. J. R. Anderson's brigade from North Carolina to Virginia.[84]

On May 13, General Lee contacted the governor of North Carolina. Almost apologetically, he told a skeptical Henry Clark, "The surest way to protect North Carolina from invasion is to drive the enemy from Virginia."[85] Lee told Clark that further reductions of Holmes's force would be necessary. Lee was aware that conscription was compelling

Brigadier General James Deshler. Holmes kept Deshler on his staff or in his commands in Virginia, North Carolina, and Arkansas. When exchanged after his capture at Fort Hindman, Deshler was promoted to brigadier general and transferred to Patrick Cleburne's division, Army of Tennessee (Library of Congress).

thousands of enlistments in North Carolina. He reminded the governor that Holmes's veteran regiments sent to Virginia could be replaced with the new regiments assembling at Raleigh. Like Holmes, Clark was worried about the Union army at New Bern. He remained frustrated that he could not stop the transfer of North Carolinians to Virginia.[86] By the end of May, only two of Holmes's five brigades were still in the state.

In Virginia, General Johnston wanted the regiments stationed at Petersburg sent toward the fight against McClellan. On May 23, he requested that four more North Carolina regiments under Gen. James G. Martin be sent to Petersburg. Johnston also placed Holmes in command of the railroad lines between Weldon and Petersburg. (The rail lines between Wilmington and Weldon were already part of Holmes's command.)[87] Holmes's area of responsibility was being extended in order to facilitate the rapid movement of North Carolina men and equipment to the Richmond area. He was coming under increasing pressure to make the fight to save Richmond his primary concern no matter what Burnside might do at New Bern.

On May 30, Secretary of War George Randolph ordered Holmes to bring most of the rest of his division to Petersburg. On his arrival, Holmes was to meet with Lee in Richmond and report to General Johnston by letter.[88] Johnston was east of Richmond and about to attack the smaller part of McClellan's army south of the Chickahominy River. The battle of Seven Pines (Fair Oaks) began the next day with uncoordinated Confederate attacks. Union reinforcements counterattacked, and General Johnston was seriously wounded. General Gustavus Smith took temporary command, and the day's fighting ended. President Davis put Robert E. Lee in charge of Johnston's army on June 1. Lee ordered the army to return to its previous position.[89]

Davis had put Lee in command of the "armies in Eastern Virginia and North Carolina." In Davis's letter to Lee, the president kept his options open. In western Virginia, Lee's first combat command of the war had been a failure. Davis told Lee that his new command would be in addition to his duties as military advisor to the president, "but only so far as to make you available for command in the field of a particular army." Davis used the word "temporarily."[90] Lee's appointment to command would prove to be one of the major factors that changed the course of the American Civil War. The passage of conscription kept the Confederate army in the field and would provide enough soldiers to fight a protracted war. In short order, Robert E. Lee would use those troops to save Richmond and dash Union hopes of defeating the Confederacy in 1862.

Since arriving in Richmond and reporting to Lee and Johnston, Holmes had been traveling between Petersburg and Goldsboro as his troops moved to Virginia. On June 18, General Lee notified him that General Burnside and fourteen thousand soldiers had sailed from New Bern to reinforce McClellan. Lee warned Holmes that McClellan could send Burnside up the James River toward Richmond's key defenses at Drewry's Bluff. He told Holmes, "It will be necessary to oppose him with your whole force.... Concentrate at or near Petersburg, so as to have your command available to move speedily to the threatened point."[91] (Lee's information about Burnside and the warning to Holmes would prove to be accurate, but premature. Burnside's force did not leave New Bern until July 6.)[92] By June 21, Holmes had his division posted between Petersburg and Bermuda Hundred. Lee told Holmes to attack any Union troops that landed and to be prepared to cross the river should he be needed on the peninsula.[93]

Lee also expanded Holmes's territory to include "the south bank of the James River, including Drewry's Bluff." He ordered Holmes to "establish his headquarters at Petersburg or at some other point."[94] The order drew Holmes directly into the Peninsular Campaign. His division was to protect the southern edge of the peninsula along the banks of the James River. With half of New Bern's Union garrison believed to have been transferred to the peninsula, Holmes could worry less about defending North Carolina against a campaign launched from the coast.

During the battle of Mechanicsville on June 26, Secretary of War Randolph ordered Holmes to cross the river and join the right flank of Lee's army.[95] Just then, Randolph and Holmes received information that Union forces were landing at City Point and Bermuda Hundred. Randolph sent John Walker's brigade from Holmes's division to investigate and delayed sending the rest of Holmes's troops across the river for two days during the battle of Gaines's Mill. Randolph wanted to keep part of Holmes's division available south of the James while Walker and Holmes investigated the landings.[96] By keeping Holmes south of the river, the small Union landings prevented most of his division from getting on the Union left flank for a critical forty-eight hours. The delay proved significant. Lieutenant General Richard Taylor would later observe that Holmes "reached the Newmarket road [River Road] a day later than was intended."[97]

The Union landings proved to be insignificant. Holmes returned to Drewry's Bluff on June 28. The next day, while the battle of Savage's Station raged several miles to the northeast, the remainder of his division (minus General Ransom's brigade, which had been detached to serve under General Benjamin Huger) crossed the river on a pontoon bridge, at Warwick's Bar, two miles above Drewry's Bluff.[98] Holmes headed toward the community of New Market on River Road. His division consisted of two brigades, a total of nine regiments (five from North Carolina, two from Virginia, and one each from Arkansas and Georgia), plus artillery and cavalry. His force was strengthened the next day by Virginia Brigadier General Henry Wise's seven hundred fifty men and two artillery batteries. Holmes now had six thousand infantrymen and six batteries.[99] Cadet Theo Holmes accompanied the troops as part of his father's staff.[100] John Hinsdale was detached from Holmes's staff to serve with another brigade. Colonel Deshler was Holmes's artillery commander.

At 10:00 A.M. on June 30, in compliance with General Lee's orders, Holmes halted his division at New Market near the intersection of the River Road and Long Bridge Road. Holmes's position was "shortly afterward inspected and approved" by President Davis.[101] Colonel Laurence S. Baker of the 1st North Carolina Cavalry joined Holmes with two cavalry regiments. They took position in order to warn of any approaching Union force. Holmes's orders were to wait at New Market for the arrival of the Union army and disrupt their passage. McClellan's troops were in full retreat, heading for Harrison's Landing and the protection of Union gunboats on the river. Holmes's men

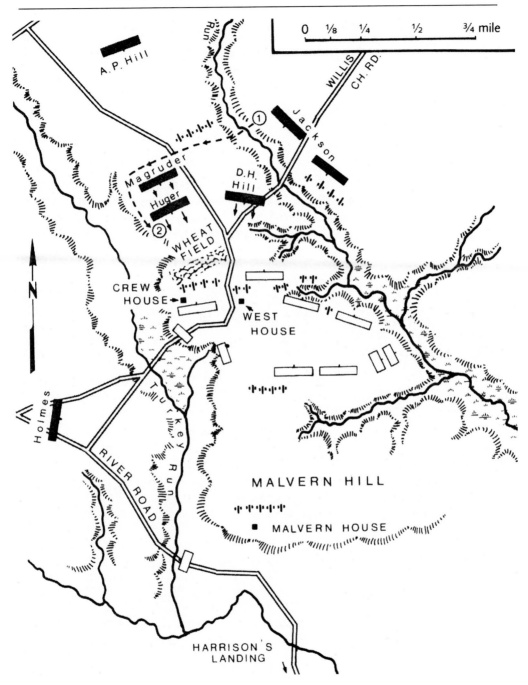

Union and Confederate positions around Malvern Hill. On June 30, 1862, Holmes's division left the position shown, advanced down River Road toward Turkey Run Creek and was bombarded by Union field artillery and gunboats on the James River. That night, Holmes returned his division to its former position (Gary Gallagher, *Stephen Dodson Ramseur, Lee's Gallant General*, 1995, courtesy of the University of North Carolina Press).

heard the battle of Frayser's Farm (Glendale) begin at 3:00 P.M., when the divisions of A. P. Hill and James Longstreet launched their attacks. He held his position for the next several hours. No retreating Union troops arrived at New Market.[102]

Confederate army engineer Maj. R. K. Meade was observing Federal activity on River Road in the vicinity of Malvern Hill. At 4:00 P.M., he notified General Holmes that the enemy was "retreating in considerable confusion along the road leading over Malvern Hill" nearly three miles distant. Meade suggested that some of Holmes's artillery, the long-range rifled guns in particular, could be sent forward to shell the hill. Meade's immediate superior, Maj. W. H. Stevens, agreed.[103] Realizing that he had been told to wait at the wrong location, Holmes ordered Colonel Deshler to move six rifled guns and a regiment of infantry toward the west side of Malvern Hill. If Deshler's artillery fire could further confuse the enemy, a follow-up attack could be made with the entire division. Soon after the artillery got underway, Holmes and the rest of his force started down River Road.[104]

After moving his command about two miles, Holmes encountered General Lee, who was personally scouting the Union position. Previously, Lee had been warned by one of Gen. Daniel Harvey Hill's staff officers that, if properly defended, Malvern Hill could be impregnable.[105] Like Holmes, Lee had heard reports of Union confusion on Malvern Hill. He approved Holmes's troop movement and instructed him to fire on the Federals when the division was deployed.[106] Lee may have been under the impression that General John B. Magruder's thirteen thousand men were approaching Holmes's position. General Longstreet had sent orders to Magruder to reinforce Holmes.[107]

Neither Lee nor Holmes knew that Malvern Hill, rather than being the scene of great confusion, was the gathering place for one hundred cannons, the Union army's reserve artillery. Two infantry divisions under the command of Gen. Fitz John Porter were deployed on the hill as well. Porter had approximately twenty thousand men.[108] His skirmishers and signal posts saw the clouds of dust created when Holmes's division started moving toward them. Flag-waving signalmen notified Union gunboats that they should steam to a point close to River Road and shell the Confederates.[109] Union sailors were spoiling for a fight. As they got underway, one gunboat hoisted a black flag.[110]

Malvern Hill was surrounded by gently sloping farmland except on its steep western side, called Malvern Cliffs. The broad top of the hill was an open plateau running approximately one and a quarter miles north to south by three quarters of a mile east to west. Generals Sykes and Morell of Porter's corps had been deploying their divisions on Malvern Hill since before noon. Hundreds of stragglers from different regiments and dozens of wagons had also crowded into the area. This was the "confusion" that was reported to Holmes and Lee.

Union officers were still positioning their regiments when Deshler's artillery shells began exploding on Malvern Hill. Soldiers caught out in the open ran for cover. Union gunners quickly brought thirty of their cannons into action. They opened fire on Deshler's artillery, which was in plain sight approximately one thousand yards away. Union army signalers notified their counterparts onboard gunboats *Galena* and *Aroostook* of

Holmes's position. From atop ship masts, signalers shouted directions and ranges to naval cannoneers on the decks below: "Fire one mile to the right." "Good shot." "Fire low and into the woods near the shore."[111]

The return fire from Union batteries told Deshler's artillerists that they were severely outgunned. Deshler held the position for an hour but was taking heavy casualties among his horses and men. He ordered a retreat. Seventeen of his artillerymen had been wounded and two caissons had been "blown up."[112] While Deshler's artillery was being driven from the field, the gunboats concentrated their fire on Holmes's infantry, which was still deploying. Many of the soldiers in Holmes's division had never been under artillery fire of any kind. The one-hundred-pound naval shells screeching overhead and exploding terrified many of them. As Deshler's artillery and some cavalrymen fled back up River Road, they ran into Holmes's infantry.[113]

The 45th and 50th North Carolina Infantry regiments were caught up in the panic produced by the bombardment and the retreating artillery and cavalry. The cavalrymen fled across a roadside plank fence and knocked it down on top of men in the 50th North Carolina Troops. They had been ordered to take shelter by lying down in the sunken roadway. While the officers and men tried to clear the road, the regiment's color-bearer, thinking perhaps to inspire his comrades, planted the regiment's flag on the crest of a nearby hill in plain view of the Union gunboats. The naval gunners immediately directed additional fire onto this part of Holmes's division.[114]

It was at about this time, according to Gen. Daniel Harvey Hill, that General Holmes came out of a nearby house where he had his temporary headquarters. He cupped his hand to his ear and remarked, "I thought I heard firing." General Hill was not present when the incident supposedly occurred. Hill later credited the story to Gen. Junius Daniel. Daniel left no record of the incident and was killed in 1864. Holmes, indeed, was quite hard of hearing, and the incident could have occurred as Hill reported. Holmes's comment could have been an attempt at self-deprecating humor about his deafness.[115]

Unlike the long, gently rising open fields over which Lee's assault on Malvern Hill would be made the next day, Holmes's avenue of attack against Malvern Cliffs faced low areas of swamp and steep hillsides. The advance down River Road had cost his division only two men killed and forty-nine wounded, but it demonstrated the danger posed by the gunboats and the strength of the Union position. Holmes had been expecting either General Huger or General Magruder to arrive with reinforcements, but those troops were still some distance away. During the afternoon, Major General James Longstreet sent Magruder a message, "Please hurry as much as possible. General Holmes has been expecting you a long time and is in much need of you."[116]

During the advance down River Road, one of Magruder's staff officers appeared and asked Holmes where Magruder should position his troops. It was too late. Additional hours would be needed for Magruder's division to arrive, deploy, and participate in the attack. Holmes was nearly speechless with rage.[117] A courier from General Huger arrived at Holmes's headquarters as well. The courier advised Holmes that Huger's troops were en route but still three miles away. Holmes told the courier, "Go back and tell General Huger that he is entirely too late. He should have been here three hours ago."[118]

Holmes called off the attack. Had he continued, his men would have charged over difficult ground, late in the day, vastly outnumbered, in the face of overpowering artillery fire. He later described that option as "perfect madness."[119] When the Union bombardment ended at sundown, he withdrew toward New Market to await orders. The area around New Market was out of artillery range and was a good defensive position should McClellan launch a counterattack. Holmes's division took no part in the larger battle the next day. Historians most commonly describe Holmes's advance down River Road as a "feeble attempt" to turn the Union flank. General McClellan was not at Malvern Cliffs during Holmes's attack. In his testimony before the War Committee about the campaign, however, he referred to the affair as "a pretty serious attack."[120]

The next day, Lee, still determined to destroy McClellan's army, was unable to make a coordinated attack. Union artillery dominated the field all day and by 3:30 P.M. had silenced most Confederate batteries. Union gunners then concentrated their fire on Lee's confused infantry attacks. The slaughter began in mid-afternoon and lasted until sundown. The Confederate army lost 5,355 men killed, wounded, and captured.[121] General Daniel H. Hill later said of the day's fighting, "It was not war — it was murder."[122] Holmes's division was idle that day. His men could only listen to the thundering Union artillery as it butchered their countrymen. In the following days, the Union army retreated to safety at Harrison's Landing. The Peninsular Campaign was over.

Under orders from General Lee, Holmes had advanced his division into a storm of land and naval artillery that was effectively coordinated by the Union army's signal corps. McClellan's chief signal officer later commented on the near-perfect coordination of communications and artillery fire. He wrote that the area and circumstances were "perhaps as perfect as could be chosen for combining[,] by the use of signals[,] the operations and the fire of land and naval forces."[123] Union general George Sykes commanded the division facing Holmes. In describing his position he said, "Nothing could have been more commanding than the line I held."[124] Without reinforcements, Holmes never had any chance to develop his advance into a successful attack.

At the close of the campaign, Lee and Davis were greatly disappointed. The Union army had not been destroyed before reaching the safety of Harrison's Landing. Lee's plan for all Confederate forces on the peninsula to converge and mount coordinated attacks had failed repeatedly. While thousands of troops did much of the heavy fighting, additional thousands did little or nothing at key battles during the campaign. Confederate soldiers were kept out of battles by their commanders or marched and countermarched within a few miles of fighting because of poor communications, bad maps, and unreliable guides.[125]

Poor generalship and the piecemeal organization of the army Lee inherited from Gen. Joseph Johnston caused most of the problems. During the Peninsular Campaign, Lee's army often operated at the division level without sufficient communication and coordination. The Confederate army suffered from bad tactics and even worse staff work.[126] Lee's commanders varied in temperament and ability. Stonewall Jackson, fresh from his brilliant campaign in the Shenandoah Valley, failed to make timely arrivals. General Huger wasted time in the woods near Malvern Hill trying to cut new roads for his artillery.[127] General Gustavus Smith suffered from bad health early in the campaign and feuded with Jefferson Davis. Magruder experienced the same difficulties of poor maps, tardy orders, and bad guides that troubled other Southern commanders. In his report, Magruder stated that he did not receive orders to reinforce Holmes until 4:30 P.M. on June 30.[128] His tardiness may have been the result of morphine prescribed for indigestion. He had become terribly fatigued and may have been drinking to excess. Consequently, he lost his "usual calmness" and displayed "an extreme irritability."[129] In his report on the campaign, General Lee did not criticize Holmes. He implied that a successful attack on Malvern Cliffs could have been made if Magruder had arrived earlier.[130]

Several of these generals, with the exception of Jackson and Longstreet, would be transferred during the next few months as Lee reorganized his army.[131] General Smith was later placed in command of a military district and headquartered in Richmond. Benjamin Huger was removed from field command and became an inspector of artillery. Later, he was sent to the Trans-Mississippi. Magruder's previously scheduled transfer to the Trans-Mississippi was blocked. Later, he was sent to command the district of Texas, New Mexico, and Arizona. The Trans-Mississippi was becoming a dumping ground for generals who had failed in Virginia.[132]

Theophilus Holmes would be sent away as well. Several generals, probably including Lee, regarded Holmes as too old and lethargic to wage the kind of war that was needed to save the Confederacy. Lee and Holmes had disagreed frequently over matters in Virginia and North Carolina. Lee was an aggressive risk-taker. He wanted his subordinate commanders to operate with general instructions and to take advantage of opportunities as they were presented. Holmes had not been that kind of general at Malvern Hill. On the morning of June 30, he could have pushed aggressively toward Malvern Hill. He could have started his attack hours earlier, but he followed his orders and stayed at New Market until later in the day.

After the Peninsula, Holmes was criticized for inattention, elderliness, deafness, and lack of aggressiveness. His decision not to press the attack at Malvern Cliffs was met with derision from Confederate veteran and historian Gen. Edward Porter Alexander, a major during the campaign. He later stated that Holmes's division could have taken Malvern Hill before mid-afternoon on June 30 had Holmes not stopped at New Market. Daniel H. Hill frequently passed along the story of Holmes's deafness during the naval bombardment. Hill also mis-characterized the times of events of June 30.[133]

Years later, when writing about the campaign, Jefferson Davis made clear his opinion of Holmes's performance. He said that Holmes had been unfairly blamed for the lack of a decisive victory over McClellan's retreating army. Davis noted that all of the Confederate generals were "ignorant of the roads" and "had no maps of the country in which we were operating." Troop movements were delayed by "erroneous answers of the guides." These circumstances, Davis wrote, caused "Lee to post Holmes at New Market, where he [Lee] was told, was the route that McClellan must pursue in his retreat to the James." As a result, Holmes waited for several hours for the Union army to appear at New Market while General Porter, with his artillery and infantry, made Malvern Hill impregnable.[134] Davis wrote that Holmes "first took position when and where he was directed, and, soon after, he moved to the last position to which he was assigned." Davis supported Holmes's decision not to continue the attack late in the day on June 30, saying, "The numerical superiority of the opposing force, both in infantry and artillery, would have made it worse than useless to attempt an assault unless previously reinforced."[135]

According to Davis, General Holmes may have innocently given his critics information about Malvern Hill that would contribute to his exile from Lee's army. After the battle, "Holmes found that a deep ravine led up to the rear of the left flank of the enemy's line." Holmes made this discovery known and expressed regret for the lost opportunity. It was then, Davis said, that Holmes was criticized "as having failed to do his whole duty at Malvern Hill."[136] Months after the battle, Davis wrote to Senator Louis Wigfall of Texas and explained that Holmes had followed orders at Malvern Hill. He advised Wigfall that even General Lee admitted as much.[137]

Several days after Malvern Hill, Lee and Davis considered attacking McClellan at Harrison's Landing, but declined to do so. Lee wrote to Davis, "I do not wish to expose the men to the destructive missiles of his gunboats." Holmes's lesson on River Road had been well learned.[138]

Other Confederate generals who failed during the final days of the Peninsular Campaign were difficult to disparage. Stonewall Jackson's inaction on June 30 was a major component in the failure of Lee's plan. But Jackson had already made his reputation at Manassas and in the Shenandoah Valley. He became Lee's "right arm" and within a year would become the Confederacy's martyred hero. Most public criticism of Lee's generalship on the Peninsula was muted by the inescapable fact that he had saved Richmond and the Confederacy. During the war and for decades to follow, he was virtually deified in the South and highly respected in the North. His death in 1870 made him essentially unassailable for generations. Although the issue was only an undercurrent during the war, years later historian James Ford Rhodes wrote, "Nearly all observers and writers agree that Lee's generalship at Malvern Hill was clearly defective."[139]

Malvern Hill was not the only factor in Holmes's fall from favor. He performed competently in the Aquia District, but his brigade rendered no real service at Manassas. There, he and General Ewell were criticized for late arrivals on the Confederate left flank. Later, in North Carolina, Holmes was given a larger assignment that he did not want. He had insufficient time and resources to defend the state or to go on the offense against New Bern. He sparred with Lee for weeks over the need for more troops, ordnance, and transportation resources. Holmes exhibited a lack of self-confidence to Lee, and Lee displayed no confidence in him. During an exchange of messages about arming North Carolina troops, Lee condescendingly lectured Holmes about the disposition of muskets and rifles within regiments, knowledge any experienced infantry officer would possess.[140]

President Davis visited Holmes at his headquarters below Drewry's Bluff on the evening of July 4. At that time, he and Holmes wanted to bombard Union positions at Harrison's Landing from the south side of the James River.[141] Davis may have told Holmes that he was being transferred. Nevertheless, Holmes likely knew that his brief service in Robert E. Lee's army was drawing to a close. His physical presence and demeanor did not inspire confidence. By 1862, thirty-seven years of service on the frontier, two wars, and Laura's death had worn him down. He was fifty-eight years old, nearly deaf, and gave the impression of an inattentive elderly man. Holmes was aware of his own strengths and weaknesses. He operated best in a stable, focused environment, implementing the plans of others. His talents were more administrative than tactical. He had informed Lee of this fact in no uncertain terms weeks before Malvern Hill.

The withdrawal of part of Burnsides's army from New Bern to assist McClellan in the Peninsula Campaign and the subsequent failure of that campaign took pressure off coastal North Carolina and eastern Virginia. President Lincoln began searching for a new army commander. The Union force at New Bern would not be sufficiently reinforced to resume offensive operations until November.[142] After the Peninsula, Lee kept Holmes's division in Virginia. He recommended, on July 13, that Holmes should concentrate his force in the area between Drewry's Bluff and the Appomattox River.[143]

On July 15, Holmes sent a message to his senior brigade commander, Gen. Samuel G. French, "Come to Petersburg immediately and assume command of the department." French's command was brief. General Daniel H. Hill was ordered to take charge of Holmes's "division and district" the next day.[144] As soon as French arrived, Holmes left Petersburg and returned to North Carolina. Magruder, French, Smith, and Huger were at loose ends after the Peninsula, but as far as President Davis was concerned, Holmes had done his "full duty" during the campaign. He was about to put Holmes in charge of military operations in the Department of the Trans-Mississippi, one-half of the Confederacy.

The official designation of the Trans-Mississippi as a military department (previously a district in Department No. 2 or the Department of the West) was made by the Confederate government in May 1862. General Sterling Price, a former governor of Missouri, wanted to command the department and retake his state. President Davis, convinced that Price was self-serving and could not be trusted, chose General Magruder instead.[145] Orders assigning Magruder to the Trans-Mississippi were issued in May but quickly rescinded as the crisis on the Virginia peninsula deepened.[146] During a meeting in June, Price and the president argued about Magruder's appointment. [147] Davis kept Price from resigning from the army by promising that Magruder and Price would be allowed to invade Missouri at the earliest opportunity. The agreement fell apart when General Magruder was charged with misconduct stemming from his poor performance on the peninsula. Davis could not transfer Magruder while the charges were pending. With Price still being out of the question, Davis chose Holmes for the Trans-Mississippi.[148]

Sterling Price came away from the incident greatly embittered. John B. Clark, a Missouri politician and friend, wrote to Price and told him of Magruder's recall and Holmes's appointment, "not to assail General Holmes by any means, but to show how determined and persistent the President is in his neglect and disregard of the interest and manifest wishes of the whole West ... as well as his continued neglect and insult to you." Clark said of Davis, "For some unaccountable cause he is your enemy, everybody knows ... that he is unfriendly to the prosperity of Missouri and totally indifferent about her success." The appointment of Holmes to command the Trans-Mississippi made Price a bitter enemy of Holmes and Davis.[149]

Holmes's appointment to the Trans-Mississippi was not without practical merit. He was a West Point graduate, not a politician or militia officer like Price and other western generals. Holmes had spent much of his career west of the Mississippi River and knew the land and people. He was familiar with Eastern tribes sent to the territory during the Indian Removal. Alliances with those tribes and the service of their warriors could be part of Confederate success in the Trans-Mississippi. There were other officers Davis could have chosen, but he trusted Holmes. He knew Holmes would be loyal to the South and, more importantly, loyal to Davis. Holmes's appointment was announced on July 16, 1862.[150]

Most of the generals Lee banished from his army after the Peninsula faded into obscurity in their new assignments, but not Holmes. Jefferson Davis had put his old friend back in the military and public spotlight, where he would be blamed, in part, for the death of the Confederacy.

6

A Disorganized Department

On July 18, 1862, from Fayetteville, North Carolina, Holmes wrote to Secretary of War Randolph and advised that he was in the process of contacting generals, commissary officers, and quartermasters in the Trans-Mississippi. From them, he was requesting information on troop strengths, supply needs, and the military situation. He also asked Randolph for several officers to be transferred with him.[1]

For his chief of staff, Holmes selected Col. James Deshler, who had fought so courageously at Malvern Cliffs. Holmes had recently heard that Maj. Julius De Lagnel had been offered a promotion to brigadier general. That being the case, Holmes wanted De Lagnel to help reorganize forces in the Trans-Mississippi and command a brigade. He and Holmes had served together at Fort Washita in the 1850s and more recently in Virginia. De Lagnel had been wounded and captured earlier in the war but had been exchanged.[2]

Holmes recommended the assignment of Maj. John B. Burton as the department's quartermaster. Earlier in the war, Burton had been on Holmes's staff and was currently serving in Virginia as Gen. John Walker's brigade quartermaster. Holmes pointed out that Burton "is from Arkansas, will be acquainted with resources of the country, is one of the best officers I know of, and is anxious to go with me, if he can be spared." Holmes informed Randolph that Lieutenant John Hinsdale, and the recently commissioned Lt. Theo Holmes Jr. would accompany him as well.[3] The same day Holmes summoned General French to Petersburg, he nominated Theo for a commission as a 1st lieutenant in the Confederate army.[4]

Enclosed in his letter to Randolph, Holmes sent a requisition for funds and asked that it be filled as quickly as possible. Holmes told him, "I sincerely hope you will not consider the demand exorbitant, when you consider the disorganized state of everything there." Mindful of recent criticism of his leadership ability, Holmes lowered expectations by pointing to his own "utter inexperience in a command of such diversified interests." Nonetheless, he was anxious to get started: "If I can get the arrangement of my staff completed I will leave here on Monday morning." In describing the Trans-Mississippi as "disorganized" Holmes was being generous.[5] The region was a military and political quagmire.

The Trans-Mississippi had been largely ignored by the Davis administration. Although focused on the war in Virginia, the government was publically committed to defending even the most distant parts of the Confederacy. The public expected no less.[6]

In devising a national strategy based on defense rather than offense, President Davis divided the Confederacy into geographic departments in 1861. The departments were sub-divided into military districts. Each department was commanded by a general or lieutenant general. Major generals or brigadier generals commanded districts. Generals could divide their commands into sub-districts as they deemed necessary. Each general was responsible for routine military operations within his respective area: law and order, defense, communication, intelligence gathering, and in varying degrees after April 1862, conscription. In the absence of large campaigns, generals were expected to defend their areas with the troops assigned to them.[7] President Davis's defensive strategy was controversial from the beginning. As early as January 1862, a Richmond newspaper editorial complained, "This defensive policy has not only cost us men, but it has cost us territory. Many counties of Eastern Virginia & important regions on the more Southern seaboards are now occupied by the enemy."[8]

The farther from Richmond the departments were, the less efficient was the departmental strategy. With so much of the war focused on Virginia, the Trans-Mississippi was too large and too far removed from the seat of Confederate government to garner the attention it needed. El Paso, Texas, was almost two thousand miles from Richmond. While the eastern half of the Confederacy was divided into nine different military departments, the Trans-Mississippi stretched from the Mississippi River across the continent to the Pacific Ocean and contained Missouri, Arkansas, Louisiana, Indian Territory (Oklahoma), Texas, and modern-day New Mexico, Arizona, and southern California. One-half of the Confederacy's territory was contained in the region, but only one-fifth of the nation's white population. The region's economy was based on agriculture. There were few railroads, factories, or telegraph connections. As the largest cattle-producing state, Texas was needed to feed the Confederate population and armies on both sides of the Mississippi River. Louisiana and Texas

Lieutenant General Theophilus Hunter Holmes, 1804–1880 (Library of Congress).

90

farmers grew the cotton needed to clothe armies and finance the war. Jefferson Davis primarily regarded the Trans-Mississippi as a source of troops and supplies for a war that would be won or lost in the East.[9]

Further complicating the Trans-Mississippi was the nature of the people. Most of the population lived on farms, ranches, and the frontier. The people were imbued with a fierce spirit of independence and individualism. In many areas there was no law, no government, and no taxation. The presence of a strong national or state government that taxed them, drafted their men into the army, and was a significant part of their lives was completely alien to their existence. It was a concept many of them would not accept.[10] Most of the men had no understanding of military discipline, the chain of command, or strict obedience to orders. In anticipation of Holmes's arrival, a Texas unit was ordered to report to Little Rock. A soldier in the company wrote, "As far as General Holmes is concerned, he can ... write his orders in a sand bank.... If we are not an Independent Co[mpany], we intend to play it a while anyway." The soldier expressed surprise that Holmes even knew where the company was stationed.[11]

The Trans-Mississippi contained fewer slaves than the rest of the Confederacy, but the Confederacy depended on cotton that slaves produced.[12] Texas cotton was needed for sale abroad and for manufacturing uniforms, tents, and civilian clothing. Rather than selling their cotton to the Confederacy at government mandated prices, Texas growers often sold their harvest at higher prices in Mexico.[13] As part of the Confederacy, the Trans-Mississippi brought international considerations into play. The border with Mexico was the Confederacy's only international boundary (other than with the Union). Slaves escaping into Mexico from Texas caused friction on that border. In Texas, Kiowas and Comanches raided between the Rio Grande and the Red River. Texas soldiers often avoided service in the Confederate army so they could remain at home and protect their families.[14]

Like President Davis, President Lincoln believed the war would be decided by land battles in Virginia. Neither president expected the war to last four years. Lincoln knew that isolating the Confederacy from European supplies with a blockade of Southern ports would eventually starve the South into submission. Additionally, cutting off the eastern half of the Confederacy from the Trans-Mississippi would deny each part support from the other. This strategy was part of General Winfield Scott's Anaconda Plan. Although never formally adopted by the U.S. government and much criticized for some of its less aggressive aspects, the Anaconda Plan's river and seaport blockade was a major component in the ultimate defeat of the South.[15] Hedging his bet on a short war, Lincoln ordered a blockade of Southern seaports in April 1861. By July 1862, the Union army and navy had made clear President Lincoln's intention to control the Mississippi River.

Well before Holmes's appointment to the department, the war in the Trans-Mississippi turned against the Confederacy. In 1861 and early 1862, the region was defended by local Confederate officers. Colonel Douglas Cooper and Brigadier Gen. Albert Pike were in the Indian Territory. Missouri State Guard Gen. Sterling Price and former Texas

Ranger Gen. Ben McCulloch commanded Missouri, Louisiana, and Arkansas troops. After their victory at Wilson's Creek in August 1861, the Confederate commanders managed to keep the Union army out of southwestern Missouri until early 1862. The generals feuded, operated independently, and were unable to secure the rest of Missouri for the Confederacy. Prices's army was forced out of the state by the end of January 1862. That same month, career soldier Gen. Earl Van Dorn (formerly of the 7th U.S. Infantry) was put in command of the Trans-Mississippi District.[16]

Before Van Dorn could organize an offensive, Union general Samuel R. Curtis pushed General Price further into Arkansas and occupied Fayetteville on February 23. On March 7, Van Dorn's Army of the West attacked Curtis at Pea Ridge (Elkhorn Tavern) with the combined troops of McCulloch, Price, and Pike's force of Cherokee, Choctaw, Chickasaw, Creek, and Seminole soldiers. McCulloch and one of his brigade commanders were killed the first day. McCulloch's other brigade commander was captured. The next day, Union attacks pounded the Confederates and forced them back. Van Dorn ordered the retreat of his exhausted army.[17] Colonel Stand Watie's Cherokee Mounted Rifles attacked a Union artillery battery, allowing the Confederates to escape. Van Dorn, Watie, and Pike retreated to the Arkansas River.

After Pea Ridge, General Curtis headed eastward with his twenty-one thousand men. He cooperated with General Frederick Steele, who, by the end of April 1862, had moved his force from Missouri into northern Arkansas. Van Dorn, still full of fight, planned another offensive, but developments in Tennessee and on the upper Mississippi River would prevent his return to Missouri and remove his army from the Trans-Mississippi.

After the Confederate defeat at Mill Springs, Kentucky, on January 19, 1862, Gen. Albert Sidney Johnston wrote to Adjutant and Inspector General Cooper. He advised that all "the resources of the Confederacy are now needed for the defense of Tennessee."[18] The Confederacy did not react quickly. The February capture of seventeen thousand soldiers at forts Henry and Donaldson cost the Confederacy southern Kentucky and part of middle Tennessee. In northwest Tennessee, the Union army and navy worked for weeks to isolate Island Number 10 on the Mississippi River, near New Madrid, Missouri. On April 7, seven thousand Confederates with fifty-two artillery pieces surrendered the island to Gen. John Pope. As Island Number 10 was being surrendered, the battle of Shiloh ended in a bloody draw. Shiloh and the defeats at forts Henry and Donaldson and Island Number 10 resulted in the loss of most of Tennessee. The fall of Island Number 10 ended Confederate control of the Mississippi River as far south as Fort Pillow.[19] Albert Sidney Johnston was killed at Shiloh, but this was precisely the situation he had warned Richmond about in January.

In April 1862, General Van Dorn and most of his army, including General Price, were sent to serve with General Beauregard in Tennessee. When Van Dorn left Arkansas, his army removed huge amounts of military stores, weapons, food, and machinery from the state. Even sick and wounded Confederate soldiers in Arkansas hospitals were ordered to rejoin their regiments across the Mississippi River as soon as they were well

Missouri and Arkansas (Robert Lee Kerby, *Kirby Smith's Confederacy*, 1972, Columbia University Press, reprinted with permission of the publisher).

enough to travel. The withdrawal of Van Dorn's troops allowed generals Curtis and Steele virtually a free hand in the state.[20]

Like North Carolina, Arkansas did not secede until President Lincoln's call for troops after Fort Sumter. Many Arkansans were ambivalent about secession and the Confederacy. All of Van Dorn's troops were volunteers who had entered the army during the first year of the war. After Van Dorn left, any officer who took command in the state would have to rebuild the Arkansas army almost exclusively through conscription.[21] More often than not, Trans-Mississippi conscripts would prove to be good soldiers, but not having a core of volunteers upon which to build would change the nature of the army.[22] With Van Dorn and his soldiers gone, Arkansas was practically defenseless. The public and politicians interpreted the situation as an abandonment of their state by Confederate authorities. Governor Henry Rector contacted President Davis and threatened to secede from the Confederacy if his state was not vigorously defended.[23]

The strategic implications of Rector's threat were immense. If the Confederacy lost Arkansas, the war in that part of the Trans-Mississippi would shift from southern Missouri and northern Arkansas to the Red River Valley in southwest Arkansas, Louisiana, and Texas. Louisiana and Texas would likely demand the return of their troops serving in Virginia. Those two states could threaten to secede from the Confederacy as well. With the Trans-Mississippi out of the war, Union resources would be sent East to fight Lee. The fate of the Trans-Mississippi and perhaps the entire Confederacy hinged on Arkansas.[24] President Davis had to do something to reassure the public and keep the state in the war.

On May 31, 1862, General Beauregard (in command of the Confederate Department of the West since the death of Albert Sidney Johnston) appointed Gen. Thomas Hindman to command the Trans-Mississippi until General Magruder could arrive. Hindman was a Tennessee native with Mississippi and Arkansas political connections. He had served in the Mississippi militia during the War with Mexico, represented Arkansas in the U.S. Congress, and led a division at Shiloh.[25] Hindman was a Westerner and acceptable to the politicians and people of Arkansas. Like Albert Pike and Sterling Price, Hindman was a politician turned general. When he arrived at Little Rock, he saw that Arkansas was on the verge of collapse. He declared martial law on June 30, rigidly enforced conscription, and established wage and price controls. He ordered the destruction of resources he could not protect from the Union army.[26]

Major General Thomas Carmichael Hindman Jr., 1828–1868. A lawyer and politician, Hindman fled to Mexico after the Civil War when his pardon was denied. He returned to Arkansas in 1867 and became politically active in promoting a controversial coalition of former slaves and Democrats. In 1868, as he sat reading a newspaper with his children at home in Helena, Hindman was fatality wounded by shots fired through a window. His killers were never brought to justice (Library of Congress).

In the meantime, Union generals Curtis and Steele in northern Arkansas were threatening to capture Little Rock but were operating a long way from their supply base. Local militia forces attacked their wagon trains and disrupted communications. At the end of June, Steele was at Jacksonport on the White River. General Hindman sent a force under Gen. Albert Rust to trap them before they could be re-supplied by the Union navy. Rust was defeated at the battle of Cache River (Hill's Plantation) on July 7 but managed to keep his force between Curtis's army and Little Rock. By then, Curtis was more interested in getting his army to a river port, where he could refit and strengthen his force. His attempts to be resupplied on the White River were stymied when the U.S.S. *Mound City* was damaged by Confederate artillery fire on June 17. Falling water levels prevented Union ships from moving further upstream. On July 12, Curtis's soldiers occupied the port city of Helena on the Mississippi River.[27]

As a result of the fighting, much of Missouri, Indian Territory, and Arkansas was without any semblance of law and order. Hindman needed time to enforce conscription and rebuild the army. He also wanted to keep the Union army off balance. To accomplish these goals and reassure the population, he authorized pro–Southern partisan units to operate freely. Their assignment was to attack Union supply and communication lines, gather intelligence, and defeat similar partisan units acting on behalf of the Union. Undisciplined guerrilla warfare became the order of the day. Murder, home burning, and robbery were visited upon the population by both sides. William Quantrill's raiders became active in Missouri during this period.[28]

Between May and Holmes's arrival, Hindman held on to Arkansas and rebuilt the army. He managed to improve war materiel manufacturing in the state. Arkadelphia, Camden, and Washington became production centers for lead, iron, musket caps, small arms, and ordnance machinery.[29] His wage and price controls, martial law, and methods of conscription enforcement, however, made him unpopular with the Richmond military establishment and Arkansas civilians and politicians. They called for his removal. While Hindman labored to rebuild Arkansas, other regions of the department were demanding attention as well.

Texas and most of western Louisiana were still under Confederate control, but the Union army and navy were active in the Gulf of Mexico and Mississippi River. New Orleans, Baton Rouge, Natchez, and Memphis were occupied by Union troops. Part of the Confederacy's River Defense Fleet was destroyed near New Orleans in April 1862. Flag Officer David Farragut's gunboats arrived at Vicksburg in May, but the city refused to surrender. The Union vessels sailed back down river. The Confederacy's ability to contest control of the upper Mississippi River ended when the remaining ships of the River Defense Fleet were destroyed at Memphis on June 6. After restoring Confederate control to part of the lower river in July, the Confederate ironclad *Arkansas* had to be scuttled on August 5.[30]

The Trans-Mississippi was being rapidly isolated. The Confederacy needed to act quickly before the river and entire region were lost. By May 1862, when Magruder was appointed department commander, consolidating the region under a single commander was long overdue. By July 30, when Holmes assumed command, the Confederacy had lost control of both ends of the Mississippi River. Most of the major river ports were in Union hands except Vicksburg, Mississippi, and Port Hudson, Louisiana.

The same day Holmes was chosen to command the new department, the Union army's District of West Tennessee was expanded to include the Department of the Mississippi. Ulysses S. Grant was placed in command of Union forces in the region. Like Robert E. Lee in the East, Grant's ascension in the West would change the course of the war. Unlike Lee, Grant was hounded by personal demons. He had graduated from West Point in 1843, but after eleven years in the army, he had resigned rather than face a court-martial. He fell into depression and alcoholism. In 1861, after failure at every turn, he offered his services to the Union.[31] Within two years of returning to the army, he would cut the Confederacy in half.

As bad as the tactical situation in the Trans-Mississippi was, a serious disagreement about overall military strategy was developing between Jefferson Davis and Secretary of War George Randolph. Davis's public policy of defending all of the Confederacy through the departmental strategy was failing. The Confederacy did not have the resources for a nationwide static defense. Secretary Randolph favored a more fluid strategy that would de-compartmentalize commanders' responsibilities. This approach would involve abandoning large areas, consolidating armies under regional commanders, and attacking Union forces. Generals Braxton Bragg and Joseph E. Johnston agreed with Randolph's reasoning.

For Theophilus Holmes, this conflict meant that Davis held him responsible for ensuring an uninterrupted flow of agricultural products across the Mississippi River. Holmes also had to defend his department without significant support from the rest of the Confederacy. On the other hand, Secretary Randolph wanted Holmes to subordinate the interests of the Trans-Mississippi and participate in coordinated operations with Confederate commanders in Tennessee and Mississippi. It was into this political and military minefield that Holmes stepped.

On July 30, 1862, General Holmes, surgeon Francis D. Cunningham, and Lt. Theo Holmes arrived at Vicksburg, Mississippi. Before crossing the river, Holmes assumed command of the department and announced that Cunningham would be the department's medical director.[32] Holmes's choice for his quartermaster, Maj. John Burton, was approved for transfer to the Trans-Mississippi on July 29.[33]

On paper, Holmes's department may have contained fifty thousand troops, including the partisan units, but they were loosely organized, poorly officered, and scattered through three states and Indian Territory. Only one-third to one-half of the soldiers were combat ready.[34] Although there was considerable confusion about the chain of command, Holmes kept the current district commanders in place: Gen. Paul Hébert in Texas and the recently assigned Gen. Richard Taylor (Zachary Taylor's son) in the District of West Louisiana. Holmes retained General Hindman in the department and assigned him to command the District of Arkansas, which included Missouri and Indian Territory.[35]

In continuing the Trans-Mississippi's separate districts and commanding officers, Holmes was conforming to President Davis's static defense strategy. The size of the Trans-Mississippi department and lack of reliable communications required district commanders to operate independently most of the time. Holmes could not and would not micro-manage his subordinates in Texas and Louisiana, choosing instead to invest them with "all the authority I can confer."[36] He would hold Hébert, Taylor, and Hindman personally responsible for failure in their districts. Holmes, however, intended to take an active role in Arkansas, where he thought the fate of the department rested.

Although Hindman was not a career officer and was completely unlike Holmes in appearance and demeanor, Holmes respected him. When standing together, the two generals made an almost comical picture. Holmes was thin, six feet tall with bad posture. His uniform coat hung loosely from his shoulders to his knees. His dark, wavy hair was combed haphazardly to one side; his beard, bushy and disheveled. In contrast, Hindman was five feet one inch tall and twenty-four years younger than Holmes. He was a "dapper little man" and a flashy dresser.[37] Hindman was more aggressive and optimistic than Holmes. He characterized Trans-Mississippi troops as "generally remarkably good." Although Holmes's opinion of Trans-Mississippi soldiers would gradually improve, initially he regarded the department's army as a "crude mass of undisciplined material."[38]

Holmes realized that the controversial measures Hindman had taken in Arkansas and Missouri were necessary evils. They were required by the dire circumstances under which Hindman had taken command. While Holmes made few friends in announcing that Hindman would stay in Arkansas, there was an advantage. Holmes suspected that Hindman's controversial methods would need to be continued, at least for the foreseeable future. As unpopular as Hindman was, by remaining in command of Arkansas, Hindman would continue to take the brunt of criticism. Holmes ordered Hindman to secure northwestern Arkansas and then establish a camp of instruction near Little Rock to rebuild the army.

In Louisiana, confusion over who commanded the district was not settled until around the time of Holmes's assignment to the department. Previously, generals Hébert and Hindman commanded areas of the state west of the Mississippi River. General Albert Blanchard was sent to Louisiana in June with ambiguous orders to oversee conscription and camps of instruction. He could not figure out where he was in the chain of command. When General Taylor arrived in July, his orders from Adjutant and Inspector General Cooper were of such detail as to imply something less than overall command.[39] Holmes's recognition of Taylor as commander of the District of West Louisiana clarified the situation.

Similar confusion existed in Texas. Generals Henry E. McCulloch (Ben McCulloch's brother) and Paul Hébert had been given command at various times, but Hébert took charge in May 1862, with the creation of the District of West Louisiana and Texas. Hébert established his headquarters in San Antonio, much to the irritation of Governor Moore in Louisiana. That same month, Governor Moore complained to Davis, "Three months since New Orleans fell and no Confederate officer in Louisiana yet.... This persistent neglect is incomprehensible.... Have not heard from you since 16th of May."[40]

Hébert contacted Holmes in late August to advise him of the conditions in Texas. By then, Gen. Henry H. Sibley had withdrawn Confederate troops from Arizona and New Mexico, exposing northwest Texas to possible Union advances. Galveston and Corpus Christi were threatened by Union gunboats and amphibious landings. The district was later subdivided, and additional conflicting orders from Richmond resulted. The issue of command would not be settled until the assignment of General Magruder to command the District of Texas on October 10, 1862. (Magruder was finally cleared of the charges filed against him after the Peninsular Campaign. The District of Texas was expanded to include New Mexico and Arizona on November 29, when he assumed command.)[41]

In August, Holmes reported on the condition of the army he commanded. He advised Richmond that his troops were scattered and "in a terrible condition. More than half of them are sick and unavailable for duty." He said he could probably build an army of fifteen thousand men ready for combat, but the force would be "very defective in officers of experience or capability." Holmes desperately needed to arm his troops. "There are but two regiments here [Little Rock] with muskets. The others have only shotguns and country rifles."[42] The governors of several Trans-Mississippi states were requesting that Richmond send twenty thousand to thirty thousand weapons to the department.[43]

Trans-Mississippi troops were not only poorly armed, they were poorly supplied, undisciplined, and practically destitute in every way. With cold weather approaching, Holmes issued an appeal through newspapers asking the population to supply his men with blankets, shirts, coats, overcoats, hats, shoes, and "clothing of every description." He reminded the public that the Trans-Mississippi Department could expect little help from the "other side of the Mississippi River."[44]

Holmes wanted to build a more professional army. He blamed officers at all ranks for the absence of discipline he saw. They lacked training, leadership skills, and experience. Few officers below the rank of general had any formal military training. A number of officers, particularly those from Texas, had served with militia volunteers during the Mexican war. Holmes recalled the shocking lack of discipline among those troops. The department's officer corps needed to be taught what to do and how to do it.

One of Holmes's more promising officers was Allison Nelson. Colonel Nelson was an acting division commander and had recently established a camp of instruction, Camp Hope, at Austin, Arkansas. In an August 21 letter, Holmes impressed upon Nelson the serious nature of his duties: "You will please remember that we are trying to train and organize an army.... The example you set will be followed for good or for evil. Your responsibility is very great."[45]

In a crash course on basic military command, Holmes counseled Nelson: "Instruct your officers in all their duties and ... hold them responsible for the condition and discipline of their men.... Issue an order requiring stated roll calls and also requiring all officers and men to attend them.... Make the colonels responsible for the good police [i.e. control] of their Regts and camps and the captains [responsible] for the police, diet and cleanliness of their men, letting everybody know that there is no time for idleness in a camp of instruction." Holmes told Nelson that his instructions were being given in "a private letter because it is much better for the service that you should do all these things of your own accord, rather than under the spur of an order, and also because I believe you are competent to the trust and it is but right that you should receive all the benefit of success."[46]

In order to keep his most experienced officer, Holmes had to convince President Davis that General Hindman should stay in the department. Holmes knew that in keeping Hindman there, he and Davis would make political enemies. Davis was still under pressure to remove Hindman from Arkansas. On August 28, Holmes wrote a long letter to Davis. He told the president that when General Hindman arrived the previous May, Arkansas "had no troops to resist Curtis who was threatening this city [Little Rock] and could have come here without firing a gun.... There was absolutely no law in Ark[ansas.]" He told Davis that Hindman had "assumed control of everything civil and military and exercised his power with a success that places the state in a condition of tolerable order and secure." In addition to declaring martial law without authorization, Hindman had generated intense controversy with his methods of attracting volunteers and enforcing conscription. Holmes admitted to Davis that Hindman had overstepped his authority and violated numerous civilian laws, army procedures, and regulations.[47]

In attracting deserters to rejoin the army, Hindman had ordered all soldiers who were absent from regiments east of the Mississippi River to report to him at Little Rock. Seizing on an opportunity to end their status as deserters and serve close to their homes, many hundreds (perhaps several thousand) deserters turned themselves in and joined Hindman's regiments. When Holmes took command, these soldiers were still listed as deserters from their former regiments. Hindman's actions were clear violations of military regulations, but Holmes told Davis that if these soldiers were forced to return to their former commands, most of them would desert again. He requested that Davis "confirm all that he [Hindman] has done because to disturb the present status of things ... would produce a confusion that might be ruinous."[48]

Holmes requested five thousand weapons to arm Arkansas troops and six additional brigadier generals for the department. He preferred generals from the Eastern Confederacy (i.e., from West Point) but gave Davis a list of Trans-Mississippi colonels who could be promoted. Holmes told Davis that he had "accepted this command with very great diffidence" based on a "sincere distrust of my own strengths." He suggested that generals Joseph E. Johnston, Beauregard, or Gustavus W. Smith be sent to command the department. He offered to serve under any of these generals. He said that by the time one of them could arrive, "I think I shall have an army fit for the field" except for the shortage of weapons.[49]

Whether or not he was replaced, Holmes had to rebuild the mid-management of many regiments in the department. Prior to his arrival, a number of officers had tried to resign their commissions by claiming bad health. Others were such poor officers that their superiors had ordered them to submit resignations. A list of names was supplied to Holmes shortly after he took command. In early September, he sent the list and a memo to Adjutant and Inspector General Cooper. Holmes recommended that all the resignations should be accepted with the understanding that the officers remain liable to conscription. Holmes intended to keep them in the army, even as privates, and make use of them one way or another. Like all professional soldiers, particularly those trained at West Point, Holmes knew that poor discipline among officers and lack of professionalism spread to the enlisted men of any army. He had seen the results of these conditions in state volunteer and militia units during the war with Mexico. In early September, an incident occurred that demonstrated how badly Holmes's army needed training.

On August 29, Union Lt. John Noble was ordered to Little Rock by General Curtis to make a prisoner exchange. This was a routine wartime matter similar to prisoner exchanges Holmes had arranged in North Carolina. Lieutenant Noble and two other officers left Helena, Arkansas, with thirty-three Confederate prisoners. Their orders were to travel down Big Creek and up the White River on a small steamboat displaying a white flag. They were to contact Confederate authorities near St. Charles and make arrangements for the exchange.[50]

At night, near St. Charles, the party placed lanterns on the ship, "three white lights, one above the other, to indicate that our boat was under a flag of truce." The party was not challenged by Confederate pickets along the river and could find no Confederate military authorities when they arrived at St. Charles Landing. After steaming another ten miles, Lieutenant Noble made contact with a squad of Confederate soldiers and a non-commissioned officer "who received us becomingly." The Confederates promised to send a message to the next river picket post at Atkin's Bluff to inform them of the approach of the boat and peaceful nature of the mission. When they arrived at Atkin's Bluff, the Union officers and their prisoners were fired upon by Confederate pickets.[51]

Noble managed to get the shooting stopped. The pickets agreed to make the proper notifications upriver, and the party continued on its way. At the next two picket posts, Confederate soldiers fled at the sight of the boat and the white flag. On each occasion, Lieutenant Noble coaxed his confused enemies out of the woods and convinced them that the mission was peaceful. All he wanted was notification of their approach sent upriver so no one would shoot at them. At Clarendon, Noble encountered a picket who had been informed "that we were to be expected." The notification had not come from other pickets but through a "citizen from Helena." As the party continued upstream toward DeVall's Bluff, pickets along the river bank saluted. One Confederate sang "Dixie" as the boat passed. Noble remarked that the soldier "at least knew the meaning of the white flag."[52]

The party docked near DeVall's Bluff. At the nearby train station, Noble found Lieutenant Colonel Giddings of the 21st Texas Ranger Regiment. Giddings, Noble, and one of Noble's officers left the prisoners under guard at the station and headed toward Little Rock on the train, a distance of fifty miles. They arrived at Little Rock at 8:00

P.M. and began looking for Holmes's headquarters, which was located in the State Bank Building at the corner of Center and Markham streets.[53] The party was unable to locate any of the general's staff until 10:00 P.M. Holmes appeared an hour later. He was irritated by the lateness of the hour and shocked by the presence of armed enemy officers in his headquarters. Noble described Holmes as "an old man quite hard of hearing."[54]

Holmes "severely" reprimanded Colonel Giddings, in front of the Union officers, for "having allowed us to come within the pickets." According to Noble, Holmes's demeanor was indicative of "great anger and want of respect" toward him and his party. Noble tried to defend Colonel Giddings's actions by telling Holmes about the lack of "information, intelligence and attention on the part of his other soldiers and officers that had compelled Colonel Giddings to bring us to headquarters." Holmes's embarrassment at these remarks did nothing to ease the tension in the room. He lectured Noble about the "conduct" of Union forces and General Curtis in Arkansas. The conversation degenerated into an exchange of thinly veiled insults before ending with an agreement to pursue the prisoner exchange in the morning. Lieutenant Noble and his party spent the night at a local hotel.[55]

The next day, confusion at Holmes's headquarters about the number of Union prisoners at Little Rock prevented a complete man-for-man exchange. Only three Union soldiers were handed over. Noble left Little Rock a day later and began his trip back down river. On September 3, his boat, still flying a white flag, was again fired upon by Confederate pickets near Atkins Bluff.[56]

The episode illustrated how unprofessional and untrained Holmes's army was. From enlisted men shooting at a white flag, to a lieutenant colonel marching Union officers into the department commander's headquarters in the dead of night, Holmes's soldiers had repeatedly failed to follow proper military procedure. He wondered if he could ever make an army out of the mob he commanded. On September 7, he requested that Adjutant and Inspector General Cooper send him six hundred copies of infantry, cavalry, and artillery manuals and one hundred "Army Regulations" books.[57]

Initially, Holmes continued Hindman's price controls in order to manage inflation. Inflation had produced hardships on the civilian population which, in turn, led to a rise in desertions from the army. Most of the population of the Trans-Mississippi lived on small family farms. If the men did not farm, the families did not eat. With so many men in the army, farm production had fallen. The shortage of food caused prices to rise. The department was deeply in debt to soldiers who "have now been in service from six to twelve months, some of whom have received neither pay nor bounty, and have families suffering at home the extreme of destitution."[58] Families were pressuring their men to desert and return to farming. On one occasion, Holmes wrote that the wives of conscripts "come to me with starving children, begging for the release of their husbands. And in violation of all law I let them go—This is law versus humanity."[59]

Holmes needed to manage the department's production and distribution of salt, used in great quantities as a food preservative. To ensure the military got enough salt and the price did not rise for civilians, Holmes's agents seized control of the saltworks in Arkansas and Indian Territory.[60] In November, Holmes ended much of his military authority over matters "having regard only to the well-being of the people," when the Arkansas legislature went into session.[61] He also needed control over the sale of cotton. The South needed huge amounts of cotton to clothe its armies and for sale abroad to finance the war. Texas growers were selling their cotton to dealers in Mexico, thus depriving Confederate government agents of access to the market. Holmes and Texas district commanders would struggle with this problem for the entire war.

In September, General Holmes sent the Confederacy's acting agent for Seminoles, J. P. Murrow, to Indian Territory. He instructed Murrow to report on the condition of the tribes and the strength of native battalions in Confederate service. Keeping native units up to strength and in the field was crucial to Confederate goals in the region. Murrow's report was not reassuring. The "Kechees, a band of Reserve Indians near Fort Cobb," had attacked the Seminoles, stolen their horses, and driven Seminole families off their land. If the Seminoles, Creeks, and Cherokees were driven out of the area, the Confederate frontier would suffer from additional Kechee raids. With Seminole warriors in the Confederate army, their families were at the mercy of the raiders. Murrow reported that displaced Seminole women and children were starving and without shelter or clothing. The Confederate government had failed to pay the Seminole soldiers for months. As a result, they were deserting in alarming numbers to care for their families.[62] If native troops and their families did not receive reasonable support from the Confederate government, regular troops needed elsewhere would have to be sent to Indian Territory.[63]

Murrow wrote his report to General Holmes from "within a mile of old Fort Holmes on Little River, Creek Nation, which I am told you founded.... Several of the old citizens still remember you." The Seminoles asked Agent Murrow to clarify the "military standing" of Albert Pike. "I ask this for good reasons," Murrow wrote; "these Indians think the world of him and desire to know." Murrow knew Pike had become a problem for the Confederacy.[64]

In 1861, Pike organized elements of the Five Nations (the "Five Civilized Tribes") to fight for the Confederacy. He was commissioned a general, appointed to command the Department of Indian Territory, and led native forces at the battle of Pea Ridge. With the Confederate government taking a more active role in the Trans-Mississippi in mid–1862, Pike became resentful and self-serving. He clashed with Hindman and would soon become a serious problem for Holmes. Holmes endorsed Murrow's report without commenting on Pike. He referred the report to General Hindman "with the request that he cause to be paid to the Seminole Battalion at least a part of the pay due them, in order that their families may not suffer."[65]

By the end of September, Holmes had reorganized the Arkansas district forces. In northwest Arkansas, southwest Missouri and Indian Territory, he created the First Corps, Army of the West, and put Hindman in command. Hindman promptly drove "all of the Marauders out of the Indian country." Holmes then recalled him to Little Rock to organize a camp of instruction and rebuild the core of the Army. Hindman left Gen. James F. Rains and the superintendent of Indian Affairs, Gen. Douglas Cooper, in command during his absence.[66]

Separate from Hindman's corps, Holmes formed the First and Second divisions under Brigadier General H. E. McCulloch and the recently promoted Gen. Allison Nelson. General Garland's brigade was assigned to the area around Fort Hindman near Arkansas Post on the Arkansas River. General Mosby Parson's cavalry brigade would patrol and defend the White and Arkansas rivers. Holmes sent two officers from his headquarters staff to commands in the field, colonels Deshler and F. A. Shoup.[67] Later, he sent Deshler and his brigade to Arkansas Post.

During the fall, Holmes's effort to improve his army was disrupted by disease. Measles, typhoid fever, mumps, and other camp sicknesses swept through Allison Nelson's camp of instruction at Austin, Arkansas. Approximately fifteen hundred soldiers died, including Nelson, who succumbed to typhoid in October.[68] One of Holmes's early recommendations had resulted in Nelson's promotion from colonel to brigadier general. When informing the adjutant and inspector general of Nelson's death, Holmes wrote that the loss was "irreparable.... I beseech you to send me some general officers."[69] Holmes's request for the services of Major Julius De Lagnel had been stymied as well. After his year as a prisoner of war, De Lagnel was exchanged, but he turned down his promotion to brigadier general. He preferred to remain in Virginia and take a position with the ordnance bureau.[70] The five thousand muskets Holmes requisitioned from Richmond were captured while being transported across the Mississippi River. He wrote to General Hindman of the loss and lamented, "I have no idea how I shall replace them."[71]

In October, seven major generals including Kirby Smith, John Pemberton, and Theophilus Holmes were promoted to the rank of lieutenant general. Holmes learned of his promotion through newspaper reports. He immediately wrote a personal letter to President Davis saying that his promotion was "prejudicial to the interests of my country." He spoke of the tenuous hold he had on Arkansas and the danger posed by Union forces at Helena and Springfield, Missouri. He wrote, "Failure here or defeat of this army virtually gives up the entire Trans-Mississippi region." He enclosed a second, official letter "declining the appointment of Lieut. Genl." and told Davis to "do with it as you choose." He assured Davis that should his rejection of the promotion not be accepted, he would depend on a "Higher Power" to enable him to "deserve your confidence and gratify your expectations." He asked Davis to send "here the strongest hand at your disposal."[72] Holmes felt powerless to defend the more remote areas of his department. During September and October, on the Texas coast, Sabine Pass, Galveston, and Indianola fell to Union naval forces.[73]

On October 13, Jefferson Davis appointed Lt. Gen. John C. Pemberton to command the Department of Mississippi, Tennessee, and East Louisiana. Pemberton's job was to defend as much of his department as possible, keep his portion of the Mississippi River open and, most importantly, defend Vicksburg. Pemberton wanted to use Holmes's troops to help accomplish his mission. Secretary of War Randolph agreed.

7

A Grave of Ambition,
Energy and System

Two weeks after Pemberton's appointment, Randolph instructed Holmes, "After providing for the defense of Arkansas and the Indian Territory, neither of which I presume will be seriously menaced from Missouri, your next object should be speedy and effective co-operation with General Pemberton for the protection of the Mississippi Valley and the conquest of west Tennessee.... An opportunity offers, therefore, of converging three armies (General Bragg's, Pemberton's and your own) upon some central point, and of regaining Tennessee and the Mississippi Valley."[1]

Randolph chose his words carefully, but he appeared to be ordering Holmes to lead or send troops across the Mississippi River. Holmes was extremely resistant to the suggestion that he should weaken Arkansas to fight in Tennessee. He responded to Randolph on November 15. (Messages between Little Rock and Richmond routinely took fifteen to thirty days to reach their destination.) He began, "It is my painful duty to disappoint your expectations relative to my ability to co-operate with the army east of the Mississippi. If I am able to protect Arkansas against the enemy now around her border I shall think myself fortunate." He reminded Randolph of the Federal army's "30,000 men in or about Springfield, Mo., with 12,000 or 15,000 at Helena." Holmes knew that if he moved part of his force out of Arkansas to join forces with Pemberton or Bragg, the Union armies would march against Little Rock.[2]

Under additional prodding from Randolph, Holmes reminded Adjutant and Inspector General Cooper on November 22, "I could not get to Vicksburg in less than two weeks. There is nothing to subsist on between here and there, and the army at Helena would come to Little Rock before I reached Vicksburg." He sent a similar letter to General Pemberton three days later. As Holmes saw it, trying to save west Tennessee or Mississippi at the cost of Arkansas was out of the question.[3]

While Randolph and Pemberton were pressuring Holmes to send troops across the Mississippi, Major General Hindman in northwest Arkansas wanted to go on the offense. In order to undo the damage Pike had done and reverse Union advances in Missouri, Holmes sent Hindman to northwest Arkansas in September. Hindman established "a good line of defense in Southwestern Missouri where we had 7,000 or 8,000 men." Unfortunately, when Holmes called Hindman back to Little Rock to set up the camp of instruction, the two generals that Hindman left in charge, James Rains and Douglas Cooper, "retreated in a most shameful manner." It was alleged that both generals were too drunk to manage their troops. As a result, the "Choctaws and Chickasaws [who] are as true and loyal a people as ever lived ... will freeze and starve."[4]

On October 20, Hindman wrote to Holmes suggesting a campaign into Missouri. Hindman asked Holmes "to arm 4,000 unarmed infantry I have.... Send me another infantry division and two batteries, and send me all the rations of hard bread [hardtack] that can be made." Hindman wanted to move immediately and told General Holmes that a "delay will be most disastrous to our interests in Missouri and the Indian Country, unless we can then quadruple our forces upon this line."[5] Holmes was not yet prepared to risk Hindman's corps with an invasion of Missouri.

In November, President Davis put Gen. Joseph Johnston in nominal command of the newly created Department of the West (Tennessee, Mississippi, Alabama, and Louisiana east of the Mississippi River). Johnston was instructed to coordinate the movements of the Confederate armies in the region, the troops of Kirby Smith and Bragg in Tennessee, and Pemberton's army in Mississippi. Unfortunately, Davis gave Johnston no formal command authority over any of the generals. Johnston could apply pressure but could not order Bragg and Pemberton to follow his recommendations. Davis gave Johnston no authority over Holmes's department.[6] If Johnston intended to combine Holmes's army with Bragg or Pemberton, he would have to convince, rather than order, Holmes to abandon Arkansas. Had Holmes and his department been formally placed under General Johnston's command, Holmes would have crossed the Mississippi River when ordered to do so. Only a month before Johnston was assigned to the region, Holmes offered to turn the Trans-Mississippi over to him and "aid and sustain you with a zealous industry that will satisfy you."[7]

The new command arrangement was unsatisfactory for Johnston. He, Randolph, and Pemberton agreed that regaining control of the eastern side of the Mississippi River required the combination of armies on both sides of the river. Johnston wanted to be given command of a department that did not exist: the Mississippi River Valley. He reasoned that with clear authority to command armies on both sides of the river, including Holmes's Arkansas troops, he could defeat Grant, then release Pemberton to join Bragg for an attack against the Union army under Rosecrans.[8] Johnston spent several weeks trying to convince Davis, Randolph, and Bragg to adopt his plan, but Davis would not budge. He had put Holmes in charge of the Trans-Mississippi and only Holmes would decide when and where his troops would fight.

Holmes had credible reasons for his course of action. Randolph, Johnston, and Pemberton were trying to convince him to endanger his department to save another. Davis was staying with his department-based defensive strategy and refused to insist that Holmes deviate from it. General Johnston disagreed with Holmes's decision but admitted that Holmes was the final authority in the absence of a direct order from the president.[9] In November, Holmes offered Adjutant and Inspector General Cooper a way out of the dilemma. He recommended that either Johnston or Beauregard could be given "command [of] the department while I would take the corps."[10] No one in Richmond accepted the offer. Saving west Tennessee and Vicksburg would be left to

Johnston, Bragg, and Pemberton on their side of the river. In the final analysis, if either side of the Mississippi fell to Union control, the effect on the Confederacy would be the same, but Holmes intended to protect his side of the river.

On November 12, Davis learned that earlier in the month Secretary Randolph had ordered Holmes to lead his army across the Mississippi. Davis was incensed that he had been bypassed and curtly informed Randolph, "The withdrawal of the commander from the Trans-Mississippi Department for temporary duty elsewhere would have a disastrous effect, and was not contemplated by me."[11] The policy disagreement between Davis and Randolph ended three days later with Randolph's resignation.[12] Davis filled the post with James A. Seddon on November 21.[13]

In the midst of the political turmoil, Holmes's thoughts turned to family matters. Since his wife's death and the break-up of his family, he had been sending money to Laura's family and other relatives for the care and education of his children. He wanted to make sure that they would be properly cared for, "in the event of my death." He wrote to his brother-in-law, Samuel J. Hinsdale, and asked him to manage the children's education and set his sons up in some business that suited them when the time came. He sent seventeen hundred dollars to Hinsdale to cover those costs and four hundred dollars for daughter Elizabeth, presumably for a dowry. In the event of Holmes's death, family slaves Garner and Sarah would go to sons Gabriel and Wetmore, respectively. Holmes told Hinsdale, "I live economically and I shall continue to forward to you all of my savings.... You will have the means of carrying out these wishes—if I should now die[,] and GOD will surely reward you for taking care of the orphans."[14]

Holmes was also contending with military and political problems caused by General Albert Pike. Pike had retreated from Indian Territory during the winter of 1861–62, "leaving the whole country open to marauding jayhawkers." When Hindman arrived, he ordered Pike to regain the lost territory, but Pike refused to obey. When Hindman relieved him of command, Pike resigned his generalship but stayed among the tribes and spread "doubt and discontentment among them." He led them to believe "that they had been betrayed and deserted by the general in command." Pike later moved to Texas, where he continued the political intrigue, allegedly involving himself with a "disloyal society." When the plot was discovered, scores of arrests were made, and forty-six persons were executed. Pike fled back "into the Indian country where he assumed command without authority from anybody." Holmes had him arrested for treason. The affair lasted for months and interfered with Holmes's ability to defend Indian Territory, southwest Missouri, and northwest Arkansas.[15]

Throughout Holmes's time in the Trans-Mississippi, Pike would work to have him removed. He wrote lengthy and insulting letters to and about Holmes and distributed them widely to citizens and politicians.[16] After arriving in the department, Holmes told President Davis, "Genl. Pike has ruined us in the Indian Country, and I fear it will be long before we can reestablish the confidence he has destroyed."[17] Months later, morale among Holmes's Native American soldiers had not improved. In writing to General Johnston, Holmes referred to his troops in the state and said, "Several regiments of these are Indians, upon whom no reliance can be placed."[18] Holmes had fought some of these tribes in Florida and respected their warriors. He knew their leaders could put good soldiers in the field if trust could be regained.

In the meantime, Ulysses S. Grant started a series of campaigns designed to capture Vicksburg. Union strategy in the Mississippi River valley was well developed. Grant and other generals would attack along the river, above and below Vicksburg, and keep Confederate forces widely dispersed. Beginning in October 1862, Grant worked to isolate the city.[19]

Maintaining at least one port city with rail connections on each side of the Mississippi River was crucial to the Confederacy. Between New Orleans and southwest Kentucky, Vicksburg and Memphis were the only points where eastbound rail lines had direct connections with the rest of the Confederacy. Memphis, already in Union hands, had rail lines that ran to Corinth and through Tennessee, northern Mississippi, and Alabama. Railroad lines beginning at Vicksburg went to Jackson, Mississippi, then north to Tennessee, south toward New Orleans and east to Montgomery and Atlanta.[20]

On the west side of the Mississippi River, railroad lines ran from Milliken's Bend and Young's Point (opposite Vicksburg) to Monroe, Louisiana, and from DeVall's Bluff on the White River to Little Rock. After New Orleans fell, cargo vessels from ports on the west bank of the river unloaded at Vicksburg, Port Hudson, and at smaller ports in between, but the routes often relied on wagons to carry freight to the nearest railroad depot. As long as Confederate supply ships could leave one side of the river and unload at several ports on the other side, Vicksburg was less crucial. As Union army and navy forces captured ports to the north and south, however, more and more of the Confederacy's resources had to cross the river at Vicksburg.

Holmes's ability to communicate from his headquarters at Little Rock to the rest of his department and the eastern Confederacy suffered from the same disadvantages that affected the movement of bulk supplies. He had divided most of his Arkansas forces between two key defensive positions, northwest Arkansas and Arkansas Post. Any message he sent or received at Little Rock often depended on all four modes of communication, telegraph, mounted couriers, rail lines, and river traffic. Holmes had telegraph contact in three directions from Little Rock. One line, to Hindman's command, stretched northwest along the banks of the Arkansas River to Dardenelle, then on to the Fort Smith and Van Buren area. Another ran southeast from Little Rock to Pine Bluff, then to Arkansas Post, near Fort Hindman. A third line went southwest to Camden, Arkansas.[21]

When telegrams were sent across a river, they had to be carried from a telegraph station on one side of the river to the station on the other side. From Arkansas Post, a combination of couriers, rail lines, and river traffic picked up messages and took them to the Mississippi River. As Union domination of the Mississippi became more complete, small boats or couriers on horseback had to cross the Mississippi at Gaines Landing, near the Louisiana and Arkansas border. They often did so at night while dodging Union gunboats. The farther from Little Rock communication and supply lines stretched, the more unreliable they became. Bad weather, lines cut by partisans, and captured couriers plagued Holmes's department.[22]

When he took command of the department, General Holmes inherited a vicious partisan guerrilla war. As Union and Confederate armies fought back and forth across Indian Territory, Missouri, and northwest Arkansas, both sides sought to exploit and gain control over the population. General Henry Halleck, commander of Union forces in Missouri from November 1861 until July 1862, decided that the pro–Confederate part of the population should pay for the war he was waging against them. In December 1861, he ordered that Missouri citizens "known to be hostile to the Union" should pay taxes "in proportion to the guilt and property of each individual." Those who refused to pay would be "immediately arrested and imprisoned." Anyone who could not pay had their property seized.[23]

In 1862, as Hindman began building a network of local, independent forces to defend the state, Halleck decreed that members of Confederate partisan groups would be denied the rights of prisoners of war. Due to the lack of supplies and the part-time nature of their service, most irregular Confederate soldiers in Missouri and Arkansas had no uniforms. While they often served in units commanded by commissioned Confederate officers, they armed themselves with pistols, civilian rifles, and shotguns. Halleck declared, "Every man who enlists in such an organization forfeits his life and becomes an outlaw." He implied that when captured, these soldiers would be executed.[24]

When Halleck was promoted and transferred, his replacement, Samuel Curtis, continued and expanded these policies with the backing of the Union District of Memphis commander, Major General William Tecumseh Sherman. In Arkansas and Missouri, Confederate artillery often fired on river boats thought to be carrying Union supplies. Sherman alleged that these batteries were operated by "guerrillas." In response to one such incident, Curtis ordered Colonel Crawford in Jefferson City, Missouri, to "arrest all the leading secesh, and hurry them from their homes. Give out the assurance that another attack on a boat will burn the town."[25] Curtis's continuation of Halleck's policies was the basis of Holmes's hostile remarks to Lt. Nobel during the prisoner exchange in September.

On October 11, General Holmes warned Curtis against conducting "a war of extermination." He wrote, "We cannot be expected to allow our enemies to decide for us whether we shall fight them in masses or individually, in uniform, without uniform, openly or from ambush." Holmes told Curtis, "If you go to the extreme ... of putting our men to death for refusing to conform to your notions, we shall be driven to ... retaliate man for man."[26] When dealing with Union officers, Holmes most often maintained his professional demeanor, but on one occasion he told one of them bluntly, "We hate you with a cordial hatred."[27]

In Texas, General Hébert was replaced by Gen. John Magruder. The personal difficulties that ruined Magruder's performance during the Peninsular Campaign seemed to have been resolved, along with the charges against him. Holmes welcomed

Magruder to the department and to Texas but warned him, "You will find neither system nor organization." He advised Magruder to confer "freely" with Texas governor Lubbock and if "it be necessary to do things without legal authority, let them be done with his full approbation if the rights of the people or State are to be effected by them."[28] Magruder's command in Texas had international implications. Because most of the Texas coast was under blockade, the Confederate government's control of trans–Rio Grande cotton traffic to Mexico was crucial. This trade was providing nearly enough "shoes, blankets, cloth, powder, lead, saltpeter, [and] sulphur" to maintain the state's war effort. Magruder would need to monitor the border carefully.[29]

When he arrived, Magruder found the harbors of Texas in Union possession from Sabine Pass to Corpus Christi, and the defensive line at the Rio Grande virtually abandoned. Most of the artillery and troops had been removed from the frontier to San Antonio and Brownsville (the site of the Fort Brown siege during the war with Mexico). Texas had approximately ten thousand troops, only half of which were "present for duty." Magruder was undaunted. Within weeks, he would mount a campaign against Union army and naval forces at Galveston and Sabine Pass.[30]

In late November, General Hindman saw an opportunity to destroy an isolated part of the Union army. Against Holmes's advice, he led twelve thousand men and twenty-two artillery pieces out of Fort Smith, Arkansas. His target was Union General Blunt, who had been in the northwest part of the state since October. Blunt and his division were dangerously far from their base at Springfield, Missouri, where two additional divisions were stationed. Hindman sent General John S. Marmaduke's division toward Cane Hill, Arkansas, about thirty miles from Blunt's camp. Blunt realized that he was about to be attacked. Rather than retreating toward Springfield, he pushed forward and attacked Marmaduke's cavalry. He also sent word to General Herron at Springfield for reinforcements. Marmaduke's force was driven from its position, but Blunt's men at Cane Hill were now thirty miles farther away from reinforcements.[31]

On December 1, Hindman advised Holmes that he could destroy Blunt's force before Herron's reinforcements arrived. Holmes reluctantly agreed to allow the campaign to continue. In the meantime, Blunt's call for help was being answered. General Herron got his two divisions on the road within hours of receiving the message and force-marched them for four days. Troops under generals Marmaduke and Mosby Parsons skirmished with Blunt's men on December 4 and 5. Instead of attacking Blunt's force, Hindman decided to bypass him and strike at Herron's relief column. Hindman's force was now only slightly larger than the soon-to-be-combined Union divisions. Marmaduke's cavalry collided with the lead units of Herron's column on the morning of December 7. After a ninety-minute running battle, the Confederates dug in along Prairie Grove ridge and waited to be attacked.[32] Rather than quickly defeating his adversary, Hindman was now on the defensive.

Herron began his attack before noon. The opposing forces fought back and forth for several hours. At 3:00 P.M., Blunt's force arrived on the field and attacked the startled Confederates. The battle raged until dark, with neither side gaining a clear advantage.

That night, the Union army was strengthened with additional troops. Hindman had no reserves, and most of his artillery ammunition had been expended. His men had no food, and his draft animals were "literally dying of starvation." He withdrew his battered army toward Van Buren, Arkansas.[33]

After the battle, illness swept through Hindman's corps. Holmes visited Hindman's headquarters at Fort Smith near Van Buren and returned to Little Rock on December 28. Of Hindman's troops he wrote to President Davis, "So much is his command reduced by disease and desertions, I have never seen such ravages by disease."[34] The next day, Blunt and Herron advanced and pushed Hindman's force out of northwest Arkansas. His army retreated to Little Rock. Almost half of Hindman's soldiers deserted along the way.

During the early part of Hindman's campaign, General Holmes sent a division from Little Rock toward the Mississippi River to assist Vicksburg, but changed his mind after the defeat at Prairie Grove. Prairie Grove further weakened Holmes's ability to defend his department, much less send troops elsewhere.[35] He wrote to Jefferson Davis on December 29 and explained that sending help to Vicksburg from Arkansas was still impossible. He told Davis, "If you had given me an order I should have believed it best but you leave the matter at my discretion.... If I send the troops [to Vicksburg] Ark. will fall."[36]

Desertions from Hindman's First Army Corps threatened the survival of Arkansas's army. Holmes gave Hindman a free hand in bringing the problem under control. Hindman ordered his generals to maintain permanent courts-martial in each division. A thirty-dollar bounty was offered for each deserter "captured or killed." The Texas troops were particularly troublesome. Hindman's orders stated, "In regards to the Texas troops, don't hesitate to disarm and tie or chain them all, or to turn loose your artillery and infantry upon them, should it ... become necessary to prevent them from deserting, or to suppress mutiny."[37]

While Hindman rebuilt his corps, the Union's first attempt to capture Vicksburg was underway. General Grant sent forty thousand men south along the rail lines toward Grenada, Mississippi. Confederate cavalry under General Van Dorn got behind Grant and destroyed his supply base and railroad connections at Holly Springs. Without supplies, Grant was forced to march his army back north. In the meantime, Sherman's thirty-two thousand men sailed down the Mississippi River and disembarked on the Yazoo River. He attacked Chickasaw Bluffs just six miles from Vicksburg, but was repulsed. The Union campaigns were hampered by poor coordination and the lack of a clear chain of command. The Confederate response was well coordinated and executed.[38]

In Texas, General Magruder attacked Galveston on January 1, 1863. His careful planning resulted in the surrender of the Union garrison after a four-hour battle. The Union blockade of the city was disrupted as well. A makeshift Confederate naval force drove off several Union ships, captured the *Harriet Lane,* and forced the destruction of the *Westfield.* Holmes sent a congratulatory message to Magruder and his men, but

Confederate euphoria over the victory would soon be overshadowed by a disaster in Arkansas.[39]

On January 9, Gen. John McClernand, commander of the Union's Army of the Mississippi, attacked one of Holmes's most heavily fortified positions. Arkansas Post was situated on a high bluff overlooking a horseshoe bend in the Arkansas River. The site was approximately one hundred miles downstream from Little Rock and fifty miles from the Mississippi River. The area had been strategically important throughout the state's history. The French had established a trading post on the site in 1686. Prior to the Civil War, at least ten forts and communities had existed in the area. The settlements benefitted from commerce on the Arkansas and Mississippi rivers. Confederate occupation of Arkansas Post prevented Union river access to the state's interior and was a base for the harassment of Union traffic on the Mississippi River.[40]

Soon after his arrival in the Trans-Mississippi, General Holmes ordered Col. John Dunnington to redesign and strengthen the defenses at Arkansas Post. The artillery had to be formidable in order to keep Union gunboats and amphibious troops from steaming upriver and attacking Little Rock. In addition to its garrison of artillerymen, Holmes assigned several thousand infantry and cavalry troops to the immediate area to protect the fort from a land attack. The completed fort, named Fort Hindman, was a square earthen structure, approximately three hundred feet on each side, with heavy wooden beam gun emplacements. Several miles of trenches and rifle pits protected the eastern and western approaches to the fort and ran along the northern bank of the river. A Union amphibious operation against the fort failed in November 1862. Holmes sent Gen. John G. Walker's division, recently arrived from Virginia, to Pine Bluff, where they would be within reasonable marching distance of the fort. In December, Holmes placed the garrison and supporting force, approximately five thousand men, under the command of Brigadier General Thomas Churchill.[41]

Churchill, a veteran of the war with Mexico and the battles of Wilson's Creek and Pea Ridge, was an aggressive commander. He used Fort Hindman as a base for attacks on Union supply and communication lines in the area. In late December, his troops captured a Union supply boat and two barges on the Mississippi River. General McClernand recognized that Churchill's activities and Fort Hindman threatened Union plans to capture Vicksburg.[42]

McClernand loaded forty artillery pieces and thirty-three thousand troops onto fifty transport vessels at Milliken's Bend, Louisiana. The fleet sailed up the Mississippi and White rivers and onto the Arkansas River. McClernand's troop transports were escorted by thirteen gunboats under the command of acting Rear Admiral David Porter, commander of the Mississippi Squadron. The envelopment of Fort Hindman began on January 9.[43]

In the wake of Prairie Grove, General Holmes was expecting an attack on Little Rock from northwestern Arkansas. As soon as he received word that Arkansas Post was in danger, he ordered General Hindman to gather as many troops as he could and mount a relief expedition. Since Prairie Grove, Hindman's broken army (half of

Holmes's Arkansas troops) had been scattered between Van Buren and Little Rock. Holmes also ordered General Walker's division at Pine Bluff to move toward Arkansas Post.

Heavy winter rains delayed the gathering of Hindman's soldiers. Some of his men "literally waded from Van Buren to Little Rock, without tents, without ambulances, strewing the way with mules" that died of starvation and exhaustion. His soldiers arrived at Little Rock during a snowstorm and climbed aboard ships for the trip downriver.[44] Walker's division left Pine Bluff in a freezing rain. The roads toward Arkansas Post turned into knee-deep mud under the feet of thousands of drenched, miserable Confederates. Streams overflowed and low areas turned into lakes.

On January 10, thousands of Union troops and artillery landed below Arkansas Post. Additional artillery took up positions across the river. The next day, Maj. Gen. William Tecumseh Sherman's infantry moved toward the fort as Confederate units retreated before them. Late in the afternoon, Union gunboats began shelling the fort and adjacent Confederate positions. The shelling and infantry maneuvers further crowded the Southerners back toward the protective earthworks surrounding the fort where they halted. The unequal duel between Fort Hindman and Union artillery lasted for hours and resulted in several of the fort's guns being knocked out of action. Porter's fleet and Sherman's soldiers virtually surrounded the fort. Well after dark, Porter's fleet sailed a short distance out of range, and the Union infantry camped for the night.[45]

Inside Fort Hindman, the Confederates repaired the damage and repositioned their artillery. In the pre-dawn hours of Sunday, General Churchill received a telegram from Holmes at Little Rock. Holmes assured Churchill that help would arrive within forty-eight hours. Later in the morning, Churchill told his brigade commanders (among them, Colonel Deshler) that Holmes had ordered the fort to be held "till help arrived or until all dead." Churchill instructed that the order should be carried out "in spirit and letter."[46] One of Churchill's soldiers wrote that "if granny holmes was down here where he could smell a little gunpowder, he would get better of the 'hold on' fit which has so recently seized him at little rock."[47]

Sherman and McClernand spent Sunday morning arranging their infantry for a final assault on the Confederate earthworks near the fort. At 1:00 P.M., Admiral Porter's gunboats steamed closer to the fort and opened fire. They were soon joined by Union batteries across the river. The bombardment lasted for three hours and disabled most of Fort Hindman's remaining guns. Union gunners, watching through their field glasses, observed one shell explode above a large gun on the fort's wall. Sixteen members of the gun crew were killed or maimed by the shrapnel. The observer stated that "seven of the poor fellows were literally blown to pieces," their body fragments being "scattered throughout their works." McClernand ordered the gunboats to end the bombardment so his infantry could attack.[48]

When the signal was given, Sherman's infantry moved toward the Confederate positions. Churchill's infantry and the few light artillery pieces that had not been destroyed poured out a deadly fire. The attack ground to a halt. For the second assault,

General McClernand arranged his troops in four battle lines and made a "desperate charge." A Confederate soldier overestimated the size of the attacking force but described the onslaught as a "grand sight, forty thousand men pressing forward ... all silent except the commands of the Officers." Seven attacks were made before the Confederates were worn down.[49]

Late in the afternoon, firing slowed on the right of Churchill's line and inside the fort. First one regiment, then another, raised a white flag. Union troops poured into the works. Churchill had not given the order, but he knew he was defeated. He surrendered the troops in his immediate area. Fighting continued, however, on the left of the Confederate battle line. Colonel Deshler and his brigade had not been advised of the surrender. His men were still firing deadly volleys into Federal troops.[50]

When the Union officers facing Deshler were told that Churchill and half of the Confederate force had surrendered, they called upon Deshler for a cease-fire. After the shooting stopped, they approached Deshler and informed him that Churchill had surrendered. They demanded that Deshler order his brigade to lay down their arms as well. Deshler told them that he had been ordered by Churchill to fight until the last man was dead, and he intended to do just that. The Union officers realized Deshler meant what he said. Not wishing to lose more men in an unnecessary attack, the Union officers sent a messenger to the fort. Within thirty minutes, a note from General Churchill was brought forward and handed to Deshler. He read the message and surrendered his men.[51] Admiral Porter quoted General Churchill as having said after the battle, "You wouldn't have got us had it not been for your damned gunboats."[52]

Hindman's relief column of troop transports never got any farther down the river than Pine Bluff. When informed of the surrender of the fort and the strength of the Union army, Hindman ordered the boats to turn around and steam back upriver. He disembarked his troops at Little Rock. Walker's division had gotten as far as South Bend Plantation when he heard the bad news. His division marched back to Pine Bluff.[53]

Many of the troops captured at Fort Hindman blamed General Holmes for not getting reinforcements to them in time. One soldier, confined in a prisoner of war camp, swore, "Granny Holmes ought to be hung."[54] Some months later, after reading Churchill's report on the battle, Holmes expressed regret at having issued his "hasty" order to hold Arkansas Post "till help arrived or until all dead." He agreed with Churchill's intention, stated later, to "cut my way out" if help did not arrive in time.[55]

For the second time in seven months, Union gunboats had been the undoing of Holmes's plans. At Malvern Cliffs, he managed to pull back from impending disaster, but Churchill and his men could not escape the naval bombardment at Arkansas Post. The failure of Hindman's and Walker's troops to arrive in time to reinforce Churchill's garrison may have been a blessing to the soldiers in those commands. Prairie Grove and the retreat afterward had decreased Hindman's corps to approximately four thousand men. His soldiers were in no condition to fight a battle anywhere, much less after struggling across the state in the middle of winter. Weather conditions and the shortage of draft animals reduced his ability to take artillery and sufficient ammunition on the relief mission. Hindman's and Walker's troops, even combined with those of Churchill, would still have been outnumbered two to one. The transports that ferried Hindman's soldiers downriver were defenseless against Union gunboats. The combined Confederate force would have been subjected to the maneuvering of a much larger Union army, coordinated with the firepower of the fleet. Major General Sherman later implied that it would have taken fifteen thousand Confederate soldiers to hold Arkansas Post against McClernand.[56] At the time of the battle, Holmes had only twenty thousand troops to defend the entire state. Nonetheless, during November and December 1862, Holmes had been pressured to send ten thousand troops to General Pemberton in Mississippi.[57] The battle of Arkansas Post cost the Union army approximately one thousand casualties. The Confederates lost 4,791 men captured and one hundred killed or wounded, nearly one-fourth the effective troops in the state.

The Union victory at Fort Hindman accomplished little. General McClernand wanted to advance from Arkansas Post and capture Little Rock, but only days after the battle, Grant ordered him to destroy Fort Hindman, withdraw his force, and report for operations against Vicksburg. Strategically, Holmes's Arkansas troop strength had been struck a serious blow, and any credibility he had as department commander ended. It was apparent that Union forces on the Mississippi River could attack Arkansas at will. Without a railroad system to move and supply his soldiers, Holmes could neither react quickly enough to contest Union amphibious landings at one end of the state nor conduct successful operations at the other end. (During the Fort Hindman campaign, General Marmaduke was repulsed in a raid on Springfield, Missouri.) Arkansas was at the mercy of the Union army. The primary reason McClernand did not attack Little Rock was that Grant was more interested in Vicksburg.

The Arkansas River approach to Little Rock still had to be defended. Engineers determined that the next best location for fortifications upriver from Arkansas Post was near Pine Bluff. Holmes ordered the construction of Fort Pleasants on the heights of Days Bluff. The Confederate commander in the area, Gen. Daniel Frost, requested that Arkansas Post's heavy artillery, abandoned by the Union army, should be recovered and sent to him for use at the new fort. Frost, mindful of the massive Union force that had attacked Arkansas Post, proposed that Holmes send him "a force of 10,000 to stop 30,000 at that point."[58] Holmes did not have ten thousand soldiers he could spare.

In the aftermath of his losses at Prairie Grove and Fort Hindman, General Holmes had to rebuild his Arkansas army. The nearly five thousand men captured at Fort Hindman were not paroled after the fight and would not return to Confederate service in the foreseeable future. In February 1863, Holmes had 16,990 men on the Arkansas roster, but only 8,475 were combat ready. The approaching spring would bring intensified campaigning after the winter of hard fighting. Holmes offered amnesty to all deserters who returned to their units and intensified conscription enforcement. By May, he had 22,264 men under arms in Arkansas.[59] Before the next campaign season began, however, Holmes's status as a department commander would come to an end.

During the winter of 1862–1863, social and economic conditions in Arkansas deteriorated along with the military situation. Prices skyrocketed and civilian suppliers of military goods and food were reluctant to do business with the Confederate government and army. Inflation produced additional hardships on individual soldiers and their families as well.[60]

In a January 28 letter to Holmes, President Davis again condemned the use of martial law and price controls. In approving, though conditionally, Holmes's decision against sending reinforcements from Arkansas to Vicksburg, Davis wrote, "If you are correct as to the consequences which would follow, you have properly exercised the discretion which was intrusted to you." Davis complained that Holmes's troops in Louisiana had done nothing to protect the rail connection from Monroe to the Mississippi River across from Vicksburg. He advised Holmes that Gen. Edmond Kirby Smith would take command of Louisiana and Texas. He hinted that Holmes should cooperate with plans that Smith might formulate. Davis told Holmes that the loss of either Port Hudson or Vicksburg would "inflict upon the Confederacy an injury which I am sure you have not failed to appreciate."[61]

After seven months in the Trans-Mississippi, Holmes had not been able to improve the military situation. Worse still was his political position. A campaign to replace him was well under way. The Arkansas congressional delegation wrote to President Davis in February. They joined their governor in protesting General Holmes's continuing use of martial law.[62] In paraphrasing "a variety of sources," Secretary of War James A. Seddon wrote, "The most deplorable accounts reached Richmond of the disorder, confusion, and demoralization everywhere prevalent, both with the armies and the people of that state." According to the sources, Holmes had "lost the confidence and attachment of all."[63]

Seddon's "sources" claimed that Holmes's army had "dwindled by desertion, sickness and death from 40,000 or 50,000 men to some 15,000 to 18,000." One of the informants was Albert Pike. He circulated a pamphlet alleging that Holmes and Hindman had reduced the Arkansas army "from forty odd thousand to less than 17,000."[64] With only unreliable figures available, Seddon could not credibly refute these allegations, if he had been inclined to do so. Holmes never had at his disposal forty or fifty thousand combat ready troops in the Trans-Mississippi. Only rarely, between April 1862 and the end of 1863, were there more than 32,583 troops present for duty.[65] A January 1863 report lists Holmes's "effective" and "aggregate" strength at the same unlikely number of fifty thousand men.[66] This report contained the most current figures available to Seddon when the decision to replace Holmes was being made. Seddon would have recognized these particular figures as pure fiction and not submitted by Holmes. Due to desertion, sickness, and persistent shortages of food, clothing, shoes, weapons and ammunition, the department's effective force was usually half of any total reported. (Surviving troop strength reports for the Trans-Mississippi reveal that, often, some troops were not counted, some reports were not received, and estimates were given in the absence of reports.)

In saying that no one was happy with Holmes, Seddon's sources were accurate.

Generals Johnston, Bragg, and Pemberton regarded him as an obstacle to their plans to retake west Tennessee and save Vicksburg. Holmes had continued many of Hindman's draconian measures, even in defiance of orders from Richmond.[67] Infuriating Arkansas politicians, Holmes had retained Hindman as the district commander. Both men aggressively enforced conscription, a law despised by Confederate soldiers and civilians alike.[68] Holmes had been unable to improve conditions for the civilian population. They continued to suffer in the wake of cavalry raids, fighting between opposing guerrilla bands, and campaigns conducted by both armies.

Holmes's Arkansas soldiers were under-supplied and poorly equipped, with no relief in sight. The Richmond government had provided little help from across the Mississippi. The lack of outside support, combined with insufficient transportation and manufacturing capabilities within the department, resulted in chronic shortages. Many of Hindman's soldiers could not participate in the Prairie Grove campaign because they had no weapons or shoes. During that battle, Hindman was forced to withdraw, not because he had been beaten, but because his army had exhausted its ability to continue the fight.[69] The army's retreat ruined morale and further aggravated an already high desertion rate. Holmes's Arkansas troops were hungry, poorly armed, unpaid, and knew they were losing the war.

At the department level, Holmes and his subordinates had defended or contested control over most of the Trans-Mississippi. By February 1863, the Union army had territory and the advantage in Indian Territory, northwest Arkansas, and along the Mississippi River. Many areas of the department, however, that were under Confederate control or contested by the opposing armies were largely unchanged from July 1862.[70] Federal armies poised around the Trans-Mississippi had certainly grown more threatening during Holmes's tenure. Most of the Mississippi River was lost, but much of that circumstance was beyond his control. The Confederate navy had lost its ability to defend the river when the River Defense Fleet and the ironclad *Arkansas* were destroyed during the spring and summer of 1862. In September of that year, the Confederacy controlled the Mississippi River from just north of New Orleans to just south of Helena. Six months later, only one hundred fifty miles of the river, from Port Hudson to Vicksburg, remained under Southern control. The large guns mounted on riverside bluffs at those cities held the Union navy at bay.[71]

Holmes could have strengthened the Louisiana portion of the river, but he would have done so at the expense of Arkansas. Nonetheless, Holmes realized that his command of the department was a failure. He had suspected from the beginning that turning the war around in the Trans-Mississippi was beyond his capabilities. He wanted neither the assignment nor the promotion to lieutenant general that came with it. Now, he was paying the price for having accepted both.

Not surprisingly, General Hindman wanted out of the department. Holmes had defended Hindman's prior command in the region and had given him great responsibility in Arkansas. Now, Hindman was blaming Holmes for his defeats in the state. In February, Hindman wrote to Braxton Bragg and threatened to resign from the army if he had to stay in Holmes's command. He had previously written to President Davis on the same topic. Hindman's letter revealed bitterness at having been replaced as department commander by Holmes and then being required by Holmes to remain as a subordinate district commander. He said, "Matters have not prospered since General Holmes came." Hindman was unwilling to bear the "odium of failures of which I am not justly chargeable." He referred to the situation in Arkansas as a "grave of ambition, energy, and system." Hindman asked Bragg to keep his comments confidential, saying, "The personal relations between General Holmes and myself are not unkind, and I have no wish to injure him, though he has about destroyed me."[72]

Hindman's demand to leave Arkansas was a moot point. At the end of January, the Arkansas congressional delegation unanimously demanded that "General Hindman should be recalled" from the command of Arkansas.[73] They cited the public's lack of support for him. The delegation privately expressed support for martial law, but Hindman's martial law, conscription enforcement, and wage and price controls (the same measures that Holmes defended and continued when he kept Hindman in the state) had turned the population against him. In February, Holmes told President Davis that he would have replaced Hindman earlier but had no other general with his experience. Holmes described Hindman's political enemies in Arkansas as "violent and open in their denunciations" of him.[74] Under public pressure, the delegation publically reversed itself with regard to martial law on February 17.[75]

Hindman was transferred to Braxton Bragg's army. On March 4, he issued an emotional farewell to his battered First Army Corps. He told his soldiers that he had requested to be transferred, but "not because of any dissatisfaction with you." He assured them, "No commander was ever more sincerely attached to his officers and men." Hindman did not mention any sincere attachments to General Holmes, saying only, "I refrain from all allusion to the true causes of my departure."[76] Hindman, like many of Holmes's subordinates in the army, was reluctant to publicly disparage the president's friend. After demanding Holmes's removal as department commander, Arkansas politicians requested that Davis keep him in the state: "We now respectfully add that we would guard the feelings of General Holmes, a faithful and devoted soldier and gentleman ... and feeling a personal confidence and regard for him, would prefer that you continue him among us."[77]

On February 26, Davis wrote to Holmes. Less than a month had passed since Kirby Smith had been given command of half of the department. Now, Davis was informing Holmes that he had put Smith in command of the Trans-Mississippi. As reasons for relieving Holmes, Davis cited the fall of Arkansas Post and General Hindman's abandonment of northwest Arkansas after Prairie Grove.[78]

Lieutenant General Edmund Kirby Smith assumed command of all Confederate forces west of the Mississippi River on March 7.[79] In reporting to President Davis on the condition of the department, Smith criticized Holmes's preoccupation with Arkansas and Indian Territory at the expense of the Texas and Louisiana districts. He stated that the "defect" in Holmes's administration was "no general system, no common head, each district was acting independently." However, Smith complimented Holmes on rebuilding Arkansas troop strength, saying, "Men were returning to their colors" and regiments were rapidly restoring their numbers through "the wise and energetic measures taken by General Holmes, in bringing back absentees, providing for the comfort of his men, and dispersing the bands of disaffected throughout the Dist of Ark."[80]

Smith was popular with Arkansas politicians, but he disappointed them when he made Alexandria, Louisiana, his headquarters. Smith kept General Taylor in the District of Western Louisiana and Magruder would remain in Texas. Bowing to the Arkansas congressional delegation, Smith appointed Holmes as district commander of Arkansas.[81]

On March 2, just prior to Holmes's reassignment, one of his spies was arrested by police officers in St. Louis, Missouri. Twenty-one-year-old Samuel Clifford (alias Samuel Stafford, alias Samuel Kibble), a native of Ohio, was found "lurking within the military lines of the United States in the disguise of a citizen." Union authorities found documents in his possession listing "the dispositions of the forces" of the Union army in Kentucky and a letter addressed to "General Holmes, C.S.A., Little Rock, Arkansas." Union provost officials charged Clifford with "Being a Spy" and noted on one document that he was also a "Horse Thief, etc." The following July, Stafford was found guilty and sentenced to be "hanged by the neck until he is dead." The death sentence was eventually reduced to "imprisonment and hard labor" for the duration of the war.[82]

One of Holmes's first acts as district commander was to warn, again, Union authorities about their treatment of Confederate prisoners of war. Union troops, acting on orders from Admiral Porter, had posted notices at Columbia, Arkansas, advising that "persons taken in the act of firing on unarmed vessels will be treated as highwaymen and assassins, and no quarter will be shown them." In his March 12 response to Porter, Holmes reminded the admiral of the "legitimate belligerent right" of destroying enemy property whether it was on board ship or on land. He warned Porter that "every violation of the rights of [Confederate] prisoners ... will be visited in kind" upon Union prisoners "without regard to rank."[83]

Holmes wrote to his daughter, Elizabeth, in March. His thoughts had turned to his deceased wife, Laura, and how he missed her "purifying influence." He referred to Laura as the most "perfect woman your father has ever known." Holmes missed his daughter and was grateful that his work kept him busy: "Was it not for my constant occupation I should be very lonely and sometimes almost wish I had brought you with me. You would have been warmly greeted by many friends who would have made much of you for the General's sake but ... you would soon have learned and felt the difference between the General's friends and the generous & affectionate relatives that now surround you." He lamented the impact of the war and Laura's death on his family: "It grieves me that my children are growing up strangers to each other." He hoped that someday he could "gather my children around me in my old age." Holmes wrote of the "sufferings of thousands of others for our beloved country" and reminded his daughter that "we cannot be too grateful in terrible times like these we live in."[84]

Toward the end of the letter, Holmes's mood brightened. He talked of family and friends who were serving with him. Theo Jr. had been ill and was "convalescing but slowly.... If he is careful, I hope he will soon be as strong as ever." He mentioned John W. Hinsdale, who had been promoted to captain the previous September. Holmes even displayed a rare attempt at humor in writing, "John is going to make a first rate adj.[utant] Genl. He is industrious and very quick. His promotion did not give him the big head though it made [him] two inches taller."[85]

Another of Holmes's nephews, Charles Wetmore Broadfoot, arrived in Little Rock on March 18. The general had been working for months to secure a commission and transfer for the twenty-one-year-old sergeant. Broadfoot joined the 1st North Carolina Volunteers in June 1861 and served with that regiment until it was disbanded the following November. He joined the 43rd North Carolina Troops in July 1862 and was promoted to 5th sergeant in October. By then, Holmes had already recommended his promotion to 2nd lieutenant, but the commission was not approved until January 1863. Broadfoot joined Theo Jr. on Holmes's staff as an aide-de-camp.[86]

Holmes's reduction from department to district commander did not affect his rank. He remained a lieutenant general. Although the affair had caused him embarrassment, he was genuinely grateful to President Davis for making the change in command. In April, he wrote to Davis and observed that Kirby Smith's appointment "has given great satisfaction to everybody and I have great hope that his usefulness will not be marred as mine has been by the political complications of the country."[87]

In advising the president on the disposition and condition of the troops in Arkansas, Holmes reported that deserters and conscripts were "being rapidly brought in." He wrote at length regarding the hardships faced by the "Indian troops" of various tribes that were fighting for the Confederacy. Holmes was reminded of his days on the frontier. As a participant in the Indian Removal, he had witnessed the wretched conditions endured by the tribes. Sons and grandsons of the "Trail of Tears" were now fighting for the Confederacy in Indian Territory. He described the hardships they and their families were enduring. Of them he wrote, "With all this there are no people in the Confederacy more loyal and few more tolerant.... Too much praise cannot be awarded to Stand Watie and the other chiefs who have inculcated a spirit of obedience & confidence that is perfectly admirable."[88]

Holmes kept his headquarters in Little Rock. Previously, he had left mundane military matters to General Hindman. Now, he was more closely connected with day-to-day operations in Arkansas. Even the most routine personnel matters came to his attention. One soldier, twenty-seven-year-old William Glenn, a shoemaker and leather tanner by trade, wrote directly to Holmes. After ten months in the army, Glenn deserted from the 36th Arkansas Infantry because he "cant stand it much longer." Glenn knew that shoemakers were often exempted from combat assignments. He told Holmes, "I mint no harm.... Pleas send me to taning[,] if I was a stout man I woodent ask.... I am a bout bare footed now." Glenn signed the note adding that he was "a privet and all wasie has bin"[89] On April 19, Private Glenn was transferred to the army quartermaster at Jefferson, Texas, and detailed as a shoemaker.[90]

In preparation for the approaching campaign season, Holmes needed firsthand information on the Union army's activities in northwest Arkansas. In early spring, he ordered Capt. Joseph Peevy into that area on a reconnaissance mission. After an eleven-day expedition between Dardenelle, Arkansas, and Cassville, Missouri, Peevy reported on the position, strength, and movements of the Union army. He also brought disturbing news about atrocities committed against pro–Confederate citizens in the area. According to Peevy, Union forces or their partisans had "murdered every southern man that could be found." In Carroll County, a fourteen-year-old boy and four adults were killed, and fifteen houses were burned. Peevy said that Union forces "seem to have hoisted the black flag, for no southern man, however old and infirm or however little he may have assisted our cause, is permitted to escape them alive." Peevy told General Holmes that the pro–Confederate civilians in the area "look to you as the avenger of their wrongs."[91]

In taking command of the department, Kirby Smith came face to face with the same circumstances that had broken Hindman and Holmes. He realized that the estimates of troop strength used to smear Holmes "had been greatly exaggerated." Smith was more supportive than Holmes of operating along Louisiana's western bank of the Mississippi to reduce pressure on Vicksburg. To that end, he shifted "all the disposable force of the department ... to the relief of Port Hudson and Vicksburg." Smith ordered two of Holmes's brigades "to the Mississippi, above Lake Providence, to break up the Federal system of planting, and to annoy, and if possible, destroy their transports."[92] In Arkansas, Holmes's forces would launch two attacks, Cape Girardeau and Fayetteville, during his first weeks as a district commander.

In mid–April, one of Holmes's brigade commanders, Gen. William L. Cabell, learned that Union soldiers at Fayetteville were preparing to begin a campaign from that city. Just that month, Cabell had been promoted from major to brigadier general (on Holmes's recommendation) and sent to northwest Arkansas.[93] The Union army's intention was to march out of Fayetteville, reinforce General Phillips, and move against Confederate general William Steele in Indian Territory. Rather than allow the combination of the two forces, Cabell wanted to attack Fayetteville with his brigade. General Steele approved the plan.

Cabell and his brigade of nine hundred mounted soldiers and two artillery pieces left Ozark, Arkansas, on April 16, and attacked Fayetteville at dawn two days later. After three hours of hard fighting, much of which took place in town, General Cabell withdrew his brigade and returned to Ozark. He blamed his repulse on inefficient officers and poorly armed soldiers. Many of his troops carried "Arkadelphia rifles" that were "no better than shotguns." He stated flatly, "Had I had 500 long-range guns, with good cartridges, I could have taken the place in an hour."[94] Cabell was eager to make another attempt on Fayetteville, but would not need to do so. Union troops abandoned the town within a week.

Cabell's raid provided General Holmes with some disturbing information. Federal army recruiters were having success at enlisting Arkansas men and Confederate deserters. Some Confederate commanders and politicians had, in the past, been publically dismissive of these reports. In his communication to Holmes, Cabell said that although the Union regiments he attacked were composed of "disloyal citizens and deserters from our army ... they resisted every attack made on them, and, as fast as driven out of one house, would occupy another and deliver their fire." He reported that the Union force at Fayetteville was composed of about two thousand men and that they "fought as well as any Federal troops I have seen." He also noted that his artillery ran out of ammunition during the fight. Additionally, he was forced to exclude part of his command from taking part in the raid. Three of his cavalry companies had to remain at Ozark because they were "badly armed with horses unshod."[95]

A second raid began on April 18. Marmaduke's division departed in two columns from Arkansas and moved into southeast Missouri. He had five thousand men and ten cannons, but twelve hundred of his men were unarmed and nine hundred soldiers had no horses. (One reason he took the dismounted soldiers along was to keep them from deserting as soon as he left.) His plan was to catch Union General McNeil's two thousand cavalrymen at Bloomfield, destroy them, and resupply his division with captured weapons and horses. Thus resupplied, he could draw out Union troops for another fight.[96]

During the campaign, Marmaduke's brigades fought skirmishes at Patterson, Frederickstown, Jackson, Bloomfield, and Chalk Bluff. Instead of getting caught out in the open, General McNeil withdrew his force toward Cape Girardeau, which was heavily fortified and designed to resist land and river-borne attacks. McNeil arrived there on April 24. He was re-enforced by two gunboats that brought additional troops and evacuated women and children from the town. McNeil now had approximately three thousand troops at his disposal. With gunboats defending the river, he removed artillery from two riverfront forts and strengthened the two forts on the land side.[97]

When Marmaduke saw that McNeil was dug in at Cape Girardeau, he decided not to make a serious attempt to storm the town. Instead, he ordered brigade commander Joseph Shelby to make a demonstration, then withdraw. Shelby's feint developed into an attack that lasted for several hours on the evening of April 26. Initially offering a chance of success, Shelby's cavalry attacks were stalled by heavy artillery fire. This prompted Marmaduke to bring up his other brigade. By the time the division was consolidated, Marmaduke had decided that any attack he could make would fail. He called off the campaign and was back in Arkansas on May 2.[98] Reports soon surfaced that Marmaduke's cavalrymen had engaged in looting and various other depredations against civilians during the raid. Holmes disciplined Marmaduke by reassigning half of his division to Gen. Lucius "Marsh" Walker. Marmaduke's wrath was directed at Walker rather than Holmes. Hatred between the two men would reach into the fields north of Helena, Arkansas, and beyond.[99]

While Holmes's troops conducted raids, Gen. Kirby Smith, now headquartered at Shreveport, searched for ways to relieve pressure on Vicksburg. Milliken's Bend was located just upstream from Vicksburg on the west side of the Mississippi River. Union troops had occupied the area since late 1862. Confederate control of the area would allow supplies to reach Vicksburg and perhaps divert Union troops away from the siege. In June, Smith sent Major Gen. John G. Walker's division to attack Milliken's Bend and Young's Point, nearby. One of Walker's brigades advanced on Young's Point but was delayed for several hours. The attack was canceled. At Milliken's Bend, the attack was made, but difficult terrain and a stubborn defense by African American troops produced heavy casualties. The arrival of Union gunboats stalled the attack. Seeing their position untenable, the Confederate commanders withdrew. Louisiana district commander General Taylor reported that "the officers and men of this division were possessed of such a dread of gunboats.... This circumstance ... attributed to the meager results of the expedition."[100] If Kirby Smith was to help Vicksburg from his side of the Mississippi River, he would need to look elsewhere.

8

The Battle of Helena

Since its capture by Union General Samuel Curtis in July 1862, the city of Helena had posed a threat to the interior of Arkansas and the defense of Vicksburg. Because the Union army could strike deep into Arkansas using men and supplies brought by the navy, Holmes and Kirby Smith had to keep troops in the vicinity of Helena rather than use them elsewhere. In supporting Grant's operations against Vicksburg, Helena served as an important link in the Union supply chain.[1] Helena had also become a gathering place for runaway slaves. This prompted plantation owners in Arkansas to complain to the government. The Union army began recruiting African American regiments at Helena in April 1863.[2]

Secretary of War Seddon had wanted the city recaptured since his appointment to Davis's cabinet. If recaptured, Union efforts to retake Helena would distract Grant from his Vicksburg campaign. General Joseph Johnston was responsible for efforts to relieve Vicksburg from the east side of the river. After March 1863, Seddon prompted Johnston to use his influence and coordinate efforts with General Kirby Smith. On May 25, Seddon urged Johnston to see that the idea of attacking Helena would be "voluntarily embraced and executed."[3]

Union troop strength at Helena was subject to change on short notice. There were frequent rumors that the city had been weakened in order to send reinforcements to the Vicksburg campaign. Holmes was aware that pressure was building for an attack on Helena. General Smith, from his headquarters in Shreveport, offered little more than moral support for operations in Arkansas. In early May he advised Holmes to "attack the enemy, should the opportunity offer for doing so with hope of success. You can expect no assistance from this quarter."[4] Holmes was skeptical of the idea of attacking Helena but decided to pursue the possibility further. An attack on Helena would require Sterling Price's division.

Major General Sterling Price returned to Arkansas in March 1863 after an unsuccessful year east of the Mississippi. He had been in command of the District of Tennessee and had fought at Iuka and Corinth, Mississippi. While there, he lobbied to be returned with his Missouri troops to the Trans-Mississippi. His ultimate goal was to retake Missouri. He implied that he might lead his troops back across the Mississippi River with or without President Davis's permission. For months, there had been rumors that Price would lead several states to form the so-called Northwestern Confederacy, a separate nation that would, presumably, ally itself with the Confederacy but could pursue a separate national agenda.[5]

President Davis and his cabinet became thoroughly disgusted with Price and finally ordered him and his staff back to the Trans-Mississippi, without their troops, in February 1863.[6] Price arrived at Little Rock in March. General Holmes put him in charge of Hindman's old territory, northern Arkansas and Missouri. Holmes gave him command of a division consisting of two brigades under generals Dandridge McRae and Mosby Parsons. In June, Price and his division were headquartered at Jacksonport, Arkansas.[7]

On June 8, Holmes left Little Rock for a meeting with Price. His mobile field office and quarters, a modified army ambulance wagon pulled by four mules (a common conveyance for senior officers) broke down while en route. Holmes often traveled in his ambulance when his duties took him more than a day's ride.[8] By courier, Holmes sent a message to Price asking if his division was strong enough to lead an attack on Helena. Price replied that his troops were ready and that he wanted to attack Helena even if there were as many as five thousand Union soldiers there.[9] Holmes was still skeptical. On June 13, he wrote, "4,000 or 5,000 men in Helena, fortified as they are, to take it would cost too much." Two days later, he received information from General Marmaduke that the garrison at Helena was "less numerous" than previously reported and was "very weak." Marmaduke advised that a portion of the force had been sent to reinforce Grant.[10] Given this information, Price's enthusiasm, and the pressure he was under to take action, Holmes decided to make the attack.

Helena would be a gamble for Holmes. He told Price, "I risk much in this expedition; you have a great reputation with the public." He extracted a promise from Price to publically support the decision to attack Helena should the effort fail.[11] If Holmes converged his forces quickly, struck hard, and managed the affair well, the plan might work. He knew that a victory at Helena could restore his reputation and credibility as a general. Back East, the perception of his earlier failures had become fact. Two weeks after Holmes decided to attack Helena, an article in the Richmond *Daily Dispatch* referred to him as one of the "officers who did mischief around this city" during the Peninsular Campaign. The article also criticized Holmes for diminishing a forty-thousand-man army in the Trans-Mississippi to twelve thousand and for leading an army that was "doing nothing."[12]

Holmes gathered his divided eastern Arkansas forces. General Price's division at Jacksonport consisted of two infantry brigades: General Dandridge McRae's three Arkansas regiments, General Parsons's four Missouri regiments, and a battalion from Arkansas. Brigadier General John S. Marmaduke, also at Jacksonport, had five regiments and one battalion of Missouri cavalry. At Little Rock, Brigadier General James F. Fagan had a brigade of four regiments. Brigadier General Lucius "Marsh" Walker commanded two Arkansas cavalry regiments and was already in the vicinity of Helena on picket duty. A large part of Holmes's army was cavalry, but he planned to use most of them as infantry during the attack.[13]

On June 18, Holmes issued marching orders. He wanted his generals to move quickly, arrive near Helena, and strike before the city could be reinforced. He ordered that only ammunition and necessary supply wagons would accompany the troops. Each soldier was to "march without baggage except one blanket."[14] The divisions of Price and Marmaduke left Jacksonport on June 22. General Holmes, most of his staff (including Theo) and Fagan's brigade started toward Helena from Little Rock on June 26. Governor Flanagin and Adjutant General Gordon Peay of Arkansas accompanied Holmes on the campaign. Their party traveled by train and steamboat as far as Clarendon.

The first thing that went wrong for Holmes's plan was the weather. Several days of torrential rain came to eastern Arkansas. Creeks spilled over their banks and rivers rose dramatically. River fords were not useable, and bridges washed away. Marmaduke's and Price's columns suffered the most during their ten-day march. The area between Jacksonport and Helena became one vast swamp, broken only by swollen rivers. Thousands of marching feet turned the soft roads into knee-deep mud. Wagons and artillery bogged down and had to be pushed or carried for miles. General Marmaduke, in describing the area of Flat Creek Bayou, wrote that he "found the Bayou a quarter a mile wide, fifty yards of which is swimming water." Millions of prairie flies and black gnats tormented the mules, horses, and men.[15] The soldiers and draft animals were miserable and wore down quickly. Price's division linked up with other elements of Holmes's army completely exhausted and four days later than planned.[16]

On July 3, Holmes gathered his commanders at a farmhouse five miles west of Helena. By then, his scouts and spies had informed him that the city was stronger and more heavily fortified than he had been led to believe. Nonetheless, he decided to proceed with the attack.[17] His plan called for simultaneous "daylight" assaults on the city from the west and north.[18] Holmes had 7,646 troops at his disposal. General Price's division, three thousand men, would make the main attack. Price's brigadier generals, McRae and Parsons, would take their brigades toward Helena from the west, down Spring Creek Road, and attack Graveyard Hill.[19] General Fagan's fourteen hundred men were to advance along the Upper Little Rock Road, on Price's right, and attack Hindman Hill. Marmaduke's cavalry was to move down the Old St. Francis Road and attack Rightor (or Reiter's) Hill north of town. General Walker and his fourteen hundred men were ordered to protect Marmaduke's left from counterattack by advancing down Sterling Road, closest to the river.[20] According to Holmes, all of his senior commanders approved the plan.[21] At the end of the meeting, perhaps remembering Kirby Smith's "You can expect no assistance" remark, Holmes told Sterling Price, "This is my fight. If I succeed, I want the glory; and if I fail, I am willing to bear the odium."[22] No doubt, Price felt free to criticize Holmes if the attack failed.

Helena's garrison commander, Major General Benjamin Prentiss, had suspected for several days that an attack was imminent. At 2:30 A.M. each day, his men were up and at their posts. In the days leading up to the attack, his troops worked to obstruct roads leading toward the city and improve the earthworks.[23] The land around Helena was covered with dense forest. Deep ravines with steep sides cut through the countryside around the town. Union soldiers chopped down hundreds of trees and placed them as barriers in the roads and ravines and on what level ground there was. More than four

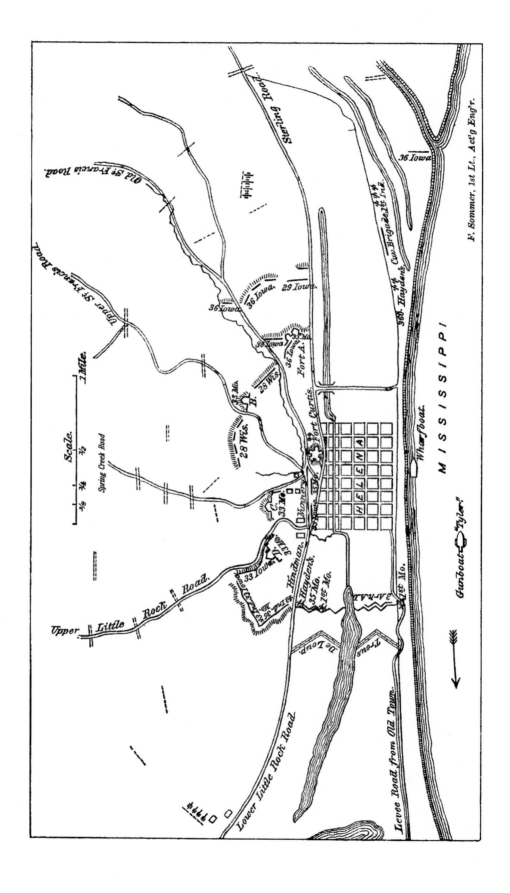

thousand Union soldiers occupied the fortifications. The Union navy was also close at hand. At Helena, the Mississippi River was almost two miles wide. The U.S.S. *Tyler*, a timber-clad gunboat, patrolled the river's edge. The *Tyler* was 189 ft. long, had a crew of sixty-seven sailors, and was armed with sixteen 8-inch smooth-bore cannons and three 30-pounder Parrott guns. *Tyler* could shell any target in or well beyond the town.

The main feature of Helena's defenses was a star-shaped earthen fort, Fort Curtis, near the northwest corner of town. The fort had walls thirty feet tall and was armed with heavy artillery, five 24-pounders and two 32-pounders. These guns could reach anywhere in the surrounding area. Arranged in a protective semicircle less than a mile from Fort Curtis were four smaller forts. Battery A was on Rightor Hill, one half mile to the north between Old Saint Francis and Sterling roads. Battery B was a third of a mile from Helena to the northwest on Upper St. Francis Road. Battery C, on Graveyard Hill, was just west of town between Upper Little Rock Road and Spring Creek Road. Battery D was on Hindman Hill near Upper Little Rock Road at the southwest edge of town. Each hilltop fort was armed with field artillery, and each position could lend supporting fire to adjacent positions. All of the area in front of the forts, and much in between was fortified with trenches and rifle pits. Hindman Hill had five lines of earthworks protecting battery D.[24]

Holmes ordered Fagan and Sterling Price's division (the brigades of Parsons and McRae) to capture Hindman and Graveyard hills, then converge on Fort Curtis. The attacks on the two hills needed to be quick and successful early in the battle. If the soldiers did not keep moving, Fort Curtis would pour a deadly fire down on them. Parsons and McRae would need substantial support from Confederate artillery. North of town, Walker and Marmaduke could expect heavy opposition once they reached Union earthworks in front of Rightor Hill. Holmes wanted Marmaduke to make his attack directly on Fort Rightor, then proceed to Fort Curtis. Walker was to stay on Marmaduke's left flank, prevent the reinforcement of Fort Rightor, and oppose counterattacks.

Shortly after dusk on July 3, Fagan started his march toward Helena approximately three miles distant. As he approached the town, he sent part of his artillery and Colonel William Brooks's 34th Arkansas Infantry to Lower Little Rock Road. Brook's assignment was to protect Fagan's right flank, engage Union troops stationed south of town, and draw their attention and fire away from the main attack.[25]

Approximately one mile from the outermost Union works, Fagan's main force found Upper Little Rock Road impassable, blocked by felled trees for the entire distance to Hindman Hill. On either side of the obstructed road, a thick forest laced with ravines ran all the way up "to the very entrenchments of the enemy." Fagan ordered his mounted officers to leave their horses behind and advance on foot. He also had to leave behind some of his artillery and ammunition wagons.[26] North of town, Marmaduke's division of 1,750 men and Walker's brigade advanced along Old Saint Francis and Sterling roads.

Opposite: Helena, Arkansas, 1863. Defenses and approaches to the city (*Official Records*, Series I, v. 22., pt. 1, p. 394).

Both columns ran into the same roadway obstructions and rough countryside that troubled Fagan, but Marmaduke's troops made better time. At 4:30 A.M., his skirmishers began exchanging shots with Union pickets approximately three-quarters of a mile from Fort Rightor. His lead units quickly pushed the Union soldiers back to their trenches, within one hundred fifty yards of the fort.[27]

At dawn, the rest of Marmaduke's infantry and artillery approached the fort. When they were two hundred yards away, he formed his battle line and sent them forward. As they advanced, Union infantry and artillery appeared on and behind their left flank and began pouring out a deadly fire. Marmaduke had to halt the attack. He knew that General Walker was supposed to be protecting his left flank but could see no indication of Walker's brigade on the field. Walker's soldiers, having encountered obstructions and difficulties on Sterling Road, had not kept up with Marmaduke's advance. They had managed to push Union pickets back until daylight, but stopped to clear the road for their artillery. This delay allowed Union reinforcements to come up. Soon, Walker's force was engaged in simply trying to hold its position. He never got his soldiers far enough forward to protect Marmaduke. Twice, Marmaduke sent messages to Walker requesting him to advance and drive the enemy away so the attack could continue. In failing to close the gap between the two forces, Walker allowed Marmaduke's left flank to remain exposed. Neither Marmaduke nor Walker made any further progress.[28]

Through a similar tangle of forest and undergrowth, in the dark of night, Fagan's skirmishers clawed their way for nearly a mile along Upper Little Rock Road. When he got close enough to see the enemy's position on Hindman Hill, Fagan saw that the

Fort Curtis. This 1863 photograph shows the interior of the fort and the fort's flagpole (from the collections of the Arkansas History Commission).

Union defenders were "on the alert, and evidently awaiting and expecting an attack."[29] As soon as his infantry got into position, Fagan began his attack "at 20 minutes after daylight," according to Holmes. The two attacks, the first by Marmaduke, the second by Fagan, began within minutes of each other.[30]

During the final approach to their objective, Price's two brigades had run into the same terrain and forest difficulties that had so troubled Fagan, Marmaduke, and Walker. Like Fagan, Price left his cannons behind and proceeded on foot with his infantry and artillery soldiers. He instructed his gunners to be prepared to use the Union cannons he "expected to capture" on Graveyard Hill.[31] After struggling for three miles through the darkness, Price decided to halt his division approximately one mile from town. He thought he was ahead of schedule and wanted his soldiers to rest before beginning the final push toward Helena. Upon resuming the march, Price's troops ran into Union pickets approximately one-half mile from Graveyard Hill.[32]

As his skirmishers pushed the Union pickets toward town, Price brought up his two brigades and arranged them in two deep, narrow columns, in order to move through the forest. Parsons's brigade was on the right and McRae's on the left of the road. Local guides who were leading the brigades through the woods soon disappeared, and the distance between the two brigades widened. The advance was delayed until the correct line of march could be determined. Once McRae's and Parsons's brigades reached their assigned positions, Price ordered another halt. His soldiers were completely exhausted from their difficult passage.[33]

As a dense morning fog rose, General Holmes arrived and demanded to know why Price's attack had not gotten underway. Holmes knew that Fagan was engaged and assumed Marmaduke and Walker were attacking as well. After exchanging messages with McRae and Parsons, Price realized that each officer was waiting for the other to advance. The two brigades were separated by intervening forest and hills. Neither general had any idea where the other was. Price ordered both brigade commanders to "make the assault without further delay."[34] According to Holmes, Price was "at least half an hour behind his time."[35] The spearhead of the entire operation, General Sterling Price's attack on Graveyard Hill, was the last to begin.

The fog that had enshrouded the opposing armies for three hours dissipated as the sun rose and would be gone by 8:00 A.M. The day would be brutally hot and humid. Price's brigades emerged from the woods on either side of Spring Creek Road and moved forward in "perfect order." The 28th Wisconsin regiment, on picket duty north of the road, retreated as Price's division approached. One of their lieutenants stated later that some of the Confederates fired on a "camp of negroes who had camped just inside our picket line."[36] As the fleeing Wisconsin pickets reached their earthworks, Price's division came within range of most of the Union line. Graveyard Hill was in a recessed part of Helena's fortifications. Price's soldiers began receiving fire, not only from Graveyard Hill in their immediate front, but also from Hindman Hill to the south and from Union infantry and artillery positions on Upper Saint Francis Road. Despite heavy casualties, Price's brigades gave a "rebel yell" and charged forward. As the Union defenders fled, the Confederates stormed over Graveyard Hill and planted their flags on the summit. It was approximately 8:00 A.M.[37]

Having gained the immediate objective, Price's attack stalled. He brought his artillerists forward and ordered them to turn the captured guns against Union positions on Hindman Hill and Upper Saint Francis Road. The artillerymen soon found that the guns were useless. Union gunners had "shot-wedged" the bores and retreated with the friction primers. While Price's men worked to get the guns back into the fight, Union fire from all sides intensified. When the fog cleared, the U.S.S. *Tyler* moved into position along the river bank and began firing huge naval shells over the town onto Graveyard Hill. Price saw that his force was being decimated by the incoming fire. He could not stay where he was for long, and he could not advance on Fort Curtis without Fagan's help.[38]

Wanting the attack on Fort Curtis to be pressed immediately, General Holmes and his staff rode onto Graveyard Hill. Foolishly, he gave direct orders to one of Parson's regimental commanders to move directly on to Fort Curtis. As the colonel led his men toward the fort, several other colonels began to advance with their regiments as well. All of the regiments were still mixed together as a result of converging on Graveyard Hill. General Parsons was trying to get them reorganized and had no idea what Holmes was doing until it was too late. As the disorganized attack spilled down Graveyard Hill,

The U.S.S. *Tyler*. Built in 1857 as a commercial side-wheel steamship, the *Tyler* became part of the U.S. Western Gunboat Flotilla in September 1861 as a "timberclad" gunboat. After distinguished service on the Upper Mississippi, Ohio, Tennessee, White and Yazoo rivers, the *Tyler* was decommissioned and sold at public auction in August 1865 (courtesy Naval Historical Foundation).

into Helena, and toward Fort Curtis, the *Tyler* lobbed more shells into the confused Confederates. The artillery and infantry at Fort Curtis also cut deeply into their ranks. The attack dissolved. Some of the dazed Confederate soldiers ended up wandering through the streets of Helena, down to the river, looking for water. One-half of the men making the attack were either killed, wounded, or captured.[39]

While Holmes was sending Parsons's men toward Fort Curtis, Price could see that General Fagan's attack on Hindman Hill had run into trouble. Fagan's assault had started well. His three regiments pressed forward through ravines and fallen timber, under heavy fire, and captured the first line of Union rifle pits atop a ridge several hundred yards west of Battery D. Four more ridges, running north to south, stood between them and the battery, each topped with a line of rifle pits. Between the ridges ran deep ravines filled with fallen trees. Fagan's men fought their way up the next ridge to a second line of rifle pits, now reinforced by Union soldiers who had been rushed to the scene. Fagan wondered why Price had not attacked on time. He ordered his attack to continue until four lines of earthworks had been

Major General James Fleming Fagan, 1828–1893. After the war, Fagan served as a United States marshal and agent for the U.S. Land Office (courtesy UALR Center for Arkansas History and Culture).

captured, all the while suffering increasingly heavy casualties from Battery D and Union infantry. Each position his men carried brought them under increased artillery fire. Fagan was trying to prepare an assault on the last ridge when he heard Price's attack get underway. Heartened by the sight of Parsons's and McRae's capture of Graveyard Hill, Fagan led his exhausted men forward toward the last line of works closest to the battery.[40] The Union soldiers fought stubbornly and held their ground until some of the attackers broke through their position. Fagan's exhausted men tumbled down into the ravine at the base of Battery D, where they were trapped. Union infantry quickly regrouped and began closing around them on three sides.[41]

Prior to Fagan's final assault, Price, who was still receiving fire from Hindman

Hill, decided to send reinforcements to Fagan. He sent word to General Parsons ordering him to take his brigade to Hindman Hill and support Fagan. Parsons and McRae were together when the order arrived. They decided that, instead, McRae should assist Fagan and that Parsons's stronger brigade should defend Graveyard Hill against the Union counterattacks that were sure to come. While these plans were being made, a courier from General Holmes arrived and ordered Parsons to attack Hindman Hill. Shortly afterward, Holmes further complicated and delayed any help for Fagan by returning to Graveyard Hill and issuing verbal instructions for troop movements to Parsons, Price, and McRae. By then, Fagan's men had made their final charge against Battery D but found themselves unsupported and pinned against the outer walls of the fort by enemy fire. Some of them tried "to go into the enemy's lines" and surrender but were shot down by their own comrades.[42]

The Confederates now occupied only one of their three initial objectives, Battery C on Graveyard Hill. They had failed to capture Batteries D and A on Hindman and Rightor hills, respectively. Holmes's troops were worn out, out of water, low on ammunition, and without reinforcements. Most of the Confederate artillery never got into action. Guns that arrived on the field were driven from their positions by Union artillery. Union guns at Fort Curtis and on the U.S.S. *Tyler* were pounding Graveyard Hill. Naval shells were exploding above the Confederates, showering them with iron fragments weighing ten pounds or

Major General John Sappington Marmaduke, 1833–1887. Marmaduke attended Yale and Harvard before entering the U.S. Military Academy. He graduated from West Point in 1857 and served under Albert Sidney Johnston in the 2nd U.S. Cavalry. After his service in Arkansas with General Holmes, Marmaduke was captured and sent to Johnson's Island prison. He was promoted to major general while still a prisoner. After the war, he became a "reformer" politician and was the governor of Missouri at the time of his death (Library of Congress).

more. One of Fagan's officers lost both arms just below the elbows to a single shell fragment.[43] Neither Marmaduke nor Walker had made any progress north of town. Both were now under attack, with Marmaduke's soldiers taking the heavier casualties. Well before 10:00 A.M. Holmes's attack had stalled on all fronts.

Union infantry and artillery commanders, seeing Holmes's predicament, began counterattacking Hindman Hill and Graveyard Hill. As their infantry advanced, they trapped small groups of Confederates huddled in the ravines, capturing many of them. Artillery was being repositioned to fire into the ravines as well. Holmes could do nothing but watch his men being hammered; that, or retreat. At 10:30 A.M., he began sending orders to brigade commanders to withdraw. Fagan, McRae, and Parsons had to fight advancing Union troops to avoid being surrounded as they abandoned their positions. Many Confederates were too tired and thirsty to retreat and were captured without resisting. From 11:00 A.M. through early afternoon, Holmes's brigades disengaged. North of town, General Walker did not receive word of the withdrawal from Marmaduke until 2:00 P.M. By then, Marmaduke, disgusted with Walker's performance, had already left the field. Walker was very nearly surrounded before he could withdraw.[44]

South of town, on Lower Little Rock Road, Colonel Brooks's regiment and artillery had kept that part of the city's defenders out of the main fight. They had also drawn fire from the U.S.S. *Tyler* early in the battle and lost several men. Brooks received orders to retreat at noon. As his men withdrew, they burned a number of "negro quarters" along with five thousand pounds of bacon and fifteen hundred bushels of corn.[45]

Holmes would later report that his retreat "was effected in the most perfect order and without the slightest demoralization of any kind."[46] His men made their way five miles from Helena before making camp for the night. They left wounded and worn-out soldiers along roadsides and at every farmhouse.[47] The next day, Holmes sent a letter to General Prentiss inquiring about several officers who had not been seen since the battle. The men were from regiments commanded by Fagan, who delivered the letter under a flag of truce. Ruling out (for Prentiss) the possibility that the officers had deserted, Holmes's letter assured him that they were "gentlemen of the highest character & social positions."[48] Prentiss made no serious pursuit of Holmes's broken army and did not send out patrols until two days after the battle. He was under the impression that Holmes had fifteen to eighteen thousand men.[49] He also knew that his own obstructions, placed to slow Holmes's approach to the city, could be used as defenses by the Southerners as they retreated.

General Holmes mis-characterized his retreat and the battle's effect on morale. On July 6, Prentiss reported that his patrols were finding wounded Confederate soldiers "in whatever direction we search." Other Confederates, too tired and demoralized to keep up with the retreat, simply surrendered when discovered by Union scouts.[50] Holmes had sent 7,646 men into action and lost 1,590, including those captured.[51] Of the 4,129 Union soldiers in the fight, Prentiss reported losing 220 killed and wounded.[52]

By every measure, the campaign was a Confederate disaster. Strategically, the attack on Helena was flawed at its inception. To the extent the campaign had been designed to relieve pressure on Vicksburg, the Confederacy and Holmes had waited too long. Pemberton surrendered Vicksburg to Grant the same day Holmes attacked Helena. Whether Vicksburg fell or not, Holmes could not have held Helena. The Union army and navy were very skilled at large, coordinated attacks. Even if Holmes had captured the city, sooner or later Union gunboats and infantry would have driven him out. For success at the tactical level, Holmes needed to move quickly, strike hard at Helena's outer defenses, then manage the various attacking columns well enough to capture Fort Curtis. He failed in all three requirements.[53]

The attack should have been launched on June 30. Price's four-day delay, due to the weather, gave Prentiss additional time to harden Helena's defenses. Holmes realized that Prentiss knew of the impending attack on June 29, but proceeded with the campaign.[54] On the day of the attack, Prentiss had his troops in place before 3:00 A.M. His pickets were more than half a mile out from town and engaged Confederate skirmishers as early as 4:00 A.M. Prior to July 3, Holmes's cavalry commander in the area, General Walker, should have reported on the nature of the countryside and the amount of obstructions that had been placed on the approaches to town.[55] These conditions greatly fatigued Holmes's troops and kept much of his artillery out of the fight.

Rather than being a simultaneous, overpowering blow, Holmes's assault on the town was uncoordinated. Marmaduke and Fagan attacked on time or very nearly so. Walker was late and ineffective. Price's attack was later still. Price allowed his men to stop and rest prior to reaching their final pre-attack position. To cover for his tardiness, Price blamed Holmes for not objecting to the halt and for designating the vague attack time of "daylight." (Apparently, Holmes, Marmaduke, and Fagan had one understanding of what "daylight" meant, but Price had another.) Price also failed to coordinate the initial attack of his two brigadier generals. Either he or they should have ensured that communications between the brigades were maintained. As it was, Parsons and McRae waited for each other to start the attack.[56]

The lopsided artillery contest during the battle was much of Holmes's undoing. With several of his batteries left behind before the fight, he could not protect his infantry from Union artillery, which already out-gunned him. Confederate gun crews arriving on the field took heavy casualties, notably on Graveyard Hill, while they were working to repair "shot-wedged" Union guns. Other Confederate artillery crews got onto the field with their guns, but were driven off before they could open fire (see Appendix A). The town's mutually protective artillery positions allowed several batteries to concentrate fire on a single target. Because the Confederate attacks were not simultaneous, Union gunners could bombard first one target, then another. Union field artillerists had shorter distances to travel when they repositioned their guns during the battle. They also had more ammunition than the Confederates. One four-gun Union battery fired 456 rounds during the fight.[57] The big guns on the U.S.S. *Tyler* inflicted heavy casualties on Confederates and demoralized many more. *Tyler* reportedly fired 413 shells.[58]

In his attempts to manage the battle personally, Holmes caused more problems than he solved. Early newspaper reports praised him for having "acted gallantly" when he rode onto Graveyard Hill "under a heavy fire."[59] Holmes, however, was not a lead-from-the-front general, nor, as a corps commander, should he have been. Nonetheless, he allowed himself to be drawn into the middle of the fight just long enough to cause chaos. He should have remained in the rear and let Price manage his and Fagan's brigades. On Graveyard Hill, Price was trying to sort out the confusion between Parsons and McRae. They were working to send help to Fagan so that all three brigades could advance on Fort Curtis together. Holmes arrived on the scene, added to the confusion, and then returned to the rear. He also violated the most fundamental military principle, the chain of command. Without Price's or Parson's knowledge, he ordered a colonel to attack Fort Curtis.[60] As a result, the disorganized and uncoordinated attack on Fort Curtis failed. Helena could not be taken without the capture of Fort Curtis.

Holmes's worst mistake was in allowing himself to be talked into an uncertain tactic that was designed to achieve a doomed strategic goal. He had little personal experience organizing this kind of expedition. A more resolute man, a man not so eager to please his superiors and not so desperate to rebuild his damaged reputation, would have declined to make the attack on Helena. Certainly, he would have suffered from the same whispers of timidity that had followed him since Malvern Hill, but the fall of Vicksburg made Helena a moot point. The news of Vicksburg and Lee's defeat at Gettysburg (the day before) would have overshadowed a non-attack on Helena, just as it did the attack.

The inevitable process of generals blaming each other for a defeat began immediately. Holmes told Jefferson Davis, "Genl. Price is utterly and entirely useless in the field." He blamed Price for his late attack and for failing to control his troops after the initial victory on Graveyard Hill. Price blamed Holmes for allowing him to be tardy. Holmes criticized Walker for not assisting Marmaduke. He also filed charges against General McRae, claiming that McRae was "two or three hundred yards in rear" of Graveyard Hill until late in the fight, and that he had failed to attack Hindman Hill in support of Fagan.[61] (Later, a court of inquiry, no doubt appreciating the confused communications among Holmes, Price, McRae, and Parsons, much of which was caused by Holmes, exonerated McRae.)

The most bitter recriminations about Helena occurred between generals Marmaduke and Marsh Walker. Marmaduke was convinced that he could have captured Fort Rightor had Walker supported him properly. Marmaduke did not see Walker's force on the field until after 7:00 A.M. Long before then, Union infantry and artillery attacked Marmaduke's left flank. Marmaduke contended that Walker never came to his support and, instead, remained a mile and a half to the rear all day. Walker's failure allowed Fort Rightor to be reinforced, stopped Marmaduke's advance, and caused his men to be killed and wounded.[62] Major Robert Smith, Marmaduke's quartermaster and close friend, was killed during the fight. Marmaduke and Walker grew to hate each other. Their feud deepened and finally ended the following September in a duel with revolvers. Each man fired and missed. Marmaduke fired again, mortally wounding Walker.[63]

In his final assessment of the Helena battle, Secretary of War Seddon understated the level of conflict among the Confederate generals who participated. Seddon observed that the reports of the campaign indicated to him "some want of confidence and good understanding between some of the superior officers."[64]

The seeds of hostility about Helena fell on fertile ground. Marmaduke and Walker already disliked each other. Holmes, well before the campaign, was not held in high esteem by several of the generals. He had been accused of jealousy regarding generals Pemberton and Kirby Smith. The problems between Holmes and Sterling Price were well known. United States Military Academy graduates, including Holmes, often regarded non–West Point graduates as amateurs. Certainly, Holmes was not unique in having bouts of jealousy and pettiness. Price and other non–West Point generals often complained of the "West Point clique."[65] Later in the war, John Tyler wrote to an apparently acquiescent Price and expressed hatred for President Davis, Adjutant and Inspector General Cooper, and all "West Pointers." Tyler referred to them as fools and knaves and criticized Confederate leadership, saying, "The West Pointers have indeed counseled and generaled us to the verge of death itself."[66] The close friendship between Jefferson Davis and Holmes, along with Holmes's inclination to deal directly with the president, caused resentment. Generals commanding other departments contacted the president directly, but Holmes was no longer a department commander. His relationship with Davis was a source of envy and irritation for many of Holmes's detractors.

Rumors of Holmes having been killed at Helena began circulating within days of the fight. Confederate prisoners told at least one Union soldier that Holmes was dead.[67] The Richmond *Daily Dispatch,* in referring to articles in other newspapers, mentioned Holmes's death twice in August. By then, the story was that he had died of pneumonia after the battle or from "drinking intoxicating liquors." The newspaper reports likely came from Union general Clinton B. Fisk, who said, "Holmes died on Sunday, August 2, of delirium tremens." Fisk wrote to his superiors, "One informed [witness] assures me that he saw [Holmes's] body lying in state at headquarters, and that he is very dead."[68] One supposed witness stated flatly that he was present at Holmes's death.[69]

The false reports of Holmes's death from "intoxicating liquors" are the likely source of rumors, later used against him, that he was a heavy drinker.[70] Holmes went into seclusion after Helena and may have had a bout of drinking, but there are few, if any, other reports of his heavy use of alcohol. On August 15, the *Daily Dispatch,* perhaps still assuming Holmes was dead, credited him with "much gallantry on the field."[71] The *Daily Dispatch* did not confirm that Holmes was alive until September 9. One Confederate soldier, aware that Holmes had survived, wrote, "The whirring 64 pound bombs was too much for him. He is at L[ittle] R[ock] verr[y] sick, in which condition I leave him and hope he will stay so."[72]

While some newspapers reported Holmes's death, others called for him to be replaced. There can be little doubt that he would rather have died at Helena. He rode onto Graveyard Hill twice and was exposed to enemy fire for some time. Major John Edwards wrote that Holmes became so distraught that he "certainly did expose himself throughout the day recklessly and gallantly, seeming by his actions to be courting death." According to Edwards, Holmes "remarked gloomily, afterward, that to him death upon the field was preferable to disaster, and that he had prayed for it earnestly when the attack proved a failure."[73] Holmes's death wish was very nearly granted. His horse was killed during the battle.[74]

In his report on Helena to President Davis, Holmes would admit that the expedition "had resulted disastrously for me," and said, "I write this report with deep pain."[75] On July 23, he turned command of the District of Arkansas over to Sterling Price, the next ranking general.[76] Holmes continued correspondence into the first week of August, but mentally and physically, he was broken. Lieutenant General Kirby Smith granted him a leave of absence for illness. One noted historian and contemporary of Holmes stated that the general's exposure in the swamps of Arkansas during the campaign "resulted in serious illness."[77] Holmes traveled to Hot Springs in southwest Arkansas to recuperate. The warm waters there were known for their healing properties. Descriptions and rumors of Holmes's collapse, demeanor, and physical appearance during this period would follow him for the rest of his life.

In diary entries for August 12 and 13, 1863, Dr. R. J. Bell, a surgeon in Parson's brigade, recorded his impressions of generals Holmes and Price. Price, he wrote, was a man "gracefully proportioned ... amiable countenance.... I never saw [a general] so handsome and so soldierly in appearance as Major-General Sterling Price. His presence among his troops awakens a thrill of joy and confidence." Holmes, in contrast, is described by Dr. Bell as having a "sallow complection .... hunchbacked, and makes a very ungraceful appearance, either on foot, or on a horse. He is in his dotage, and is apt to insult his best friend."[78] The drawing of contrasts and comparisons between Holmes and Price was common among observers during Holmes's time in the Trans-Mississippi.

Another contemporary description of Price stated that "it was impossible to find a more magnificent specimen of manhood in its prime than Sterling Price."[79] While Holmes and Price were of approximately the same age, they were strikingly different men. Price was a robust, handshaking politician, full of confidence, enthusiasm, and self-promotion. Holmes was a "plain, quiet man, makes no show."[80] He was an introvert, distant, and dour, and projected a lack of confidence in himself and generated the same opinion in others. By August 1863, his temperament, thirty-eight years of army life, and the defeat at Helena had reduced him to a shambles. At no time in his career could Holmes have been at more of a disadvantage in a side-by-side comparison with a man such as Sterling Price.

In response to the twin disasters of Helena and Vicksburg, the Alabama General Assembly passed a resolution demanding that generals Holmes and Pemberton be replaced. The resolution stated, "The people and the army have lost confidence" in them.[81]

When Price assumed temporary command of Arkansas, Holmes's army was certainly not "without the slightest demoralization of any kind" as Holmes had initially reported. An inspection of the district was conducted in August by Major W. C. Schaumburg of the department's adjutant and inspector general's office. Schaumburg noted early in his findings that he could "only hope to point out a few general evils ... remedies for which it will be hard to find save in an entire reorganization of the troops and a more rigid enforcement everywhere of regulations and orders."[82]

Schaumburg stated that Price's division and Fagan's brigade were in better shape than other troops in the district. He noted, however, the lax disciplinary atmosphere tolerated by officers in these regiments and that there was "too little pride and effort at soldierly bearing" on their part. He observed that familiarity between officers and enlisted men bred lethargy, dissatisfaction, and lack of respect. Infractions were not sufficiently punished by company officers, and they were not held responsible for the actions of their men. As a result, incidents of repeated desertion by enlisted men were common. Schaumburg credited some of the district's morale problems and desertion to the recent Helena campaign, which he called "a fatiguing and harassing march." He also stated, "General officers of the command are zealous and competent, but are in a measure paralyzed in their endeavors by a lack of hearty co-operation from their subordinate officers."[83]

As the department's immediate past commander, then as district commander, Holmes can be blamed for some of the long-standing problems that Schaumburg reported. Troops in Arkansas, however, were necessarily scattered throughout the state. They were under the more immediate command of Price as a division commander and brigadier generals such as Fagan, McRae, Marmaduke, and Walker. Some of these officers had little respect for each other, and less for Holmes. It was they who allowed the lax disciplinary atmosphere among regimental and company officers to continue over a long period of time. The lack of discipline in Price's division can be attributed to his management style. General McCulloch and Governor Reynolds of Missouri, among others, criticized Price for pandering to his troops and being a weak disciplinarian.[84] Holmes had little power to replace generals who had political influence in the region and were popular with their troops. Few replacement officers with the training and experience that Holmes preferred could be found. Capable generals, serving east of the Mississippi River, had no desire for a transfer to the Trans-Mississippi.

General Price knew his command of Arkansas would be brief; only until Holmes recovered his health. Price had neither the inclination nor the aptitude to reorganize Holmes's army and retrain the mid-management officers. With Vicksburg lost and Union forces under General Steele increasing at Helena, Price was expecting an attack into the heart of the state. Two weeks after Helena, Union General James G. Blunt's army in Indian Territory attacked and routed General Douglas Cooper at Honey Springs. Cooper was preparing to attack Blunt's base at Fort Gibson, but the plan fell apart when Union forces attacked before Cooper started his campaign. Price was concerned that General Blunt might move into northwest Arkansas in coordination with a campaign by General Steele from Helena.

Price wanted to fight and save Little Rock, but he had only eight thousand men available. He told Kirby Smith that his troops were "eager to meet the enemy" but that he "did not believe it would be possible for me to hold it [Little Rock] with the force then under my command."[85] Price estimated that sixty thousand Union soldiers would soon converge on Little Rock. Saving the state capital was important to Price, but more important was keeping his army intact. In order to do both, he wrote to Kirby Smith and recommended concentrating all Confederate forces in the state along the south side of the Arkansas River.[86]

Union threats in Texas, Louisiana, and Indian Territory required Kirby Smith to think beyond Arkansas. Unlike Holmes, he was willing to give up most of Arkansas to save the department. If necessary, he could retreat from the Arkansas River and concentrate his troops along the Red River. He could then counterattack advancing Union forces when their supply lines were longer and more exposed.[87]

Price did what he could to strengthen Little Rock. On September 4, he issued a circular in Pulaski County (Little Rock) warning the population of an impending attack. He called on all men to volunteer and "rush to the side of the undaunted men who crowd the entrenchments and eagerly await the coming of the foe." The volunteers could join any company of their choice or "organize to-night under the call of your Governor." Officers at Little Rock were authorized to "arrest every able bodied man tomorrow who may be absent from his post, whether he be officer, man or citizen, and whether he belong to commands elsewhere or not, and place him wherever his services be most required." Officers and soldiers at "the front" were ordered to "arrest, and to shoot down, if necessary, every one who may be found attempting to pass toward the enemy under any pretext whatever, either with or without a pass."[88]

The large, coordinated Union offensive that Price predicted was not forthcoming. Instead, a Union force of about six thousand men and thirty-nine pieces of artillery left Helena on August 11. They were joined by six thousand cavalrymen on the White River at Clarendon and proceeded toward Little Rock. On September 10, after several large skirmishes and an intimidating tactical advance on the city by the Union force, Price abandoned Little Rock. General Holmes was with Marmaduke during the retreat. He predicted the Union army would not pursue them because there was no reason to do so. Holmes told Marmaduke, "We are an army of prisoners and self supporting at that."[89] Holmes had spent more than a year protecting the Arkansas River valley and Little Rock. Now he was leaving as little more than a spectator.

The Union commander, Maj. Gen. Frederick Steele, briefly considered chasing Price's army, but as Holmes had foreseen, decided against it. As they retreated, the Confederates set fire to their pontoon bridges on the river. This delayed the Union infantry from crossing in a timely manner. Steele's cavalry made only a half-hearted pursuit. It was getting late in the campaign season and bad weather would soon be a factor. Steele's army was a long way from its supply base, and Price had skillfully removed almost everything useful to the Union army.[90]

In saving his army by abandoning Little Rock and the Arkansas River valley, Price was hailed by Kirby Smith as having acted "wisely." A newspaper in southwest Arkansas agreed, saying that Price had saved his army "for the protection of South Arkansas and the good of the Department." Not everyone approved of the retreat. The exiled governor of Missouri, Thomas C. Reynolds, observed, "General Holmes and all the general officers under Price at Little Rock, except General Frost, considered the evacuation a blunder, and that Steele could have been beaten back." A major in Col. Joe Shelby's command said, "The capitol of Arkansas was abandoned without a blow ... to inferior numbers of the enemy."[91] Price wrote to a friend on September 27 and complained that Holmes and "many others" had been critical of the abandonment of Little Rock. He said they had misrepresented the number of troops at his disposal and the number of Union soldiers he faced.[92]

General Kirby Smith believed that Price and Holmes were on the "eve of a most dangerous quarrel." (Marmaduke had killed Walker less than a month earlier.) He asked Governor Reynolds to meet with each general and defuse the situation. According to Reynolds, Holmes was moderate but critical of Price, while "Price was very much excited against Gen. Holmes, and in the course of his remarks said to me: if Gen. Holmes attempts to degrade me, I'll put him in chains and send him to his master, Jeff Davis."[93]

Losing the state capital without a serious fight was an emotional blow for Price's troops. The high morale he had previously reported was no longer in evidence. The countryside was full of Confederate deserters as his army retreated toward Arkadelphia. General Steele described them as "greatly demoralized, and deserted almost by regiments."[94] The Union army settled in at Little Rock. Price halted his retreat at Arkadelphia on September 14.

Anticipating Holmes's return to duty, Gen. Kirby Smith wrote to him on September 21. He reminded Holmes of Arkansas's situation as it related to larger Union designs, particularly in Texas, Indian Territory, and western Louisiana.[95] Holmes resumed command of Arkansas on September 25. His army was in terrible condition. He had Price's infantry division, the cavalry divisions of Marmaduke and the recently deceased Marsh Walker, and other troops scattered around the state. There were twenty thousand men on the rosters, but Holmes could muster only about eighty-five hundred for duty. By this time, he had developed a deep respect for the resilience and fighting spirit of his soldiers. He referred to them as "the remains of one of the best little armies in the world." He directed his subordinate generals to meet with him at headquarters each day except Sunday, "when practicable."[96] Holmes wanted to get his army back in fighting condition.

Desertion and illness among Holmes's troops had continued unabated since Helena. The loss of Little Rock and the subsequent retreat to Arkadelphia had further demoralized his men. As for Holmes, he had always felt Arkansas was the key to success or failure in the Trans-Mississippi and that the Arkansas River valley was the key to success in the state. Even with the defeats at Arkansas Post and Helena, most of central and southwest Arkansas was in Confederate hands when Price took over. Now, during the two months Holmes was not in command, most of the state had fallen to Union control. September also brought the sad news that James Deshler had been killed in Georgia. After his capture at Arkansas Post, Deshler was exchanged in June 1863. He was promoted to brigadier general and commanded a brigade under Patrick Cleburne. Ironically, Deshler, who had graduated from West Point as an artillery officer and served on Holmes's staff as chief of artillery, was cut nearly in half by a Union artillery shell at the battle of Chickamauga.[97]

Late in September, Kirby Smith reported to President Davis on the conditions in the Trans-Mississippi. He was despondent. Fort Smith, Arkansas, had fallen. Union armies held Missouri and were active in Louisiana. The Mississippi River was under Union control. In Arkansas, most of the state was occupied. There were twenty-five thousand Union troops at Little Rock. Smith was expecting them to go on the offense as soon as their stockpile of supplies would permit. An additional fifty-five thousand Union soldiers were arrayed at various points in and around the department. When they began to move, Smith would have only about fifteen thousand men to resist them. In addition to Holmes's army, Smith's forces were scattered in the Indian Territory, Texas, and the District of West Louisiana. Smith estimated Holmes's troop strength at "less than 7,000." The Trans-Mississippi Department needed weapons and payroll for its troops, neither of which General Smith expected to receive. He lamented to Davis, "Cut off as we are, I know not what aid you can give us."[98]

The one bright spot for the Confederacy, in an otherwise bleak fall in the Trans-Mississippi, was a raid conducted by Col. Joseph Shelby. On September 22, Shelby led eight hundred cavalrymen, two pieces of artillery, and twelve supply wagons on a month-long raid into Missouri. During their one-thousand-mile ride, Shelby's little force inflicted thirty-five hundred casualties on the Union army, captured three hundred wagons and six thousand draft animals, and destroyed eleven small forts.[99]

General Holmes's two months away from active command of the district had done much to restore his spirits. In early October, General Smith ordered him to move his command to a better tactical position at Camden, Arkansas. Smith wanted to have the option of attacking Little Rock or moving toward Louisiana if the need arose. Holmes, long realizing that time was not on the South's side, particularly in the Trans-Mississippi, did not want to withdraw to Camden and do nothing. He still wanted to fight. He told Kirby Smith, "*we must fight some where* soon or all *will be lost.*" He was worried that remaining inactive at Camden would further sap his army's morale.[100]

Holmes was troubled by his desertions and by the public's lack of faith in the Confederacy: "There is no doubt that the Federal force in Ark. is being already greatly increased by our own deserters and the disaffection among the people." Holmes recommended that he and the West Louisiana Department commander, General Richard Taylor, combine forces to recapture central Arkansas or mount an offensive in Louisiana.[101] Holmes wanted to start a campaign or go into winter quarters and rebuild his army. General Smith wanted to reposition his forces to meet Union advances from Arkansas and Louisiana. At the end of October, he ordered Holmes to be prepared to abandon Arkansas and leave only a small force behind. He wanted to be able to combine

Holmes's army with Taylor's force on the Red River between Shreveport and Alexandria, Louisiana. Smith ended his order by criticizing Holmes for not keeping him informed about Union activity in the Little Rock area.[102]

General Smith believed that Holmes was not being sufficiently aggressive in contesting the area between Little Rock and Camden. In a November letter, Smith again prodded Holmes to keep him better informed and criticized him for inactivity. He mentioned General Taylor's daily skirmishes with Union troops in Louisiana as an example.[103] Smith also wanted Holmes to protect Arkansas cotton plantations along the Mississippi by sending a brigade there.[104]

Kirby Smith was still concerned about the friction between Sterling Price and Holmes. Holmes continued to blame Price for the defeat at Helena. Price charged that Holmes was conducting a slander campaign against him. The approaching spring campaign season would require the cooperation of all the department's generals. Governor Reynolds got involved and recommended to Smith that he should replace Holmes. Smith regarded Holmes as a better general than Price, but in October he wrote to President Davis, "Whilest I respect and love General Holmes for his unselfish patriotism and purity of heart, I believe the public interests would be advanced by removing him."[105] When President Davis saw Smith's recommendation, he suggested that, rather than transferring Holmes, Price should be removed to "Kansas and Western Missouri."[106] Earlier in the month, Smith had antagonized Holmes by separating Indian Territory from the District of Arkansas and putting General William Steele in command.[107]

Except for an unsuccessful attack on Pine Bluff by Marmaduke's cavalry on October 25, Holmes's forces made few aggressive movements during the fall. Winter rain slowed campaigning for both armies. The state settled into raids, ambushes, and skirmishes. Holmes's army went into winter quarters in the vicinity of Spring Hill, Washington, and Camden.[108]

As it became apparent there would be no offensive operations until spring, Holmes used the time to rebuild his army. By November, his efforts were meeting with some success. An inspection report by the Trans-Mississippi adjutant and inspector general's office noted that Holmes and his subordinate officers were "zealous and sober and efficient" and the "morale of the army has greatly improved in the last month, and the ranks are again filling up slowly." The men in the ranks were described as "well fed, and the clothing generally good." The report cited problems that Holmes and his generals could not solve: "The great wants of the district are men, arms and money. With 3,000 or 4,000 re-enforcements, the commander would be able to reoccupy the valley of the Arkansas [River], which is of the first importance to the Trans-Mississippi Department." The report stated that ten thousand sets of weapons and accouterments were needed immediately. Holmes's troops had not been paid in six months.[109] They and their families at home were destitute. For the month, Holmes reported a total of 25,623 officers and enlisted men in the state. Only 13,905 were present for duty.[110]

On November 30, General Smith wrote to Holmes and suggested that he "occupy

Pine Bluff with your whole force." Smith thought this move would induce the Union garrison to abandon Little Rock or advance toward Holmes and attack. In the event the Union force should come out to fight, Smith left it up to Holmes whether to give battle or retreat. In the same message, Smith advised Holmes that generals Taylor in Louisiana and Magruder in Texas had "their hands full" and would not be able to support the proposed movement.[111] Holmes had suggested a similar but more aggressive campaign to Smith in October. At that time, he wanted Smith to bring reinforcements and take command of the operation in person. Smith had not adopted that plan.[112]

Still lacking support for a November attack, Holmes did not advance on Pine Bluff. Winter weather could spoil the best-laid plans. Holmes's army, though improved since Helena, was still weak and poorly armed. Perhaps Helena had taught Holmes that acting alone, rather than in concert with a larger offensive, was not something he wanted to do again. Perhaps he remembered Kirby Smith's pre–Helena words, "You can expect no assistance from this quarter" and Smith's reluctance to reinforce Holmes for an attack on Little Rock. Smith's moral support, alone, was not enough to make Holmes gamble again with what was left of his reputation or the lives of his soldiers. Holmes notified Governor Flanagin in late December, "Gen. Smith has decided not to advance" on Little Rock.[113]

Price's division was at Camp Sumter near Spring Hill, Arkansas. On January 1, his division had 8,285 officers and enlisted men, but only about five thousand were fit for duty. Union forces were centered around Helena and Little Rock. Their generals planned a spring offensive. Kirby Smith tried to consolidate and strengthen his positions and anticipate the next attack. While he and other Confederate generals fantasized about retaking Missouri, in reality they knew they would be fortunate to hold the territory they had. General Taylor concentrated his strength along the lower Red River valley between Simsport and Alexandria, Louisiana. Winter sickness and desertion had reduced his division to sixty-five hundred effective soldiers. On December 31, 1863, Kirby Smith reported the Trans-Mississippi Department's "present for duty" troop strength at 34,581.[114]

On Christmas eve, General Holmes answered a letter he had received from Jefferson Davis. He thanked Davis "from my heart" for his support. Holmes was critical of Kirby Smith's abandonment of the Arkansas River valley, although he told Davis that Smith was "honest, devoted & zealous" and that "I have no idea you have an officer who would do as well in the administration of [the Trans-Mississippi Department's] officers." Holmes believed Smith would never give him an opportunity to recapture Arkansas. He recommended that Davis promote Brigadier General Fagan to major general and put him in command of what was left of the state. Holmes pointed out to Davis that Fagan was "an excellent officer, a fighting man who distinguished himself at Helena & Prairie Grove and who has the confidence of the troops." With Kirby Smith in command of the department and Arkansas lost, Holmes saw no reason to remain in the Trans-Mississippi.[115]

In the early winter of 1864, President Lincoln approved the Red River Campaign, a plan that was designed to capture southern Arkansas and northern Louisiana, and invade Texas. General Steele with fifteen thousand soldiers at Little Rock was to advance against Arkadelphia, then start toward Kirby Smith's headquarters at Shreveport. A second army, led by General Nathan P. Banks with seventeen thousand men, would move through Louisiana to Alexandria. They were to link up with another ten thousand soldiers sent by General Sherman. Those forces would then move on to Shreveport. After defeating Smith's forces along the way, the combined Union armies could then invade east Texas. The campaign was the next logical move, not only to the Union generals who devised it, but also to Confederate generals who were already working to defeat it.[116]

General Smith and two of his district commanders, Holmes and Taylor, agreed that southwest Arkansas and northwest Louisiana would be the most likely battleground. Confederate troops in Texas and Indian Territory would be needed to reinforce those areas. In Texas, General Magruder disagreed. He was convinced that Union forces were more likely to invade the coast of his district. Nonetheless, Magruder reluctantly agreed to send troops toward the Red River valley. General Taylor knew that his troops and fortifications on the Red River could not be made strong enough to resist the Union fleet and land forces. Still, he made the preparations that Kirby Smith ordered.[117]

Except for a brief period of illness, Holmes spent January and February preparing for Gen. Frederick Steele's anticipated spring attack from Little Rock into southwest Arkansas. He strengthened Camden's defenses by building extensive earthworks around the city. He wanted to hold Camden but knew that he might need to withdraw his army before reinforcements could arrive. He established a series of supply depots toward Shreveport in the event that Camden would have to be temporarily abandoned. He made arrangements for the evacuation of civilians and the destruction of immovable supplies that would be useful to the Union army.[118] By the end of February, he felt confident enough to attack Little Rock "single handed," but Smith would not approve the campaign.[119]

Although Holmes was building his forces and hoping to reclaim Little Rock, he suspected that he would not be part of the approaching campaign. Rumors of a command change in Arkansas had been making the rounds since December. Anticipating his exit from Arkansas, Holmes wanted his son and nephew to rejoin him at Camden. Theo Jr. had been temporarily assigned to the 4th Confederate Engineers. John Hinsdale had also been on temporary assignment. On February 25, Holmes issued orders to have them report to him for duty at Spring Hill near Camden.[120]

Holmes had learned that he was the target of political intrigue orchestrated by Kirby Smith. On January 20, Smith had written to Davis and recommended "placing a younger and more energetic officer in command." Smith said of Holmes, "Time also tells upon him, lessening his activity and impairing his memory."[121] Holmes's record since the defeat at Helena had not been impressive. He had been absent from command of his troops for two months. During that time, his army had been pushed out of Little Rock. Smith was displeased with his performance between Little Rock and Camden.

Holmes was angered that command changes made by General Smith had reduced his responsibilities. His bitter feud with Sterling Price had only worsened with the passage of time. In an effort to make a graceful exit, Holmes wrote to Smith and requested transfers for himself and his staff. He offered as his reasons the hopeless situation in Arkansas and the "feeling of depression that has come over me."[122]

Other communications were passed between the two generals, but Holmes received no response regarding his request for the entire month of February. His anger toward Smith simmered. He knew that Smith, Governor Flanagin, and the Arkansas congressional delegation had contacted President Davis months earlier and demanded his dismissal. He felt betrayed by the politicians who had spoken so kindly of him only a year earlier. Under the circumstances, he could see no excuse for Smith's failure to grant the transfer or to acknowledge having received it.

On February 28, Holmes vented his frustration to Kirby Smith's chief of staff. He wrote of the "want of confidence & respect he [General Smith] has so frequently manifested towards me." He again requested General Smith to order him back to Richmond, "to the War Dept. for duty."[123] General Smith's March 5 response was not conciliatory. He justified the changes in command he had made and demanded from Holmes "an explanation of the charges he makes against me."[124]

Holmes realized the insubordinate nature of his letter and apologized on March 8 for his "unjust and intemperate" remarks. He suppressed his rage, politely offered his reasons for requesting the transfer, and asked to be excused for the "temper shown in my letter." Holmes might have honestly regretted his display of anger, but he wanted out. He ended his message by saying, "I hope you will consider this as a renewal of my application and act upon it for the benefit of our sacred cause."[125] Smith wrote a less hostile response to Holmes on March 11. He admitted to recommending a transfer behind Holmes's back and advised him that his first transfer request had been approved and sent to Richmond.[126]

While Holmes and Smith quarreled, the anticipated Union offensive had begun. Smith advised Holmes on March 5 that Union gunboats had run past Confederate batteries on the Ouachita River and were heading toward Monroe, Louisiana. General Banks's army and Admiral Porter's fleet were moving up the Red River toward Shreveport. General Steele's troops would soon march out of Little Rock toward Washington, Arkansas, sixty miles west of Camden.[127]

On March 16, the day Union troops occupied Alexandria, Louisiana, Holmes resigned his command of Arkansas. General Sterling Price again assumed control of the state by virtue of rank and seniority.[128] Ironically, the transfer requests that Holmes had submitted on February 1 and 28 (and reiterated on March 8) had been granted by the war department on March 11.[129] Given the slow communications between Smith's headquarters at Shreveport, Louisiana, the Confederate capital, and Arkansas, Holmes resigned before he was notified that his February transfer request had been forwarded to the war department by General Smith.

As much as he disliked Sterling Price, the farewell message Holmes issued to the soldiers and people of Arkansas urged them to do all they could "to sustain him." In referring to his own troubles and demise, Holmes said, "No man knows better than myself how perfectly the most honest and zealous endeavors may be paralyzed by a want of confidence."[130] Theo was particularly distressed about leaving. During the previous months, he had fallen in love with a sixteen-year-old Arkansas girl. The couple announced their engagement but were to be separated by the war. The wedding would never take place.[131]

General Holmes left the Trans-Mississippi during the early stages of a Union campaign that was ultimately defeated. Steele's army marched out of Little Rock on March 23. Six days later, he occupied Arkadelphia and prepared to push on toward Shreveport. General Banks's army and Admiral Porter's fleet advanced up the Red River, intending to link up with Steele. The converging Union forces were hampered by low river water, poor communications, and lack of coordination. Banks was defeated by Gen. Richard Taylor at Mansfield, Louisiana, on April 8. The two generals fought again the next day at Pleasant Hill. Taylor's attacks were repulsed with heavy casualties. Steele moved out of Arkadelphia but was defeated at Camden on April 18. With Steele defeated, Banks began withdrawing downriver. Banks's retreat caused Porter and his fleet to start back downriver as well. He lost several vessels to Confederate attacks along the way.[132]

The expedition was a Union disaster. Admiral Porter nearly lost his fleet in low water. General Banks's reputation was damaged. The two men became bitter enemies and a congressional investigation was called. On the Confederate side, Kirby Smith was credited with the Confederate victory, but he relieved General Taylor of his command over an angry exchange of correspondence concerning the tactics of the campaign.[133]

The South was heartened by the first good news to come out of the Trans-Mississippi in some time. Holmes's exit at the very beginning of the Red River Campaign sustained the nearly universal opinion that he should never have been sent to the West. As department commander, he had failed to save Indian Territory or recapture Missouri. He refused to reinforce Confederate armies that were trying to save Vicksburg. He lost Arkansas Post. As Arkansas district commander, he failed in his attack on Helena.

As a department and district commander, Holmes had followed Jefferson Davis's static defense strategy. His responsibility was to defend the area assigned to him. While Davis often urged Holmes to cooperate with Confederate armies east of the Mississippi River, he never ordered Holmes to do so. Davis forced Secretary of War Randolph out of office for ordering Holmes to cross the river. Davis always left the decision to Holmes.[134] In the final analysis, Holmes was sent west not to save Vicksburg or fight in Tennessee and Mississippi, but to save the Trans-Mississippi. Later, as a district commander, his primary task was to defend Arkansas.

Under withering criticism and pressure from secretaries of war and influential generals, Holmes steadfastly used all his assets to defend his department and district. He regarded Arkansas as the key to the Trans-Mississippi. He had come to this conclusion soon after being assigned to the department. In late 1862, he reluctantly told Texas

Governor F. R. Lubbock that Texas and General Magruder would get no additional troops from Arkansas. Holmes had decided on his priorities. He told Lubbock, "If we leave the valley of the Arkansas [River] the whole Trans-Mississippi region goes with it."[135]

In protecting Arkansas, Holmes was never able to concentrate his meager forces. He always had to contend with Union armies operating in the Indian Territory, northwest Arkansas, Missouri, and Louisiana. In eastern Arkansas, the large Union garrison at Helena was always a threat, forcing Holmes to keep troops nearby. The Arkansas River was a path that led into the heart of the state. Union threats and constant pressure on the river required him to keep thousands of soldiers at Arkansas Post and later, at Day's Bluff. His army was always divided among several vulnerable areas. When Kirby Smith took command, he saw Holmes's dilemma. Before the battle of Helena, Smith wrote of the insurmountable problem facing any commander of the Trans-Mississippi, "This immense empire is without an army. Were all the troops concentrated, they would scarcely be more than sufficient for operating at any one point threatened.... No effectual concentration can be made at any one point without the abandonment of all others."[136]

After Holmes's departure, the Trans-Mississippi came to be known as "Kirby Smithdom," in part because of its isolation from the rest of the Confederacy.[137] But the region stayed in the war, defended itself, and tied up vast Union army and navy resources. Had the loss of Arkansas occurred earlier in the war and been quickly followed by the loss of the entire region, those Union resources would have been sent to fight in the eastern Confederacy. Isolated as the region was, the last Confederate soldiers to stack arms and surrender were those in the Trans-Mississippi. Native American Confederate soldiers lived up to Holmes's high regard for them as "no people in the Confederacy more loyal and few more tolerant." Stand Watie was the last Confederate general to surrender his troops, doing so on June 23, 1865. Hindman, Holmes, and Kirby Smith can be credited with maintaining the Trans-Mississippi as part of the Southern war effort.[138] In retrospect, President Davis should have given Gen. Joseph Johnston command of both sides of the Mississippi River in late 1862.

In a February 1864 report, Holmes's old friend Adjutant and Inspector General Samuel Cooper evaluated Holmes and the perception of him as a commander in the Trans-Mississippi: "This officer impressed me with the purity of his motives and his great devotion to our cause. He is temperate in his habits; the reports circulated against him in this respect are without the slightest foundation. The dissatisfaction with him, both in the army and among the people, is very great, and I fear has become so firmly fixed that his usefulness as the commanding general of this district is greatly impaired."[139]

The undertones of dissatisfaction with Holmes started early during his tenure in the department. Sterling Price wanted command of the region and was obsessed with recapturing Missouri. Albert Pike did his best to undermine both Hindman and Holmes. Holmes, with his retention of Hindman, made political enemies in Arkansas and Richmond. Like Hindman, Holmes believed that only through totalitarian measures could the region be mobilized and the war fought effectively. Holmes and Hindman enforced conscription and often managed the civilian economy well beyond any legal authority. These methods contradicted the state's-rights philosophy that Southerners thought they were fighting to uphold, particularly in a region that was accustomed to little or no government intrusion. Holmes's lack of success on the battlefield destroyed his image as a general. His refusal to send help across the river to Vicksburg turned many high-ranking Confederate generals and politicians against him. Behind the scenes maneuvering and whispering campaigns dominated much of his Trans-Mississippi career. No doubt, on more than one occasion, his deafness was a blessing.

9

The Forlorn Hope

The shortage of manpower that bedeviled the Confederacy throughout the war had reached a crisis in late 1863. During the first year of the war, only about one-third of the Confederacy's physically fit, military-age men volunteered for the army. The first conscript law kept the twelve-month volunteers in the army for a total of three years and required the enrollment of all others eighteen to thirty-five years of age. As conscription laws were amended, more and more of the Southern white male population was pressed into service. By the end of 1863, the Confederacy was drafting white males from eighteen to forty-five years of age.[1]

Conscription bureaus were established in each state, complete with camps of instruction, guards, supporting forces, and networks of local enrolling offices. The bureaus administered the system, gathered conscripts, and hunted deserters. For a variety of reasons, Confederate conscription was enforced somewhat differently in the three geographic areas of the South: the eastern Confederacy between the Appalachian Mountains and the east coast, the central Confederacy between the Mississippi River and the Appalachian Mountains, and the Trans-Mississippi. As war weariness set in on the armies and the civilian population, desertion became a serious threat to the South's ability to continue fighting. Estimates as high as one hundred thousand were given as the number of deserters and draft dodgers at large in the Confederacy.[2] Occupational exemptions and exemption fraud allowed thousands of additional men to avoid military service altogether.

By early 1864, all white men in the Confederacy between the ages of eighteen and forty-five were either in the army, avoiding army service, working at wartime production, or exempted on health, occupational or religious grounds. The Confederate Bureau of Conscription estimated that there were approximately 64,000 men between the ages of forty-five and fifty-five that could be brought into the army. There were seventy thousand additional men in the population, between the ages of eighteen and forty-five, that could not be accounted for by the bureau.[3] Men who refused to appear for their initial enrollment were classified "absent without leave" and hunted along with deserters.

The untapped sources of manpower in the South were younger and older white males and African American men, most of whom were slaves. By the end of 1863, politicians and military leaders realized that for the South to have any hope of winning the war, conscription had to be overhauled. President Davis summoned General Braxton

Bragg to Richmond in January 1864 to be the advisor for military operations in the Confederacy.[4] Congress was about to expand the number of men covered by the conscription laws, but Bragg had additional plans for the system. He knew the Confederacy was not efficiently classifying and accounting for men not currently serving in the army. In addition to the thousands of soldiers who were deserters, there were additional thousands who were avoiding military service by manipulating the Confederacy's confusing system of exemptions and wartime industrial and agricultural deferments. The new law would provide Bragg with a framework to implement his remedies.[5]

On February 17, 1864, the Confederate congress expanded conscription by requiring the enrollment of all white males between the ages of seventeen and fifty. The law created two new classes of conscripts, "state defense" and "detailed men." The position of general of the Reserves was created for each state. The Reserve generals would administer the assembly of forces authorized by the new law. Seventeen-year-old males were to be conscripted and assigned to Junior Reserves units. Forty-five- to fifty-year-old men were to serve in the Senior Reserves. Men currently in the army but "unable to perform active service in the field," referred to as "light duty" soldiers, were to replace guards, soldiers who enforced conscription laws, and able-bodied soldiers assigned to other duties. The Junior Reserves were not to be used for light duty assignments. The law specified that the new organizations "shall not be required to perform service outside the State in which they reside."[6] Once organized, the Reserves would replace regular Confederate regiments serving within their states. Those regiments, in turn, would be sent to reinforce Lee's army in Virginia or General Joseph Johnston in Georgia.

The law, as it pertained to detailed men, was designed to keep government agencies staffed and maintain a civilian work force that could sustain the Confederacy's wartime economy. A variety of exemptions and deferments from army service was provided. These provisions would undergo an endless series of revisions beginning within a few months. Responsibility for enrolling the Reserves and organizing the detailed men was given to the conscription bureau. Orders were issued to state conscription bureaus on March 1.[7]

Two weeks later, orders were issued for the enrollment of twenty thousand free African American men or slaves. They were to be assigned to non-combat duty as soldiers and laborers. If an insufficient number of these men were enrolled voluntarily, slaves could be seized (i.e., drafted) from their owners.[8] The conscription of free African Americans for non-combat duty was not a new concept. Shortly after the Peninsular Campaign, the city of Richmond began conscripting "free negroes" to work in the city's overflowing hospitals.[9]

The February law was sweeping in its extension of the national government's control. According to one Confederate assistant adjutant general, the law made the Confederate government "the custodian and director, to a large extent, of the agricultural and industrial interests of the country."[10] Braxton Bragg was delighted, but he was determined to further streamline conscription and its enforcement. His plan was to use the overlapping responsibilities of state conscription bureaus and the generals of the Reserves. Bragg's friendship with Davis and Holmes would soon put Holmes in a position to render his most significant service to the Confederacy.

Between mid–February and the end of May, the adjutant and inspector general's office and the superintendent of conscription set the law in motion. President Davis appointed generals of the Reserves in Georgia, Virginia, South Carolina, Alabama, and North Carolina. In North Carolina, Davis approved Braxton Bragg's recommendation and appointed General Holmes on April 18.[11] Initially, Reserve generals had no direct connection with conscription. They were, however, "held responsible in all matters relating to the efficiency and permanent organization of their commands."[12] In order to enroll the new regiments, Reserve generals would utilize conscription bureaus in their respective states. General Bragg intended to eventually consolidate the Reserves, conscription, and other military functions under the generals of Reserves.

North Carolina's conscription bureau had been functioning efficiently for two years, but by the end of 1863, the state had exhausted its population of draft-age men. Most of the bureau's resources had turned toward apprehending deserters and draft dodgers. Conscription camps at Raleigh and Morganton were staffed with supporting companies commanded by former drill masters (lieutenants). Rather than processing incoming draftees, the camps had become jails for deserters awaiting transportation or trial. The camps' support companies scoured the western part of the state for deserters and transported them back to units in the field. Congressional district and local enrolling officers kept track of soldiers who were home on leave and coordinated the search for men who were absent without leave from the army.

If managed properly, the enrollment of men aged seventeen to eighteen and forty-five to fifty could supply approximately ten thousand additional North Carolina soldiers for the Confederacy. General Holmes's job was to push these men through North Carolina's conscription system and organize them into battalions and regiments. The process would involve sorting out additional thousands of men seeking medical exemptions, deferments, and job assignments, called "details," as civilian workers. One Confederate officer who would serve in the Junior Reserves stated later that General Holmes's "capacity for a work of the kind was unquestionable."[13]

Holmes finally had an assignment that suited his organizational and administrative talents. He was back in his native state, where he was still held in high regard. He had family, political influence, and would be working closely with his friend, Col. Peter Mallett, commander of North Carolina's conscription bureau. Holmes had considered retiring from the army in late 1863 but changed his mind in early 1864.[14] By then, he knew about the new conscription law and impending creation of the Reserves. It is likely that he, Bragg, and Davis communicated about a new assignment during that time.

For decades before the war, the Mallett and Holmes families had lived near Fayetteville and traveled in the same social circles. In the 1850s, Peter Mallett moved to New York City and became a successful businessman. He was a lieutenant in the 7th New York State Militia regiment while Holmes was stationed at Governors Island. When the war started, Mallett, at the age of thirty-seven, returned with his wife and children to Fayetteville. He offered his services to his native state and became a captain in the 3rd North Carolina State Troops. His regiment was under Holmes's command in the Aquia District in 1861 and 1862. Mallett served in Virginia until the beginning of the Peninsular Campaign, when he was appointed, through General Holmes's influence, to command the bureau of conscription in North Carolina. Mallett left his regiment, established his headquarters near Raleigh, and began organizing his bureau in June 1862. He showed Holmes his appreciation for the assignment (and promotion to major) by naming North Carolina's first conscription camp, located near Raleigh, "Camp Holmes." Mallett used suggestions from General Holmes to begin the enrollment process.[15]

While Holmes was in the Trans-Mississippi, Mallett created a state-wide network of conscription offices and operated one of the South's most efficient and productive conscription bureaus. With the cooperation of Governor Zebulon Baird Vance and the state militia, North Carolina provided nearly one-fourth of all army conscripts collected east of the Mississippi River.[16] Governor Vance recommended Mallett for promotion to colonel in November 1862. As was the accepted practice, Mallett assumed that rank, pending confirmation by the Confederate senate. The next month, Mallett's camp guard battalion fought at the battles of Kinston and Goldsboro during General Foster's expedition from New Bern. Mallett was wounded at Kinston and partially disabled. During 1863, his bureau kept Robert E. Lee's army well-supplied with North Carolina conscripts. His battalion chased draft-dodgers and deserters in the troubled western half of the state.

The February 1864 law designated the Confederate Bureau of Conscription as the implementation tool for gathering the Reserves, but there was confusion in the military over the relationship between the bureau and the Reserve generals. General Order No. 26, issued by Adjutant and Inspector General Cooper on March 1, attempted to clarify the responsibilities of each. Reserve generals were to be ultimately responsible for Reserve troops, but conscription bureaus in the states were directed to assemble the men and organize them in military units. Holmes would command the Reserves until he transferred them to the field. In addition to the Reserves, thousands of civilian workers, including African Americans, had to be enrolled as well. Mallett's bureau was the perfect instrument to accomplish Holmes's mission.[17]

Holmes arrived in North Carolina during an attempt to drive Union forces out of Plymouth, Washington, and New Bern. For the operation, General Lee authorized the detachment of part of General Robert F. Hoke's brigade while the rest of the Army of Northern Virginia was in winter quarters. The off-and-on campaign under General George Pickett suffered an initial repulse at New Bern in February. Pickett returned to Virginia, but Hoke's forces captured Plymouth and forced the evacuation of Washington in April. As Union soldiers abandoned Washington, they looted and burned most of the city. Hoke's force was recalled to Virginia before he could mount an attack on New Bern.[18]

On April 28, Holmes rented five rooms in Raleigh and established his headquarters not far from Colonel Mallett's conscription offices. Two days later, a Raleigh newspaper commented favorably (and generously) on Holmes's return to the state, "Lieut.-Gen. Holmes ... has filled many responsible and difficult positions, with credit to himself and with success to our arms where success was in the range of possibility. His appointment to duty in his native state will be highly acceptable to our people."[19]

Most of Holmes's Arkansas headquarters staff stayed with him in the new assignment. Captain John Hinsdale was the assistant adjutant general. Lieutenants Charles W. Broadfoot and Theo were aides-de-camp. Holmes chose West Point graduate Lt. Col. Frank S. Armistead as his assistant inspector general. These officers would see that the scores of orders, circulars, and directives issued by Holmes and Adjutant and Inspector General Cooper were properly distributed and enforced throughout the state.[20] Holmes appointed Capt. A.W. Lawrence as the ordnance officer for the Reserves. It would be Lawrence's responsibility to arm and equip North Carolina's young boys and old men. Dr. Thomas Hill was chosen as the Reserve's medical director. Hill would see to the health of the men and conditions in the

Colonel Charles Wetmore Broadfoot, 1842–1919. A member of General Holmes's staff for much of his military career, Broadfoot is shown here wearing his 1st lieutenant's uniform with "buff" (off-white) trim, denoting his staff assignment. After the war he became a successful lawyer, served on the board of trustees of the University of North Carolina and was a member of the state legislature (courtesy Mr. Hal W. Broadfoot Jr., Mrs. Hal Broadfoot Sr., and the North Carolina State Archives).

camps where they assembled. Almost immediately, Theo began pressuring his father for a transfer to a combat unit in Virginia. Holmes wrote that his son was "perfectly restless here in inaction" in continuing to serve in a staff assignment.[21]

Mallett and Holmes conferred about assembling the Reserves, conscription, and other manpower resources in the state. Most North Carolinians who had been exempted from military service were excused because of their age, bad health, professions (such as sheriffs and postmasters) or their assignment to wartime agricultural and industrial production. They were not organized other than being in the North Carolina State Militia, the North Carolina Guard for Home Defense, or both.

In the case of the state militia, Holmes had no authority. The militia was commanded by Governor Vance through the state's adjutant general, Richard C. Gatlin. Although the Home Guard was authorized to enforce Confederate conscription and arrest deserters, like the militia they were state troops and not subject to Confederate authority. Holmes and Governor Vance knew each other and each was disposed to assist the other when possible. But Vance jealously guarded his authority over the militia and Home Guard. Throughout the war, he steadfastly refused to allow the Confederacy (i.e., Mallett) to conscript his militia officers. That situation would not change. Fortunately, Adjutant General Gatlin and Holmes were friends. They had served together in the 7th U.S. Infantry in Florida and Mexico. Within parameters set by Vance and Gatlin, Holmes could expect some level of cooperation.

The Department of North Carolina and Southern Virginia was under the command of General P. G. T. Beauregard. Beauregard had approximately fourteen thousand men, the majority of which were in Virginia.[22] His troops in North Carolina were stationed in the Wilmington and Fort Fisher area, near Kinston along Southwest Creek, and guarding the Roanoke River bridge at Weldon. Neither Holmes nor Mallett was under Beauregard's command, but the three officers would be working closely together. Conscripts enrolled by Mallett's bureau were to be organized into Reserve regiments by General Holmes. Those regiments would then be assigned to Beauregard to replace the veteran regiments he would send to Virginia.

Mallett told Holmes about problems in western North Carolina. Conditions there had deteriorated significantly since Holmes left the state two years earlier. With the Union army's occupation of Tennessee, western North Carolina was experiencing frequent raids and the possibility of invasion. The Department of Western North Carolina (the Appalachian Mountains between Asheville and Tennessee) was defended by sixteen hundred troops under the command of Colonel John Palmer. Palmer had all he could do in guarding dozens of mountain passes. He did not have enough soldiers to deal with growing civilian unrest in the area.[23]

Like other Southern states, there was considerable opposition to conscription in North Carolina, particularly in the western half of the state. Confederate conscription was controversial at the time of its passage in 1862. By mid–1863, simple draft dodging had escalated to armed resistance in North Carolina's "Quaker belt" and mountains. The counties of the "Quaker belt" included Randolph, Davie, Yadkin, Moore, Montgomery, Davidson, Alamance, and Forsyth.[24] Anti-Confederate, even pro–Union sentiment, had taken hold.

At the core of the unrest in western North Carolina was a group known as the Heroes of America. They were also referred to as the "red strings," so named for an identifying piece of thread they occasionally wore on their clothing. Mallett's second-in-command, Maj. James McRae, had spent enough time in western North Carolina to know that there was organized resistance to Confederate authority. Unlike other groups, the Heroes of America were not simply anti-conscription or anti–Confederate. They worked to defeat the Confederacy militarily and install a pro–Union government in the state.[25]

Mallett, Governor Vance, and others expressed their concerns to Richmond during the first half of 1863. Conscription Superintendent John S. Preston sent Col. George W. Lay on an inspection tour of the area. That August, Colonel Mallett sent two companies of his battalion to Morganton and opened a new conscription camp, Camp Vance. Colonel Lay's report was alarming and verified for Preston what Mallett and McRae already knew. Lay reported that in some counties, well-armed, semi-military organizations, comprised of deserters and draft resisters, had gathered. These groups were killing state militiamen and Mallett's enrolling officers. Militiamen and pro–Confederate factions were retaliating with atrocities of their own. Colonel Lay warned that "something like civil war" could result in western North Carolina if decisive action was not taken.[26]

Lay's report and pressure from Vance resulted in the creation of Major McRae's cavalry battalion at Asheville in September 1863. McRae's assignment was to break up bands of deserters and suppress pro–Union activities. At the same time, two regiments of Gen. Robert F. Hoke's brigade were sent to North Carolina from Lee's army. Hoke's orders were to capture and return to the army several hundred deserters that infested the Quaker Belt. During the next several months, Mallett's companies, Hoke's regiments, and McRae's battalion had a positive effect on the lawless conditions in the region. They arrested hundreds of deserters and reduced civilian violence. Hoke's regiments were withdrawn from the area in January 1864, and later participated in the attacks on New Bern, Plymouth, and Washington.[27]

When Holmes returned to the state, four of Mallett's companies were at Camp Holmes, near Raleigh, and two were at Morganton's Camp Vance. McRae's battalion was operating in the Department of Western North Carolina but was helping Colonel Palmer defend the border against Union raids more often than arresting deserters. Soon, Mallett's and McRae's battalions would no longer be available. Under the February conscription law, provost troops, hospital guards, and troops assigned to conscription duty had to be sent to the regular army. They would be replaced by the light duty battalions.[28] If Holmes and Mallett coordinated the handover well, there might be no serious interruption of security. Still, they worried about replacing two battalions of experienced veterans (nearly one thousand men) with soldiers not fit for field service. Furthermore, putting light duty troops in the field, so soon after their organization, was a gamble. If a significant lapse in coverage occurred, Colonel Lay's "civil war" in western North Carolina could erupt.

In April, as Holmes and Mallett discussed coordinating their responsibilities, the governor of North Carolina nearly upset their plans. Zebulon Vance wrote to Secretary of War Seddon requesting that the Reserves not be called into the army until after August. Vance wanted the state's crops harvested before the seventeen and forty-five- to fifty-year-old farmers were mobilized. He warned that taking the farmers "from their crops at any time between this and August would be followed by the most distressing consequences."[29] If Seddon approved Vance's request, Mallett's companies and McRae's battalion would be disbanded in June but not replaced by light duty men until after August. Western North Carolina would be defenseless except for Palmer's troops. As a remedy, Holmes devised a plan that provided for the partial mobilization of the Reserves and left Vance with enough farmers to harvest the year's crops.

Holmes wrote to Adjutant and Inspector General Cooper and made two suggestions. He wanted authority to "use any troops that may be available" (i.e., Colonel Palmer's troops) for suppressing the "insurrectionary spirit" in western North Carolina. He also recommended calling the Junior Reserves into service on schedule and using them to replace the two battalions that were to be disbanded. The absence of the younger men would "take but little from the agricultural interests" of the state. Holmes suggested that the older men could be called into the army after the harvest.[30]

The recommendation was shuffled back and forth among Cooper, his assistant, H. L. Clay, Secretary of War Seddon, and General Bragg. Part of Holmes's plan was attractive to Richmond. Vance's concerns about the harvest could be mitigated by delaying the call-up of the Senior Reserves. Holmes's request to use Junior Reserves and "any troops that may be available" to hunt deserters and suppress civilian violence was another matter. The law that created the Junior Reserves expressly forbade their use for conscription enforcement. Bragg could also foresee friction if Holmes was allowed to use Palmer's troops for that purpose. Palmer and his soldiers had a specific geographic assignment. They were responsible for defending the North Carolina and Tennessee border. Palmer would surely object to having any of his soldiers diverted from that task.[31]

Holmes's intention to use a military force to suppress pro–Union civilian activity was also met with skepticism. Uncharacteristically, Bragg was troubled by the prospect of taking direct military action against civilian political factions. In commenting, Bragg wrote, "It is especially objectionable that military officers should be at all mixed up with the unfortunate political dissensions in our States." A compromise was struck during a meeting between Seddon and General Holmes. They agreed that Holmes's separation of the Reserve mobilization would be adopted. Some limited use of the Junior Reserves in western North Carolina would be allowed, but Palmer's troops would not be involved.[32]

General Holmes began enrolling his Reserves pursuant to Bureau of Conscription Circular No. 13. Confederate authorities gave North Carolina a quota of eight Reserve regiments or approximately eight thousand men. Mallett's enrolling officers placed notices in newspapers throughout the state. Men covered by the law were ordered to report to designated rendezvous points for enrollment.[33] Militia officers were to oversee the process. Men applying for medical exemptions would be examined by surgeons employed by the conscription bureau. Even with the delay granted to the older men, hundreds of the seventeen-year-olds filed petitions for exemptions as farmers. Some of the enrolling officers were entirely too generous in approving the requests. One officer in Forsyth County, Lt. W. A. Albright, granted thirty-one out of thirty-two petitions filed.[34]

At their rendezvous points, the Juniors were organized into companies, elected company officers, and were sent to one of Mallett's conscription camps or other designated locations. At the camps, companies were combined into battalions, and company officers elected the battalion commanders. The elections were supervised and certified by Mallett's "Enrolling and Mustering" officers. The resulting paperwork was sent through Colonel Mallett to General Holmes for final approval.[35] When the officers' commissions were approved by Holmes, the battalion was accepted for service. The soldiers were issued uniforms, arms, and equipment. On May 26, one of Holmes's aides-de-camp, Lt. Charles Broadfoot, was elected major of the 1st Battalion North Carolina Reserves.[36] Holmes and Mallett sent Lt. Col. Armistead to command the Reserve rendezvous at Wilmington.

At the conscription camps, Mallett's drill instructors trained the young men in the manual of arms, company drill, and battalion maneuvers.[37] As the novice Reserve officers became more confident of their skills, they conducted daily drills of their men. No one knew when General Holmes would send them to the field, but the war was drawing closer every day. A long and bloody summer was beginning in Virginia and Georgia.

On May 15, Secretary of War Seddon ordered the Reserve generals to employ the "utmost activity and energy ... in collecting and organizing the reserves, and hurrying them into positions to relieve every trained soldier that can be spared for service in the field.... This by the President's direction." Lee's army was fighting General Grant near Petersburg and Richmond. General Johnston was resisting Sherman's campaign to capture Atlanta. President Davis and General Bragg were deciding how to deploy Reserve regiments so Lee and Johnston could be reinforced.[38]

The 1st, 2nd, 4th and 6th battalions of North Carolina Reserves were organized at Camp Holmes during May and June. The 3rd (Seniors), 5th, 8th and 9th battalions were formed during the same period at Goldsboro, Wilmington, Morganton, and Asheville. Most battalions contained three companies.[39] As soon as possible, the battalions would be combined into regiments. General Holmes commanded Reserve units until he released them from camp and turned them over to General Beauregard. By law, Reserves were required to serve within their home states. Beauregard would then transfer his veteran regiments to Virginia.

Junior Reserve officers found themselves responsible for dozens of fellow teenagers who were away from home for the first time. Major Broadfoot complained in June that his soldiers came to him for everything: "One wants a furlough, one has broken his gun and expects me to mend it for him; another wants to go home to get married, etc." Briefly, Broadfoot had to tend to the medical needs of his battalion until a surgeon could be assigned. A medical officer from Major Hahr's battalion gave Broadfoot "some medicines with full directions how to use. To-day I dosed about thirty [soldiers]."[40]

By May 26, Davis and Bragg had decided where the Reserves should be assigned. Holmes's counterpart in Georgia, Gen. Howell Cobb, was ordered to send five of his regiments to Atlanta, three to Andersonville, and two to Savannah. General Chesnut, in South Carolina, was to assign three regiments to Charleston and three more to the western part of the state along the Georgia border. General James Kemper, in Virginia, was ordered to assign "ten to fifteen regiments for Richmond, two for Petersburg, and two for Danville railroad." General Holmes was to divide five regiments between Wilmington and Weldon and assign "two in the mountain district."[41]

While the organization of the Junior Reserves was being completed efficiently, the Senior Reserves were a different matter. After the agreement to delay their organization until the season's crops were gathered, debate about the postponement continued. The delay had been approved some time after notices went out ordering all Reserves to assemble. The 3rd Battalion (Seniors) was organized at Goldsboro by the end of May. Hundreds of additional older men who reported for duty were sent back home or assigned to part-time duty with the Home Guard. Under the pressure of North Carolina's need for troops in all areas of the state, Holmes vacillated and contributed to the confusion. Debate about when and how to deploy the Seniors, and inefficiency, would continue through much of the summer.[42]

Since his appointment as President Davis's military advisor, General Bragg had been working to reorganize the conscription process. To that end, on May 28, orders were issued to the Reserve generals by the adjutant and inspector general's office. In addition to Holmes's command of the North Carolina Reserves, he was given authority over Colonel Mallett's conscription bureau as it related to the formation of the Reserves. He was also given command of all companies raised in the state for "local defense and special service" (excluding the militia and Home Guard). Confederate quartermasters, commissary officers, ordnance and medical departments were "required to furnish all necessary facilities" in support of Holmes's duties. He was also put in charge of the Invalid Corps and all other Confederate officers and enlisted men not assigned to a specific unit or duty.[43]

Mallett was still North Carolina's commandant of conscription, but now he had two masters. He and his bureau answered to Holmes regarding gathering the Reserves, but to Adjutant and Inspector General Cooper (through Superintendent of Conscription John Preston) on non–Reserve conscription matters and deserter apprehension. Because of his close relationship with Holmes, the change made little difference to Mallett, but some of his enrolling officers were confused. For a time, they refused to obey orders from Holmes's headquarters until after their Reserve companies were organized and sent to the camps of instruction.[44]

Mallett's officers were not alone in their confusion. Conflicting orders from Richmond, designed to sort out spheres of command among department commanders, district generals, and Reserve generals, frustrated others as well. On June 17, the lieutenant colonel in command of the Junior Reserves at Goldsboro, Frank S. Armistead, was ordered by district Gen. Laurence S. Baker to send two of his battalions to Weldon. Armistead complied with the order but complained to General Holmes's adjutant that he was still under orders to "report directly to Lt. Gen. Holmes and having been instructed to obey *only* his orders." Armistead stated that he "would probably have disobeyed the order" were it not in the best interests of the service.[45]

As the Union army's siege of Petersburg tightened, threats along the railroad between Petersburg and Weldon became more frequent. Generals Grant and Meade wanted to cut the railroad lines that supplied Lee's army and provided him with an escape route. The railroad bridge across the Roanoke River at Weldon, North Carolina, was the vital link for supplies moving from Wilmington to Lee's besieged army at Petersburg. Concern for the bridge's security had been a major part of Confederate defensive plans since early in the war. In 1862, Fort Branch, an extensive earthwork mounted with heavy artillery, was built on the Roanoke River near Hamilton, North Carolina. The fort kept Union gunboats from steaming upriver and shelling the bridge. At Weldon, more earthworks were built on both sides of the river to protect the bridge from infantry and cavalry raids. One Confederate officer estimated that, depending on where the earthworks were built, between eight hundred and five thousand men should be permanently stationed near the bridge.[46] In May, the 68th North Carolina Infantry was ordered by General Beauregard to occupy the defenses around the Weldon bridge. The regiment was well uniformed and equipped, but a Confederate deserter reported that the 68th was "composed of conscripts, many of whom are old soldiers"[47] (see Appendix B).

In addition to being a rendezvous for Junior Reserves, Camp Holmes was the last stop for officers and enlisted men in Mallett's and McRae's battalions. By the first week in June, most of both battalions was gathered at Camp Holmes to be disbanded. The soldiers were issued new uniforms and equipment and sent to North Carolina regiments in Virginia and Georgia. Union activity south of Petersburg disrupted some of the transfers. General Beauregard ordered Mallett to postpone disbanding several companies and strengthen Weldon. The plan to use Mallett's men to reinforce other army units was further thwarted by a loophole in the February law. Mallett's soldiers were allowed to choose their new units. Nearly one hundred of them, having lost their enthusiasm for the army, joined the Confederate navy.[48]

Holmes was in the midst of his most productive service to the Confederacy and was extraordinarily busy organizing the Reserves. Consistent with Bragg's long-term plans, his authority in North Carolina's conscription bureau was expanding. But the months of May and June brought correspondence and newspaper reports that recalled his difficulties in Arkansas. A letter from an appointment seeker, W. S. G. Andrews, reminded Holmes that, after Helena, reports of his death had been "frequent and confirmed." On May 13, the Richmond *Dispatch* reprinted an article from the *Atlanta Appeal* that referred to Holmes as an "incubus."[49] In June, Congress considered a resolution of thanks to Gen. Kirby Smith for his victories in the Red River campaign. During the discussion, Representative Clark of Missouri publically insulted Holmes by stating that the "former commander of the Trans-Mississippi had not been very successful." Clark then sarcastically added that he "thought his name was Holmes."[50] After the first week of June, however, personal insults could not have further injured Holmes. His worst fears were realized in Virginia on June 3. Nineteen-year-old Theo was killed during the Battle of 2nd Cold Harbor.

More than two years earlier, at the boy's insistence, General Holmes had appointed him as a civilian volunteer and cadet on his staff. Theo was later commissioned a lieutenant and served with his father at the battles of Malvern Cliffs and Helena. He held a staff position in Arkansas and, briefly, at Reserve headquarters in Raleigh. Not satisfied with a non-combat assignment, Theo went to Virginia (with his father's permission) and joined the 5th North Carolina Cavalry. Within two weeks, the 5th Cavalry's colonel informed General Holmes that Theo had been killed while "leading a line of sharp shooters to dislodge the enemy's skirmishers in the Battle near Ashland.... He was brave, gracious & true."[51] One of General Holmes's relatives wrote that Theo had "died a glorious death," and "his poor father and sister are almost heartbroken."[52] Holmes was devastated, but unlike his collapse after Helena, remained at his post.

In mid–June, Holmes contacted General Lee about the North Carolina Reserves and military conditions in the state. He implied that there was confusion in the chain of command. He renewed his April request to take control of Colonel J. B. Palmer's department in western North Carolina. He also complained that Palmer had improperly assumed command of Junior Reserves in that part of the state. In passing the information along to President Davis, Lee recommended that Holmes be given "supreme control" of the state's Junior and Senior Reserves "unless General Holmes is incapacitated for these duties" (a reference to Theo's death and the persistent rumors of Holmes's alcoholism and frail health).[53] The matter was settled in July when Colonel Palmer and his troops were put under the command of Gen. James G. Martin. Martin was given command of the Reserves in western North Carolina but was ordered to report to Holmes.[54]

In the wake of Theo's death, Holmes came under pressure from his next oldest son, Gabriel, for an appointment as a Confederate cadet. With mixed feelings, Holmes wrote a letter to the war department and recommended Gabriel's appointment and assignment to a North Carolina artillery unit. In Richmond, Holmes's request generated a "Memorandum for the President" from an officer in the adjutant and inspector general's office. The memo informed Davis that Gabriel "has just attained his 16th year and has not been in service." Both documents specifically mentioned that Gabriel's older brother had been killed in action. The reminders of Theo's death served to inform everyone of General Holmes's difficult situation. The memorandum to Davis specifically mentioned that Gabriel wanted to be assigned to the "Third District of North Carolina." Holmes's request did not mention the 3rd district. Apparently, other information had been received at the war department.[55] Holmes was in Richmond when he submitted the request. He may have gone to Virginia in an effort to recover Theo's body.

Everyone in Richmond dealt very carefully with the request. One officer wrote that granting the application was contrary to current rules governing cadet appointments. He also noted that the matter was subject to "other considerations." When the documents arrived on President Davis's desk, he directed one of his aides to "write a friendly letter explaining the rule[,] the reason of which will be perceived."[56] The petition was disapproved on July 27, but Holmes knew that a presidential rejection would only delay the inevitable. Gabriel would be seventeen years old on January 25, 1865, and subject to conscription in the Junior Reserves.

Toward the end of June, fighting in Virginia threatened Weldon. On June 21, General Meade ordered an attack to cut the rail line south of Petersburg. Two Union corps moved forward but became separated as they maneuvered. Confederate forces attacked, and a three-day battle ensued. On June 23, Holmes received orders from President Davis to "proceed to Weldon with all the reserve forces you have collected, or may collect, and assume command there for the protection of that line of railroad to Petersburg." On the 27th, Holmes ordered Lieutenant Colonel Armistead and his Junior Reserves to move from Wilmington to Weldon.[57] They reinforced the 68th North Carolina Troops and part of Mallett's battalion commanded by Maj. Franz Hahr. Hahr had been sent to Weldon three weeks earlier by General Beauregard.[58]

Holmes caused a reshuffling of the 1st Junior Reserves' leadership shortly after their arrival at Weldon. He wanted his former chief of staff, Frank S. Armistead, to lead the regiment instead of the recently elected Col. Charles Broadfoot. Broadfoot and the other officers, Lt. Col. Walter Clark, and Maj. Nathaniel Gregory, complied with Holmes's wishes. Another election was held, and Armistead was elected. The incident produced some bitterness among the young officers. Walter Clark, in particular, felt that Holmes had ruined his chance for advancement. Clark wrote to his mother after the incident and complained, "Gen'l Holmes was much opposed to my election — I was too young. He doubtless thought 65 the right age to qualify a man for my position tho' it doesn't seem to fit him for Lt. Genl by the way."[59]

Major Walter McKenzie Clark, 1846–1924. General Holmes thought Clark was too young to be a lieutenant colonel. Clark thought Holmes was too old to be a general. After a notable career in the Confederate army, Clark became a distinguished lawyer and served three terms as the chief justice of the North Carolina Supreme Court. Among his many writings is a multi-volume history of North Carolina Confederate regiments, *Histories of the Several Regiments and Battalions from North Carolina in the Great War, 1861–1865,* known was *Clark Histories* (from Aubrey Lee Brooks and Hugh Talmage Lefler, eds., *The Papers of Walter Clark: V. 2, 1857–1924,* copyright 1948, University of North Carolina Press, renewed 1976 by Hugh Talmage Lefler, courtesy University of North Carolina Press).

While Holmes was in command at Weldon, a raid from Tennessee into western North Carolina began. Some weeks earlier, Union General John Schofield initiated plans for an attack on Morganton's Camp Vance. Colonel Mallett had established the camp in August 1863, to enroll the forty- to forty-five-year-old men President Davis called into service that month. Western North Carolina had become infested with deserters and draft-dodgers from North Carolina, Tennessee, South Carolina, and Virginia. Mallett sent two companies of his battalion from Raleigh to work with Major McRae's cavalry battalion, which mustered at Asheville during the same period. Despite the best efforts of Mallett, McRae, and Colonel Palmer, the area was vulnerable to raids by Union cavalry and mounted infantry units from Tennessee. When McRae's battalion and Mallett's companies left the area and returned to Raleigh to be disbanded, all that remained at Camp Vance were several enrolling officers, a few guards, and approximately 240 unarmed, untrained Junior Reserves.[60]

Shortly after dawn on June 28, Capt. George Kirk and one hundred thirty mounted Union soldiers appeared at Camp Vance. Kirk, who had a fearsome reputation in the mountains, demanded the immediate surrender of the camp. His regiment, the 3rd Regiment North Carolina Mounted Infantry, U.S., consisted of veteran Union soldiers, Native Americans, Confederate deserters, and runaway slaves. Most were armed with Spencer repeating rifles. Kirk and his men were products of the vicious mountain warfare on the Tennessee and North Carolina border. They were the source of "growing legend and fear" in the mountains and could be expected to slaughter the young soldiers if a battle took place.[61]

The camp's enrolling officers, lieutenants Walter Bullock and Edward F. Hanks, conferred briefly and decided to accept Kirk's terms, which included the immediate parole of Confederate officers. As soon as Bullock and Hanks surrendered the camp, Kirk's men rounded up the entire garrison and held them at gunpoint while the camp buildings were set on fire. Kirk's men burned a nearby train station before starting back toward Tennessee with two hundred seventy-seven prisoners. Local Home Guard units chased the raiders for several days, skirmishing with them along the way. Kirk's men passed through Mitchell County, stopping long enough to burn Colonel Palmer's home. Approximately half of the prisoners escaped during the pursuit.[62]

Holmes was enraged at the news. "I am astounded at the neglect [in] permitting such a raid," he wrote. He wanted Mallett to go to Camp Vance and "take command in person," but Mallett had already dispatched a company of McRae's cavalry that had not been disbanded. For an investigation of the surrender, Holmes sent a disabled captain from the 30th North Carolina Troops, Charles N. Allen. Allen arrived at the burned-out railroad station the day after the raid. In addition to destroying much of the camp, the railroad station, a locomotive, several flatcars, and capturing the Junior Reserves, Kirk's men had burned 250 bushels of corn, 6,500 pounds of forage, 150 bushels of rye and oats, 1,500 rounds of small arms ammunition, and 250 sets of weapons and accouterments. When Mallett received Allen's report, he wrote to Holmes and remarked that the episode was "by no means creditable to the officers present."[63] Using Captain Allen's observations, Mallett reported on Kirk's raid to the superintendent of conscription, Colonel Preston. In a not-so-subtle "we told you so," he reminded Preston that without reliable supporting forces, parts of North Carolina were in a "defenseless condition."[64]

The Heroes of America assisted Kirk's raiders in their mission. Holmes, Mallett,

Major McRae, and even Governor Vance had known of the group for sometime. Two weeks before the raid, Holmes and former North Carolina governor Thomas Bragg (also a former Confederate attorney general and General Braxton Bragg's brother) had sent a letter about the Heroes of America to General Bragg in Richmond. At that time there was no information about Kirk's plan to attack Camp Vance.[65] The Weldon crisis and the destruction of Camp Vance occurred almost simultaneously. Only days later, another raid began, this time in the eastern part of the state.

On July 3, Union cavalry left New Bern and headed toward the Wilmington and Weldon Railroad depot at Magnolia. During five days in the saddle, they captured Confederate cavalrymen, couriers, and pickets. At Kenansville, their commander, Lt. Col. G. W. Lewis, reported destroying a saddle factory and armory along with a "large quantity of sabers, saber bayonets, knives." At Magnolia, his men tore up several miles of railroad tracks. During the raid, a total of one million dollars in property was destroyed and "between 40 and 50 prisoners" were taken, along with one hundred horses and mules; "nearly 500 contrabands ([African American] men, women and children) were also brought in."[66]

On July 10, General Whiting requested that Holmes send Colonel Armistead's 1st North Carolina Reserve regiment to Kenansville, where he expected another raid.[67] On July 18, the immediate crisis at Weldon was thought to have passed and Holmes returned to his headquarters at Raleigh.[68] Major Hahr's battalion remained at Weldon until it was disbanded later in the month. His men were replaced with two companies of light duty soldiers.

By late July, 1864, Holmes had two regiments and six battalions of Reserves organized. The two battalions of light duty men, commanded by majors Hahr and Jesse McLean, were stationed at Camp Holmes and Weldon. Enough of the older men had reported for duty to organize the first of the Senior Reserve regiments. During the month, Colonel Mallett received some disappointing news. The secretary of war notified Mallett that he was, in fact, not a colonel. Commandants of state bureaus of conscription were authorized by law to be majors. Mallett's promotion to colonel in November 1862 was the result of a recommendation from Governor Vance, but was never confirmed by the Confederate senate. General Holmes and Thomas Bragg wrote to President Davis on Mallett's behalf, to no avail.[69]

Holmes realized that one requirement of the Junior Reserve program was counterproductive to the maintenance of well disciplined regiments. Upon reaching the age of eighteen, all Juniors were required to leave their regiments and transfer, as privates, to regiments in the field. The rule was applied regardless of their rank in the Reserves. While the requirement provided a steady supply of enlisted men to the army, it robbed Junior Reserve regiments of promising young officers. Company staffs were in a constant state of turmoil, and continuity of command was lost. In July, Holmes obtained approval from the war department to keep capable young officers in the Reserves and send the less talented ones to the field as privates. He was also allowed to fill some Junior Reserve officer vacancies with experienced but disabled veteran officers. The result was "a very decided improvement in the personnel of the company officers."[70]

Union forces attacked Beauregard's troops on the Weldon Railroad on August 18 and 19. The next day, President Davis warned Holmes that his Reserves might be needed at Weldon. Davis recommended that Wilmington should be strengthened as well. Holmes could not reinforce both threatened points sufficiently to satisfy Beauregard and Whiting. He traveled to Wilmington for a conference with Whiting, then went on to Fayetteville, arriving there on August 28. When he returned to Raleigh, he was greeted with a telegram sent from Wilmington. General Whiting was complaining that the Senior Reserves Holmes sent earlier in the month were arriving without cooking utensils and blankets.[71]

In September, Reserve generals were put in charge of "impressment as a means to provide for the immediate needs of the Army and to accumulate stores." Confederate army officers were authorized to seize crops, livestock, practically anything the army needed. Property owners were to be given receipts estimating fair prices or prices set by the government. Reserve generals or their designees were to administer the program and conduct investigations of any disputes. In overseeing the seizures, Reserve generals were admonished, "Moderation, good temper, and firmness should characterize your actions under this order." Nevertheless, should property owners refuse to cooperate, the property was to be seized and the owner reported to the Reserve general.[72]

After Atlanta fell on September 2, there remained but two campaigns that would seal the fate of the Confederacy. The siege of Petersburg would continue for seven more months. If Petersburg fell, Richmond would have to be evacuated. Lee's army might escape, but he would have to retreat along railroad lines that supplied his army from Wilmington through Weldon. If Wilmington fell, the rail lines would become irrelevant: Lee's army would starve. Wilmington had become even more crucial to the Confederacy in August when Mobile, Alabama, was captured. Union plans to close Wilmington were well underway by September.[73]

Rumors of an impending attack on Fort Fisher or Wilmington were becoming more frequent. At Wilmington, Maj. Gen. William H. C. Whiting commanded the district. His immediate superior was General Beauregard. Beauregard's troops were divided among three military district commanders: Gen. Henry A. Wise, District No. 1, southeastern Virginia, with approximately thirteen thousand six hundred effective troops; Gen. Laurence S. Baker in District No. 2 with thirty-seven hundred effectives at Weldon, Goldsboro, New Bern, Kinston, and Plymouth; and General Whiting in District No. 3 at Wilmington, Fort Fisher, and the forts on the Cape Fear River and Masonboro Sound, with approximately thirty-five hundred men. At the end of August, Whiting sent Beauregard a lengthy description of Wilmington's defenses and a plea for more troops, artillery, and laborers. At the time, Beauregard was more concerned with Petersburg, where most of his soldiers were under siege with Lee's army. He urged Governor Vance to reinforce Whiting but offered only to have troops in the 2nd Military District prepared to help Whiting in the event of an attack.[74]

In his frustration, Whiting contacted General Lee directly, asking for more troops. Lee, like Beauregard, refused to weaken the Richmond and Petersburg line. Whiting then asked Governor Vance to mobilize the state militia for ninety days. Vance was not convinced that Wilmington was in immediate danger. He was reluctant to call out the militia that time of year because most militiamen were farmers and were still harvesting crops. He refused Whiting as well. Both Lee and Vance told Whiting that he would have to rely on Holmes's Reserves and troops already assigned to the Wilmington and Fort Fisher districts.[75]

During the same period, Holmes and Vance were being pressured to send more troops to Virginia. On October 8, General Lee requested that three North Carolina regiments, the 50th, 67th and 68th, be replaced by Reserves and sent to his army. He asked if the 10th Artillery at Masonboro Sound could be sent as well.[76] Lee also wanted North Carolina's detailed men. From Chaffin's Bluff near Richmond, he telegraphed Holmes, "Are you sending the detailed men to the army[?]... We want every man we can get and at once."[77] (At the time of Lee's message, he was apparently unaware of the conscript law's restriction regarding the use of detailed men outside of their home states.)

Neither Whiting nor General Baker was likely to replace the 10th Artillery with Reserves and send the artillerymen to Virginia. The Reserves were trained as infantry. Without extensive retraining, they would be useless as artillery troops. The other troops in Whiting's district were mostly artillery, cavalry, a scattering of infantry companies, and local defense troops. He had no infantry regiments for Lee. General Baker's 2nd District was similar in composition, but contained two of the regiments Lee wanted, the 50th and 67th. The 50th North Carolina Troops served under General Holmes at Malvern Cliffs and were swept up in the panic on River Road. The unit was currently stationed at Plymouth and Washington, North Carolina, and would remain in the state until November. The 67th, a regiment of dubious quality, was in the area around Kinston. Through an agreement between North Carolina and the Confederacy, the 67th could not be sent out of the state. The 68th North Carolina infantry had been moved from the Weldon area and was currently serving under General Martin in the Department of Western North Carolina. Like the 67th, the 68th could serve only within the state. There was not much left in North Carolina that could be sent to Lee.[78] (In November, President Davis would suspend, for sixty days, the in-state service restriction on the Reserves. North Carolina Reserves served in Tennessee, Virginia, and Georgia before the war ended. See *OR*, Series I, v. 42, pt. 3, p. 1226.)

The tug-of-war over troops drew Holmes into a personal feud that was brewing between Vance and Whiting. Vance thought Whiting "drank too much" and that Whiting's "nervous system had been damaged by it." Foolishly, the governor confided his opinion to Holmes. Just as foolishly, Holmes told Whiting. Several letters were exchanged, each trying to smooth over the insult, but the damage was done. The Whiting and Vance relationship, already strained over the question of using militiamen at Wilmington, was seriously injured. Vance would, in the future, be more guarded when confiding in Holmes.[79]

Once the Junior Reserves were organized and the remaining forty-five-to-fifty-year-old men were scheduled to report in November and December, the war department's attention focused on the Confederacy's civilian workforce. In August, state commandants of conscription were required to identify and locate all men who had "obtained exemptions or details" for agricultural production.[80] The problem of how many men were needed to keep the South's farm economy running and produce an adequate supply of food to feed the army had troubled the government since 1862. The first conscription law did not provide enough industrial and agricultural details from military service to increase production as the war continued. Numerous deferments and exemptions were added, altered, or dropped in late 1862 and 1863. A confusing and ever-changing system of regulations, exemptions, and details resulted. No comprehensive count of workers deferred from military service or of men older than fifty-five years had been made.

The February 1864 law had greatly reduced the number of details sheltering Southern men from the army. For nationwide management of the civilian workforce, the law classified all white males age seventeen through fifty (those not already in the army) as "detailed men." They were to be detailed to civilian industrial and agricultural production or to one of the six supply bureaus of the Confederate army.[81] Consequently, Mallett's bureau spent weeks re-examining existing details and petitions for lapsed or new deferments. By mid–summer, his staff was receiving more than one hundred petitions each day.[82] (In February 1865, the Confederate States War Department estimated that a minimum of 15,622 white men and 37,749 African American men would be required to keep the six supply bureaus of the Confederacy running. The bureaus were Nitre and Mining, Engineers, Ordnance, Medical, Commissary, and Quartermaster. See *OR*, Series IV, v. 3, p. 1095.)

As the February law was implemented between March and July, it was found to be an incomplete remedy for the civilian workforce problem. The system was still inefficient, encouraged draft-dodging, and was resistant to the nationwide management required by the war. By then, war-weariness had settled in on the population and conscription was the most hated law in the Confederacy. In large numbers, Southerners were taking advantage of the confusion. The war department suspected that thousands of men who should have been in the army were still avoiding service through civilian job details granted by conscription officers and governors.[83]

In August, Adjutant and Inspector General Order No. 63 was issued. The order required all detailed men, regardless of age, to be organized "into companies and regiments" and commanded by the Reserve generals.[84] Men who could not produce current detail authorizations were to be arrested and sent to the army. As a result, the Confederate ordnance works at Salisbury, North Carolina, was in danger of having nearly all its workers arrested.[85] General Order No. 63 did not seek to identify fraudulent or unnecessary details. This omission would need to be corrected within weeks.

On September 22, generals of Reserves were given command of "the business of conscription and enrollment in their respective states." All army personnel who had been assigned to conscription duty were ordered to advise their respective Reserve generals of their current assignment and duties. In North Carolina, Holmes simply issued orders to Major Mallett, advising him of the change. Mallett passed the information to his subordinates. From that time forward, Mallett reported directly to Holmes rather than to Colonel Preston's conscription bureau and the adjutant and inspector general's office in Richmond. Mallett was also required to replace many of his officers and enlisted men who were capable of active duty with men from the Reserves.[86]

The problem of fraudulent or unnecessary details needed to be addressed. Most previous occupational details for men between the ages of eighteen and forty-five were revoked by the Confederacy on October 8. Men not in the army were required to be enrolled and petition anew for their assignments to war-related agricultural or industrial details. Once approved, the details often consisted of reassignment to the same jobs that had deferred workers from military service for much of the war. Again, Mallett's bureau had to reprocess hundreds of petitions. White males who were exempted from military service on grounds other than health, religion, or for a very few occupations (such as sheriffs and postal workers) were to be closely examined. Individuals whose details were found to be unnecessary or fraudulent were sent to the army.[87] Men who remained on detail were to be organized by the Reserve general in each state into the military organizations required by General Order No. 63. Later in the month, the adjutant and inspector general required the names of one-fifth of all men detailed to the Nitre and Mining Bureau (employed in mining lead, iron, copper, and coal) to be turned over to conscription officers for possible induction into the army.[88]

Mallett's officers ultimately identified 3,117 legally detailed men in the state. At the end of November, two regiments were organized. By February 1865, Holmes had a total of three regiments and two battalions of detailed men. The regiments were designated the 1st, 2nd, and 3rd Regiments of North Carolina Detailed Men. The battalions were Major Rencher's Battalion and the City Battalion of Raleigh. There was also an independent company of detailed men. Although these men were organized in battalions and regiments, their use as a military force was regarded as both impractical and unlikely for the obvious reason: If all detailed men were called out for military service, all industrial and agricultural production would cease. The order was designed to give the Confederacy an accurate count of men who were not serving in the army but were legally assigned to wartime production. Detailed men were assured by law that they would not be called out for military service "except in emergencies occurring in or near the counties of their residence ... and those contiguous thereto."[89]

On October 15, President Davis sent Braxton Bragg to temporarily command "the defenses of Wilmington and its approaches." Ordinarily, having a general with close ties to the president would have been beneficial to the state. Beauregard's focus was on Virginia. Bragg was a senior Confederate commander and a North Carolinian. Holmes served with Bragg in Mexico and had expressed high regard for him just days before Fort Sumter. But like Holmes, Bragg's reputation had suffered during the war. He was criticized for squandering the lives of his men at Shiloh and Murfreesboro. He failed to follow up on the victory at Chickamauga and botched the siege of Chattanooga. Thereafter, he resigned as commander of the Army of Tennessee. Perhaps no Confederate general was publically vilified as frequently as Bragg. A Virginia newspaper editor, upon hearing of Bragg's assignment to defend Wilmington, wrote, "Good bye, Wilmington." Since Bragg was back in his native state, North Carolina newspapers took a more optimistic view of his arrival. Like Holmes, Davis was loyal to Bragg, and like Holmes, Davis had put Bragg in positions of responsibility that were often ill-suited to his talents.[90]

Adjutant and Inspector General Cooper urged Holmes to rush the organization of his Reserve forces into "Brigades, Divisions and Army Corps." Cooper told Holmes that the formation of a North Carolina Reserve army corps would allow Holmes, a lieutenant general, to once again have a command that would "conform to that rank."[91] On October 8 and 10, Holmes sent Cooper recommendations that combined five Reserve regiments and two battalions in two brigades, and put the regiments of detailed men into a third brigade. He recommended several officers for promotion to the ranks of lieutenant colonel, colonel, and brigadier general. Because these officers would command Reserves and detailed men, the law required the positions to be filled by officers who were incapable of active field service due to wounds or other disabilities.[92]

One of the promotions to colonel that Holmes recommended was for Maj. Peter Mallett. Holmes was still annoyed that Mallett's rank had been reduced from colonel to major in July. He reminded Cooper that Mallett was "permanently disabled from field service but is an excellent officer of much experience and abundantly able to command a regiment of Reserves." He told Cooper that, if promoted, Mallett would remain commandant of conscription as well as command a Reserve regiment. Cooper saw through Holmes's patronage. Mallett would remain a major.[93]

Holmes also wrote to President Davis in October. His purpose was to advance the career of his nephew, Capt. John W. Hinsdale. The note was a gentle reminder of Holmes's original request, made "some weeks" earlier, for Hinsdale's promotion. He recounted Hinsdale's "great merit both in the field and in the office.... Few men are more capable." Hinsdale was, indeed, an exceptional young man. He would become colonel of the 3rd North Carolina Junior Reserve regiment in January 1865.[94]

Holmes was never reluctant to advocate for family and friends. He was a good judge of character and ability in his subordinates. Men whose careers he championed, Mallett, Deshler, Nelson, Hindman, and Marmaduke, among others, were brave men and good officers. He followed their careers closely. Deshler was a respected brigadier general at the time of his death at Chickamauga. Holmes's recommendation was responsible for Col. Allison Nelson's promotion to brigadier general in the Trans-Mississippi. Nelson died before the potential Holmes saw in him could be realized. Colonel Frank Armistead went on to command a Reserve brigade. Nephews John Hinsdale and Charles Wetmore Broadfoot became fine staff officers under Holmes's guidance and were developing into excellent field commanders. Theo was gone but had demonstrated great courage and enthusiasm.

The Junior Reserves were another source of pride for General Holmes. While stationed at Weldon in October, Lieutenant Colonel Broadfoot wrote to the secretary of war. He and the 1st Junior Reserves unanimously requested to be sent to Virginia "while our National Capital is threatened and its brave defenders stand in need of reinforcements." After the war, Broadfoot stated that Holmes often spoke of the incident "in highly complimentary terms."[95]

Holmes's pride in his young soldiers notwithstanding, his preference was to keep college students in school during the war. In the autumn of 1864, he supported an appeal to Jefferson Davis by University of North Carolina president David Swain. Swain wanted his senior class exempted from conscription until graduation the following June. At the time of Swain's request, there were only fourteen seniors left at the university.[96]

During October, General Bragg, Secretary of War Seddon, and others received specific information that an attack on Fort Fisher and Wilmington was imminent. Colonel William Lamb, in command at Fort Fisher, noted in his diary that Commodore Porter was assembling a fleet at Fortress Monroe. Seddon's information was more specific. He notified Bragg, Holmes, and Whiting that twenty-five large Union vessels, "including several monitors," were expected to sail for Wilmington on October 25.[97] Similar rumors and reports had been common earlier in the month. Lamb, Bragg, and Whiting wanted soldiers to reinforce Wilmington and Fort Fisher and needed laborers to improve the area's earthworks. On October 11, General Whiting telegraphed Holmes, asking, "Can you and the governor commence sending forward troops[?] You cant be too soon. Farragut is preparing his expedition. I have neither men nor labor."[98] Reports of an impending attack on Fort Fisher and/or Wilmington, accompanied by Whiting's appeals for troops, artillery, and laborers, would continue through December.

North Carolina was already detailing white men and impressing slaves for work on construction projects like Fort Fisher, but Whiting wanted to further strengthen his command. The governor of Virginia was arming civilians in Richmond. General Whiting asked Holmes to help talk Governor Vance into doing the same at Wilmington.[99] In the foreseeable future, the need for black and white men in the army could cause North Carolina's economy to collapse. Taking laborers away from their work interfered with the state's ability to maintain its railroads, agricultural production, and manufacturing. One North Carolinian wrote, "The drain of white laborers is so great that great detriment must ensue to agriculture. Black Smiths, Tanners, & Wagon Makers, etc., are taken by Whole Sale, under the last call for detailed men. Call into service the negro men, and the result must be frightful."[100] The same problem existed in other Southern states. In North Carolina, a showdown over the issue was brewing between the governor and the Confederacy.

Governor Vance had quarreled with Richmond authorities about the conscription law since its passage. Early in the war, he realized that North Carolina needed certain classes of individuals and professions to be exempted from conscription. He refused to allow his state militia officers to be conscripted. He also wanted a variety of state and local officials exempted from army service. That number grew as the Confederacy's upper and lower conscript age limits expanded and included more of the state's workers. When General Holmes returned to the state, there were approximately twenty-six hundred conscripts detailed to transportation, communication, mining, state factories, salt-works, quartermasters, and other war-related assignments.[101] Vance wanted many of those men shielded from army service through details or outright exemption. In April 1864, Vance and Holmes protected older farmers from Senior Reserve service until after the harvest season. Later, Vance refused General Whiting's request to call out the militia for the same reason.

In addition to Vance's many requests for details submitted to the Bureau of Conscription, he wanted to maintain the workforce in the state's textile industry, the largest in the South. As a result of past deferments and February's expansion of the draft-age limits, hundreds of draft-age men were working in North Carolina textile mills. North Carolina produced more than enough cloth to supply her own troops with uniforms. Once soldiers were accepted into the Confederate army, the Confederate government was responsible for uniforming them. By special arrangements with the Confederacy, North Carolina provided all of the state's soldiers with clothing. For relieving the government of this responsibility, the state received payment from the Confederacy.

In May 1863, the Confederate government borrowed, for a sixty-day period, eighteen hundred bales of cotton from the state. (Fifteen hundred bales were still owed to the state a year later.) Finding that North Carolina was a more reliable source of cloth than the Confederate government, other Southern states contracted with the state for cloth and uniforms. Governor Vance maintained cloth production by requesting that his workers be detailed to work in textile factories rather than being conscripted for military service.[102] The Confederate government grew increasingly dissatisfied with the arrangement. The Confederate quartermaster wanted to introduce a more equitable distribution of North Carolina cloth. In an attempt to gain national government control over the state's textile industry, Confederate authorities used the draft laws as a weapon. General Holmes and Major Mallett were ordered to conscript textile workers from factories that had cloth or uniform contracts with North Carolina and other Southern states. In October 1864, when Governor Vance realized what was happening, he wrote directly to Holmes saying, "I shall not submit to it."[103]

Vance was angry that the Confederate government was using the draft laws to "break down the State of North Carolina in this way and deprive her of the power to clothe her armies in the field." The governor told Holmes that he would resist any changes in the granting of textile and related details. He bluntly warned Holmes, "Should these details therefore be unreasonably refused, I shall have to try tilts with the Confederate Government."[104]

Vance and North Carolina were in the same predicament that existed in all Southern states. There were not enough men to keep state governments and economies functioning and still maintain armies large enough to win the war. The creation of the Junior and Senior Reserves had further stripped states of men who had been farming and working in wartime production. By this time, Holmes had gathered approximately 9,000 Reserves. He certainly knew the situation, but Vance summed it up for him on October 26: "I respectfully ... invoke your attention ... to the absolute necessity of retaining at least a limited number of the Mechanics, Millers, Tanners, etc. who are going off under recent orders. Anxious as I am to reinforce the Army, I am fully convinced that the Govt. is going too far in stripping the country of this class of persons." Vance ended his letter with a threat to take the workers he needed from the state's Home Guard. The Home Guard was under the control of the governor but was the backbone of Holmes's conscription and deserter-apprehension efforts. If Vance withheld the cooperation of his Home Guards, Holmes's conscription bureau would grind to a halt.[105] Holmes did his best to follow war department orders and accommodate Governor Vance's state sovereignty position. Like the Confederacy itself, both men were torn between the needs of a nation at total war and the state's-rights philosophy upon which that nation was founded. Vance and Holmes had at least one personal meeting on the issue after October 26. In the meantime, a North Carolina Supreme Court decision, Johnson vs. Mallett, seemed to sustain the state's-rights position. The lawsuit had been filed against Major Mallett and the bureau of conscription. Because there was no functioning Confederate supreme court, Mallett had no avenue of appeal when he lost the case. While the decision was a victory for Vance, the question of ultimate authority in such cases was never settled at the national level.[106]

Confederate military authorities in Richmond wanted officers like Holmes and Mallett to ignore state supreme court decisions when they were counterproductive to national defence. On the other hand, conscription officers throughout the South needed the goodwill and cooperation of governors. Governors were inclined to support decisions made by their own state courts. In North Carolina, Vance had jealously defended the state's-rights principle. While he refused to allow the conscription of his militia officers, he required those same officers to assist Mallett in gathering conscripts and arresting deserters. When that arrangement was struck down by a North Carolina Supreme Court judge in 1863, Vance created the Home Guard to enforce the draft laws. His cooperation resulted in North Carolina's supplying more conscripts to the Confederacy than any other state.[107] That fact alone gave the Governor Vance a strong bargaining position. He did not need the court decision, but he cited it as the legal basis for his actions when he wrote to Holmes in November.

In his letter, Vance said, "I regard this [Johnson vs. Mallett] as settling the whole question, and shall be governed by it accordingly." Vance enclosed a list of "necessary state officers and agents to be exempt from conscription." He informed Holmes that he would also exempt from conscription "any and all persons in the actual employment of the state," as required by North Carolina state law. In a more conciliatory tone, he stated, "It shall be my purpose to aid you by filling, as far as possible, all the departments under my control with non-conscripts, and turning over all able-bodied men who can be spared." The Confederacy was unable to resolve the legal issues, but Vance, Holmes, and Mallett kept the system functioning in North Carolina.[108]

Organizing the Reserves was putting thousands of soldiers on the rosters but did not release a like number for combat service in Virginia and Georgia. Most regiments that remained in North Carolina at the end of 1864 were not required to leave the state. As soon as regiments of Reserves and detailed men were organized, they were sent to local trouble spots. A riot occurred in November at Salisbury's prisoner-of-war camp. Two guards were killed and ten wounded. Forty-nine Union prisoners were killed or wounded as well. Reserves were needed to reinforce the camp guard. In December, an officer from the adjutant and inspector general's department called for more troops to arrest deserters in western North Carolina. He advised that men from all over the South were hiding in the area, with local women supporting and protecting them. He recommended that a Virginia regiment should be sent to replace the 62nd and 64th North Carolina regiments. He also recommended that residences of civilians who were harboring deserters should be burned. The men of the two North Carolina regiments were reluctant soldiers, suffered from low morale, and lacked enthusiasm for the harsh measures needed.[109]

On November 15, Bragg again notified President Davis of rumored Union plans for an amphibious attack on Fort Fisher. He complained of the small number of troops in the area, "not 1,000 men," and their lack of experience, "not a battalion of which has ever been under fire." Likewise, Bragg was not impressed with Holmes's Reserves stationed at Wilmington and Fort Fisher: "The reserves are undisciplined, and uninstructed. Officered from their own number, they are inefficient." He warned that Fort Fisher would be overrun and Wilmington lost if defense of the area depended on "home guards, reserves, and untried artillery.... A proper commander is needed."[110] Bragg appointed General Whiting to command the Department of North Carolina on November 23.[111]

Holmes's organization of eight Reserve regiments was substantially complete in December. Teenagers composed the 1st, 2nd, and 3rd North Carolina Reserve regiments. The 4th, 5th, 6th, 7th and 8th Reserve regiments contained the older men. Despite the initial sporadic and disorganized service of the companies and battalions that eventually became the Senior Reserve regiments, they performed valuable service during the late summer and autumn of 1864. They guarded rail lines and bridges and responded to threatened points throughout the state, occasionally relieving Junior Reserves units so they could be sent elsewhere. During the hotly contested governor's election between Zebulon Vance and William W. Holden, Senior Reserves were used to guard polling places. The 4th Reserve Regiment was sent to Salisbury to guard the prisoner of war camp. The 8th Reserves was sent to Wilmington. In December, the 7th Reserves fought against General Foster's force at Tullifinny River in South Carolina.[112]

Whiting's attempts to have the 68th North Carolina Troops transferred from western North Carolina to Fort Fisher dissolved amid conflicting orders among generals Holmes, Bragg, Whiting, and Martin. Bragg threatened to have Martin arrested if he interfered with the transfer. Ultimately the regiment was diverted to Hamilton on the Roanoke River. A combined land and river attack was expected at Fort Branch.[113] On

Dec. 14, young Gabriel Holmes enlisted in the 1st Regiment Junior Reserves one month before he was of conscription age. He joined the regiment at Fort Branch.[114]

With Bragg's concerns about Wilmington and Fort Fisher largely unresolved in late December, General Holmes volunteered his services. Bragg put him in charge of Wilmington and sent General Whiting to be with Colonel Lamb at Fort Fisher. Anticipating an imminent attack, Bragg ordered Holmes to defend the city and coordinate troop movements and the issuing of supplies.[115] The first attempt to capture Fort Fisher would occur in only a few days. The invasion force left Hampton Roads on December 18 and sailed toward the fort. General Lee detached Robert Hoke and his division, six thousand men, and sent them to Wilmington. Hoke's troops began arriving at Wilmington on the 23rd. Admiral Porter's fleet arrived off Fort Fisher the same day.

General Benjamin Butler commanded the sixty-five hundred soldiers designated to make the landing. The fleet and soldiers were battered and delayed by rough seas. The brief campaign would be further marred by dissension between the navy and army and a harebrained plan to destroy Fort Fisher with a boatload of explosives. On December 24, an old hulk filled with two hundred fifteen tons of black powder was detonated near the fort. The time was 1:40 A.M. The tremendous blast shook windows and awakened soldiers and civilians for seventy miles along the coast. The explosion, particularly loud in Wilmington, accomplished nothing at Fort Fisher, with the exception of terrifying a battalion of Junior Reserves camped on the beach.[116]

Having failed in an unconventional attempt to reduce Fort Fisher, Porter's gunboats bombarded the fort in preparation for Butler's amphibious landing. The shelling continued through Christmas day as Union infantry landed two miles north of the fort. They captured one outlying battery and approached Fort Fisher late in the day. As the first element of Hoke's division, Kirkland's brigade, arrived at Wilmington, Holmes got them through town and sent them to a defensive line located north of the fort at Sugar Loaf. There, Kirkland's brigade joined twelve hundred Reserves camped near the Cape Fear River. By then, the approach of Hoke's division and concern about high casualties forced Union commanders to reassess the mission. The next day, Union infantry began climbing back into their landing boats and returning to their troop transports.[117]

During the brief campaign, a small detachment of Confederate troops at Fort Gatlin abandoned their post without authorization. Holmes was ordered to have them arrested as soon as they arrived in Wilmington. He appealed the decision and reassigned them to the earthworks around town. He was in telegraphic communication with coastal observers about the number and movement of Union ships and passed that information to threatened points. When Home Guard units were assembled, he assigned them to earthworks around the city and at Masonborough Sound. On December 29, when the immediate crisis had passed, Holmes dismissed the Home Guard from the trenches, where they had spent several days, and sent them home.[118]

Several Reserve units were involved in the campaign but with unimpressive results. More than two hundred Junior Reserves, terrified by the shelling, surrendered during the Union evacuation. The teenagers were taken aboard transports as prisoners of war and shipped north. A number of Senior Reserves were killed during the bombardment of the Sugar Loaf line. One of Kirkland's staff officers was shocked at the sight of their grey-haired corpses.[119] The 1st North Carolina Junior Reserves, Gabriel Holmes's regiment, stayed at Hamilton during the Fort Fisher fight. Gabriel was promoted to sergeant in late December and elected lieutenant on January 9.[120]

The next attack on Fort Fisher was only days away. A reorganized landing force, this time under the command of Gen. Alfred Terry, was loaded onto transport vessels and sailed from Bermuda Landing, Virginia, on January 4. They rendezvoused with elements of Admiral Porter's North Atlantic Blockading Squadron off Beaufort, North Carolina. Terry's infantry force had eight thousand men. Porter's sixty vessels mounted a total of 627 guns, more than ten times the firepower of Fort Fisher.[121]

While the Union army and navy were regrouping for the second attempt on Fort Fisher, Holmes returned to his duties in Raleigh. On January 6, General Bragg asked him for a comprehensive list of the Junior and Senior Reserve battalions, regiments, and their officers. Six days later, Bragg informed his district commanders (along with generals Lee and Holmes) that the Union fleet was, again, off the coast at Fort Fisher. He asked Holmes to contact Governor Vance and urge the movement of General Leventhorp's Home Guard brigade to the Southwest Creek defensive line east of Kinston. Bragg was expecting an attack from New Bern on Kinston in an attempt to divert troops and attention away from Fort Fisher.[122]

Bragg ordered Hoke's division to occupy the peninsula below Wilmington and prepare for the expected Union landing. Whiting reinforced Colonel Lamb at Fort Fisher with six hundred soldiers. Lamb had forty-seven large guns and approximately two thousand men to defend the fort. Bragg told Holmes, "We must expect a desperate effort, and should bring all our means to bear."[123]

Admiral Porter's bombardment began at midnight on January 12. The shelling was concentrated on part of Hoke's division in the wooded area north of the fort, as well as on the fort itself. By 3:00 P.M. on the 13th, Terry's infantry had landed and entrenched across the peninsula facing north toward Hoke's six thousand men. When his defensive works were completed on the 14th, Terry ordered a simultaneous two-column attack against Fort Fisher's north-facing wall. Porter's gunboats were to concentrate their shelling on that part of the fort. The bombardment began at 8:00 A.M. on the 15th and continued until 3:30 in the afternoon, when Union infantry began their attack. Vicious combat, punctuated by deafening artillery fire, continued until 10:00 P.M., when the last of Fort Fisher's defenders surrendered at Battery Buchanan on the southern tip of the peninsula. Several of Holmes's Reserve units were assigned to General Hoke, but Bragg never sent Hoke's division into the fight.[124]

The fall of Fort Fisher, followed by the occupation of Wilmington on February 22, was a fatal blow to the Confederacy. Lee's army would be slowly starved of food and war materiel. Any army assembled in North Carolina to resist Sherman would face the same situation. As early as the previous September, U.S. Navy capt. O. S. Glisson correctly predicted, "The port of Wilmington is the only hope of rebeldom.... If this port is taken the rebellion will not last three months."[125]

In a January retreat from his department defense strategy, President Davis approved the new rank of "General-in-Chief of the Confederate Armies." Robert E. Lee would assume the post and coordinate all Confederate military operations. At this late stage, the change to a nationwide military strategy was almost pointless. The Trans-Mississippi was completely isolated. The Army of Tennessee, after its near destruction at Franklin and Nashville in December, was finished in that theater of the war. During the next few months, the remnants of that army would be sent to North and South Carolina to face Sherman. Lee's army was still tied to the defense of Petersburg and Richmond. The steady loss of territory and armies left little for the general-in-chief to coordinate. Lee accepted the appointment on January 31.[126] (President Lincoln had appointed Ulysses S. Grant as commander of all Union armies nearly a year earlier.)

On the day of Lee's promotion, Bragg reported on the strength and disposition of his troops in North Carolina. He had only eleven thousand five hundred men present for duty. General Laurence Baker's brigade, headquartered at Goldsboro, included the 3rd Junior Reserves and several companies of Seniors. The 1st Junior Reserves, under Col. Frank Armistead, was still at Fort Branch. The 2nd Regiment and 1st Battalion of Junior Reserves were at Weldon. The infantry in Colonel George Jackson's brigade at Wilmington was made up of Senior Reserves and Maj. Franz Hahr's two companies of light duty soldiers.[127]

During this period, General Holmes was often called upon to send Reserve units to trouble spots, but he had transferred all of them to field commanders. In response to one request, Holmes reminded Assistant Secretary of War John Campbell, "I have no men."[128] Confusion about authority over the Reserves had troubled their deployment since mid–summer. Several months earlier, even General Lee exhibited a lack of understanding concerning legal authority over the Reserves, detailed men, the North Carolina State Militia, and the Home Guards.[129]

On February 1, Sherman's army left its bases at Savannah, Georgia, and Beaufort, South Carolina, where his troops had been re-supplied by the Union navy. Confederate General William Hardee retreated with the Savannah garrison, some militia, and troops he could gather up along the way. By mid–month, General Beauregard had evacuated Columbia and Charleston, South Carolina. Sherman did not stay long in Columbia, leaving the city in flames on February 19.[130]

Adjutant and Inspector General Cooper, anticipating Sherman's advance into North Carolina, issued orders to prepare the state for another invasion. He ordered Holmes, Bragg, and officers at Yorkville and Chester, South Carolina, and Charlotte, Salisbury, and Greensboro to destroy all supplies "on Sherman's route ... as soon as they become liable to capture."[131] Holmes notified Johnston that two regiments of detailed men were available for duty when they were needed.[132] Colonel John F. Hoke, commander of the 4th Reserve Regiment (Seniors), was ordered to remove the Union prisoners from Salisbury and march them to Greensboro. The trip was plagued with straggling and inattention by Hoke's guards. After making camp near Greensboro, some of the prisoners stole away to "purchase liquor and annoy the citizens, to the subversion of all good order."[133] (Charges were filed against Hoke for "Disobedience of Orders." In April, General Holmes was ordered to bring Hoke to trial.)

Holmes's officers in the Junior Reserves were still learning the wide-ranging nature of their responsibilities. In February, Captain Hinsdale was elected to command the 3rd Reserve Regiment. Maj. Charles S. Stringfellow took Hinsdale's place on Holmes's staff.[134] When Colonel Hinsdale arrived at Kinston, he found his troops "most miserably dirty." He recommended that the current ration of soap, two pounds per hundred men, be increased. He advised his brigade commander, "The clothing of the Regiment is so filthy that water without a good supply of soap cannot make them clean."[135]

Major Stringfellow arrived at Holmes's headquarters several days later and assumed Hinsdale's duties. He was not pleased with what he found. One of his first assignments was to prepare, for the Confederate adjutant and inspector general, rosters of the eight regiments and three battalions of Reserves then in service. Stringfellow found that General Holmes's headquarters records for Reserve units were "so incomplete as to furnish no material for my use." Holmes's staff had been using forms and reporting procedures required by the state rather than those required by the adjutant and inspector general. Stringfellow was a veteran staff officer and had served generals in other commands. He began reorganizing Holmes's office and bringing the reporting formats and procedures into compliance with Confederate regulations.[136]

Toward the end of the month, Lee rearranged his army commanders. Bragg stayed in command of North Carolina, but Joseph Johnston was put in charge of troops in most of the eastern Confederacy. This change gave Johnston authority to consolidate remnants of various commands in other states and direct them as he deemed necessary. Much of the Confederate army's leadership would end up in North Carolina, but after the loss of Fort Fisher and Wilmington, Bragg's influence was being reduced.[137]

On February 23, the adjutant and inspector general issued General Order No. 8. All Reserve soldiers who had not been detailed or assigned to specific army units were to be organized into organizations of "convenient" size (companies or small battalions) and used exclusively "in arresting and returning to the army all deserters and absentees." Generals commanding armies were ordered to return any Reserve soldiers who were "not indispensably necessary" to their commands. The order gave field generals the option of keeping Reserve regiments or sending them back to the Reserve generals.[138] A number of Reserve units had proven to be of little use in the field, particularly the Senior Reserves. They had high rates of desertion and illness and were often considered useless for combat. In describing his Senior Reserves in Virginia, Major General Kemper stated that the older men were the "least effective troops.... They melt away like frost ... under the sun."[139]

General Order No. 8 made the Reserve generals almost solely responsible for controlling the Confederacy's desertion and draft-evasion problem. The order further directed that hunting deserters and draft-dodgers would be the "primary duty of officers of the reserve forces."[140] In North Carolina, the Guard for Home Defense had been specifically designated for this duty by the legislature and Governor Vance in 1863. The arrangement worked reasonably well until late 1864, but as civilian morale and support for the war sagged, the Home Guard became less and less effective.

On March 5, Assistant Secretary of War Campbell cited a report from General Holmes. Campbell expressed hopelessness concerning the Confederacy's attempt to gather twenty thousand slaves for non-combat military duty and labor. The previous December, that number had been revised to require a total of 14,500 (2,250 from Virginia, 2,500 from South Carolina, 2,250 from North Carolina, 2,500 from Georgia, 2,500 from Alabama, 500 from Florida, 500 from Tennessee, and 1,500 from Mississippi and east Louisiana combined).[141] Holmes told Campbell that the effort to draft African Americans in North Carolina had resulted in their fleeing from their plantations and produced "1,500 fugitives in one week." By March 7, the Confederacy had managed to conscript only 4,000 African Americans out of the 14,500 required. As unproductive as the effort was, Holmes and his counterpart in Virginia, General Kemper, together, had gathered three thousand five hundred. Campbell also noted, "If the use of slaves had been resorted to in the beginning of the war ... it might have been more judicious."[142]

Early in March, General Schofield, commander of Union troops in North Carolina, marched two of his divisions out of New Bern toward Kinston. His orders from Sherman were to repair the railroad as his army moved west, accumulate supplies, and meet Sherman's army near Goldsboro. Sherman's troops crossed the Pee Dee River on March 6, and entered North Carolina. Once Goldsboro was in Union hands, Wilmington and New Bern could be used to supply further operations in the state.[143] General Johnston knew Bragg would have to fight at Kinston to prevent the capture of Goldsboro.

Troops under Bragg and Robert Hoke occupied existing earthworks along the western bank of Southwest Creek east of Kinston. General D. H. Hill, with two thousand veteran soldiers from the Army of Tennessee and a brigade of North Carolina Junior Reserves, was approaching Southwest Creek to reinforce Bragg. The opposing armies skirmished at nearby Wise's Forks on March 7. Bragg had approximately nine thousand soldiers against Schofield's thirteen thousand. Hoke attacked the next day. Hill began his attack when he heard Hoke's artillery open fire.[144] The initial Confederate advance was successful, but Bragg began to mismanage the affair. A third Union division arrived before sundown. The day's fighting ended with Confederates still occupying the Southwest Creek line and Union troops digging defensive positions of their own. The next day saw little fighting as the Union force held its position and Bragg waited for reinforcements. On the morning of March 10, Hoke attacked the Union left flank while General Hill held his part of the line. When Hoke's attack stalled, Bragg ordered both divisions to withdraw and camp near Kinston. The Union army made no immediate pursuit.[145]

Wise's Forks was the first significant battle for the Junior Reserves. Under the command of Gen. Laurence Baker, they advanced well during the first day's fight and suffered casualties. But later, according to D. H. Hill, "one regiment ... broke, and the rest lay down and could not be got forward."[146] The lackluster performance may not have involved all of the Juniors. They were, however, assigned to defensive positions on the battle's second day.

Prior to Wise's Forks and convinced that Schofield and Sherman intended to unite in North Carolina to crush General Johnston, the Confederacy began repositioning troops in the state. The theater of operations was small enough for Confederate forces to be consolidated where they were needed. The railroads could still be used to move troops rapidly, but troops needed to be positioned near the lines. Lee's army at Petersburg would either hold on until Johnston's twenty thousand men arrived or retreat toward North Carolina and combine with Johnston. In compliance with his orders, General Holmes assembled all detailed men along the railroad lines for immediate service in the field. In the case of the Reserves, however, most of them were still assigned to field commanders. Holmes correctly reminded Cooper, "All the Reserves in North Carolina have long been in active service under the different commanders, and I have no men to order." Holmes also reminded Cooper that with the detailed men in the field, production of war materiel would cease. As Holmes had implied that he should, Cooper contacted General Johnston and had him order the redeployment of the Reserves.[147]

Two days later, Bragg reassigned two regiments of Senior Reserves to General Holmes's command. He told Holmes, "These regiments are so reduced as to be of little use in the field." Bragg wanted the Seniors to chase deserters, but with a total of only one hundred thirty men, he admitted that the force was completely inadequate. "The country is perfectly infested [with deserters], and the most atrocious outrages are being committed." Bragg lamented, "Nothing but an active cavalry force can accomplish the object."[148] There was no cavalry available to either general for rounding up deserters.

During the previous weeks, several thousand Army of Tennessee soldiers were making their way from the Deep South to reform their regiments in Johnston's army. Most of these men were unarmed and traveling in disorganized groups. Their arrival in North Carolina interfered with Holmes's mobilization of detailed men. As a result, Holmes wrote to Adjutant and Inspector General Cooper, saying that the arriving Army of Tennessee soldiers had been given "all the arms reserved for the detailed men." He informed Cooper that he had been forced to revoke his orders and send the detailed men back to their work.[149]

On March 14, General Lee informed President Davis that the war was all but lost. Johnston would likely lose Raleigh, and with it, the rail connection from Raleigh to Petersburg and Richmond. Lee stated flatly that when that happened, "both armies would certainly starve." As Lee saw it, the Confederacy's only hope was for Johnston to make "a bold and unexpected attack" on Sherman.[150]

Assuming that Raleigh would fall before Greensboro, Holmes worried that Camp Holmes and Major Mallett's headquarters would soon be in jeopardy. On March 12, he ordered Mallett to make arrangements to move his administrative offices and camp operations. The previous October, Mallett had closed Morganton's Camp Vance and opened a new camp of instruction, Camp Stokes, at Greensboro. Mallett's Raleigh operations would soon be located there as well.[151] On March 16, advancing Union forces under General Henry Slocum collided with Confederate troops near Averasboro. The Confederate right flank was driven back to an entrenched position, but nightfall ended the Union attack. The Confederates withdrew toward Bentonville with Slocum's cavalry in pursuit.[152]

Three days later, as forces under Sherman's overall command converged, General Johnston attacked Slocum's column near Bentonville. Slocum consolidated his position and withstood several determined attacks. Johnston, knowing that he would soon be facing Sherman's combined armies, went on the defense. On March 21, the Confederate main line held all day against repeated attacks, but Johnston realized that part of Sherman's army was about to block his only avenue of retreat. That night, he withdrew his army toward Smithfield.[153] After the battle, Maj. Gen. Robert Hoke wrote that the Junior Reserves "repulsed every charge made on them.... Their conduct in camp, on the march, and on the battlefield was everything that could be expected of them."[154]

After Bentonville, General Sherman's army camped at Goldsboro to reorganize and resupply. When his army was ready, Sherman wanted to march north, cross the Roanoke River at Weldon, and help Grant defeat Lee at Richmond. Grant, however, wanted to strike Lee quickly, before the end of March, and likely, before Sherman's army could arrive. If Lee's defenses held, Sherman would have time to join Grant. If Lee was defeated or retreated into North Carolina, Sherman could attack Johnston's army.[155]

On March 26, General Bragg gave President Davis a firsthand account of the situation in North Carolina and the Deep South. From Raleigh, Bragg wrote that he had "retired to this point where I have nothing to do but mourn over the sad spectacle ... of disorganization, demoralization, and destruction." He told Davis that General Stephen D. Lee was "somewhere in the rear" with about five thousand stragglers from the Army of Tennessee. Thousands of others were "scattered over the States of North and South Carolina, Georgia, Alabama, and Mississippi." Military discipline among these troops had disappeared. "Officers seem paralyzed, men indifferent to everything but plunder, and the people ... appear disgusted and dismayed. This state of things cannot last, and no one is so blind as not to see the inevitable result."[156] On March 31, General Martin reported from Asheville, "I regret to say I have nothing to report but disobedience of orders, neglect of duty, demoralization of the people, and desertion of both officers and men." He predicted that Asheville would be captured by Union forces within two weeks.[157] The breakdown of law and order forced Governor Vance to place warning notices in North Carolina newspapers: "Lawless Desperadoes ... if detected in committing outrage they will be shot.... Posted by order of Lt. General Holmes."[158]

The most sweeping reform of the Confederate conscription system came in the form of General Order No. 17, issued on March 29, 1865. This order abolished the Bureau of Conscription and gave complete control of the process, from beginning to

GREENSBORO', NORTH CAROLINA,

May 1st _____ 1865.

In accordance with the terms of the Military Convention, entered into on the twenty sixth day of April, 1865, between General JOSEPH E. JOHNSTON, Commanding the Confederate Army, and Major-General W. T. SHERMAN, Commanding the United States Army in North-Carolina,

Col. Jno. W. Hinsdale 3rd Reg.t Reserves nc

has given his solemn obligation not to take up arms against the Government of the United States until properly released from this obligation; and is permitted to return to his home, not to be disturbed by the United States authorities so long as he observe this obligation and obey the laws in force where he may reside.

_____ U. S. A.,
Special Commissioner.

_____ C. S. A.,
Commanding.

Colonel John W. Hinsdale's parole. Before leaving the army and heading home, each surrendered Confederate soldier was issued a parole by Union authorities and was required to keep the document until further notice. Once paroled, Confederate officers were authorized to issue paroles to soldiers in their commands or to other officers. This parole was issued to Colonel Hinsdale by Colonel Frank Armistead and was cosigned by a Union army officer (Walter J. Clark, ed., *Histories of the Several Regiments and Battalions from North Carolina in the Great War*, v. 4, 1861–1865, p. 583).

end, to the Reserve generals. The conscription bureau's local enrolling offices, congressional district medical officers, and advisory boards would remain in place. Under the revisions, conscripts had no right to appeal their induction until after they reported for duty. Unless their petitions for deferment or exemption were based on obvious medical grounds, conscripts had to serve in the army while their cases were being considered.[159]

General Johnston, unsure of Sherman's intentions, centered his army near Smithfield. From there, he could block an advance toward Raleigh or move northeast and block Sherman's possible march toward Weldon to link up with Grant. Should Grant force Lee out of Richmond, Johnston wanted his army to unite with Lee's and destroy the Union armies before they combined. At the end of March, Johnston sent General Holmes to Richmond for a conference with President Davis and General Lee.[160]

After the failed attack on Fort Stedman, General Lee knew that Petersburg and Richmond would have to be evacuated.[161] Holmes's mission was to clear up confusion about when and where the armies of Johnston and Lee should unite. Holmes told the president that conditions in North Carolina were much worse than Davis had been led to believe. Davis wanted Holmes to confer with General Lee, but part of Lee's army was fighting desperately at Five Forks. Holmes left Richmond on April 1 to report Davis's views to General Johnston.[162] While in Richmond, Holmes may have seen the

African American Confederate battalion that was reported marching in the streets.[163] During the previous few weeks, Lee and Davis had been working on the mobilization of African American men.

On March 9, the Confederate Congress had approved the use of slaves as combat soldiers. With the approval of their owners, slaves could volunteer for the army. The idea had been under discussion since early 1864, when Gen. Patrick Cleburne made the suggestion. By 1865, Lee was in favor of the plan and wrote, "In my opinion, the negroes ... will make efficient soldiers." He advocated freeing slaves who served honorably in the army. He also favored the gradual emancipation of all slaves as a part of any plan to employ slaves as soldiers.[164]

Given the Confederacy's desperate situation, the conscription of African American men as combat soldiers had been expected. The day before the measure was approved, Major Mallett requested permission to "raise a negro brigade."[165] General Lee's officers began requesting African American soldiers for their regiments in mid–March. The Confederacy's last desperate effort to avoid defeat came too late. Petersburg and Richmond were evacuated on April 1 and 2. Davis and most of his Cabinet took a special train toward Danville, Virginia.[166]

As the Confederate army marched out of Richmond, all semblance of order collapsed. On Sunday night, April 2, the army set warehouses full of tobacco, cotton, and military stores on fire. By noon the next day, the area between 7th and 15th streets, from Main Street down to the James River, had been incinerated. Perhaps as many as eight hundred buildings were destroyed. The streets of the city filled with terrified citizens, refugees, and runaway slaves. Inmates broke out of the state prison. Looting, often by Confederate stragglers, was widespread, and additional fires were set. City officials had ordered the destruction of "all the liquor in the city," but much of it fell into the hands of the mob. This began a final breakdown of law and order; "chaos came, and a Pandemonium reigned." On the James River, scuttled Confederate gunboats burned and exploded, shaking the city "to its foundations."[167]

The Army of Northern Virginia retreated westward, shadowed by Grant. On April 4, the army gathered at Amelia Court House, but found no supplies. Confusion and disrupted communications had frustrated Confederate efforts to stockpile food and ammunition. The army scoured the countryside for food and then marched toward Farmville.[168] Desertions increased dramatically.

During the retreat, Lee's decimated columns became separated while crossing Sayler's Creek. Union commanders saw the opportunity and attacked. A large part of Lee's army was captured, approximately eight thousand men. The army continued toward Appomattox Court House, where Union cavalry were blocking the route. Generals Gordon and Fitzhugh Lee attacked but soon realized they were facing enemy infantry as well. Robert E. Lee saw that he was surrounded, hopelessly outnumbered, and out of food. He surrendered his army to Grant on April 9.[169]

In the wake of Lee's surrender and President Lincoln's assassination on April 14, Johnston and Sherman began negotiations. On April 26, after several days of confusion over terms, the two generals signed a document that was similar to the surrender of Lee's army. Confederate officers and enlisted men in central North Carolina reported to Sherman's provost officers and surrendered. When General Holmes surrendered, he was allowed to keep his sword. A few days later, Major Mallett, General Holmes, and several staff officers were seen on horseback riding through Fayetteville. Holmes's forty-year military career had come to an end.

General Holmes's most significant contribution to the Confederacy was as North Carolina's Reserve general. Georgia, Virginia, South Carolina, and North Carolina sent significant numbers of Reserves to the field during the last year of the war. Holmes had mobilized approximately ten thousand North Carolina Junior and Senior Reserves. In so doing, he produced a higher percentage of Reserves from his state's military population than the other Reserve generals produced in their states (see Appendix C).

While reinforcing the army, Holmes maintained North Carolina's wartime industry and agriculture with detailed workers. Under orders from the war department, he assumed command of North Carolina's sprawling conscription bureau and local defense forces. He commanded troops in the field for brief periods at Weldon and Wilmington. His administrative and organizational skills helped maintain North Carolina's crucial role in the war. His analysis and solution of systemic problems evidence a clear mind and sharp intellect.

Like his counterparts in other Confederate states, Holmes's service as a general of the Reserves went largely unnoticed after the war. The Confederacy's conscription of young boys, old men, and African Americans was a forlorn hope born of brutal necessity. It was not the stuff of glory.

10

Living Only in the Past

Within a few weeks of the war's end, Holmes moved into the Wetmore family's "country home" near Fayetteville. Family arrangements provided him the use of the small house and some acreage until mid–1867. "After that," Holmes wrote to a friend, "I shall be perfectly abroad unless something turns up to enable me to follow some occupation or office by which I can make my living."[1] Holmes was too old to start his post-war life as a farmer. His plan was to seek some type of employment in state government. In order to be eligible for such positions, he would need to have his citizenship restored. He applied for a pardon as soon as they became available.

On May 29, 1865, President Johnson issued a general amnesty to all Confederate veterans and former government employees, with the exception of persons in fourteen specific categories. The provisional governor of North Carolina, William W. Holden, included President Johnson's exclusionary provisions in his own proclamation. Holmes, like most high-ranking Confederate military and government officers, was excluded from the amnesty by four separate provisions of the proclamation.[2] These individuals were required to submit individual petitions for pardon. The applications would go first to the petitioner's governor. The governor could grant, postpone, or reject the requests. Those approved by the governor were sent to Washington for final review.[3]

Holmes requested his pardon in early June. In putting his "situation" in the best possible light, Holmes wrote that from early childhood he had been taught that his first allegiance was to North Carolina. He stated that he attended the United States Military Academy and served in the army for more than thirty years "without an unfavorable criticism." According to Holmes, just before the war started, he received a letter from Governor Ellis of North Carolina "claiming my services for my state. This, added to the fact of perfect unanimity among all those that I loved ... induced me to resign my commission in the U.S. army and to take service with my state." Holmes said, "That I was faithful to the service thus accepted, is most certainly true," but he said that during the war he had never committed "an act of cruelty" nor any deed "by which I would be ashamed." Holmes stated that he was anxious to return his allegiance to the United States "with a view to a full and perfect adherence to its requirements."[4]

Governor Holden received 1,555 requests for pardon. He approved 1,451 and postponed the decisions on another one hundred. He rejected only four, including Holmes's, on June 12.[5] Holmes wrote of the rejection, "If I had been pardoned I would have come to Raleigh and offered [myself] for one of the ... offices, but it would have been useless as Holden is evidently the Dictator of all the Legislature."[6] Holmes's prospects for employment were severely limited. He had no choice but to farm his few acres until something better came along. His twenty-five-year-old daughter, Elizabeth, moved into the farmhouse to help her father until his circumstances changed.

Even during personal hardship, Holmes continued to further the interests of his relatives. On October 18, 1865, he contacted a friend and college administrator on behalf of his nephew, John Hinsdale. Holmes wrote of Hinsdale, "He is the son of my best friend[,] of great promise and excellent intelligence. Will you ... oblige me by extending to him your support and countenance during his connection with the Institution over which you so justly preside[?]" In alluding to the war and its aftermath, Holmes wrote, "I thank God that He has spared you to see the end of the terrible desolation of the last four years ... [and] that He will speedily relieve us from the terrible poverty incident to it."[7]

During the immediate post-war period, Holmes became increasingly provoked by the Southern adoration heaped on Robert E. Lee and the criticism of Jefferson Davis. Holmes believed that Lee had been merely the instrument of Davis's wartime genius. Holmes was concerned that Davis's eulogy of Lee on November 3, 1870, conferred, exclusively, upon Lee "the gratitude and affection of an enthusiastic & generous people." During the speech, Davis said of Lee, "This citizen! this soldier! this great general! this true patriot! left behind him the crowning glory of a true Christian." At the end of his impassioned remarks, Davis said, "His fame has gone over the water—his deeds will be remembered; and when the monument[s] we shall build shall have crumbled into dust, his virtues will still live."[8]

Holmes wrote to Davis on November 29, 1870, only a month after Lee's death. He urged Davis to rescue himself from "the 2nd place in the hearts of his countrymen." In speaking of Lee, Holmes told Davis, "What he was *you* made him.... When away from you he *failed*. When near and subject to your supervision and *authority* he succeeded brilliantly." Holmes urged Davis to write a book about the Confederacy so the truth about "the Cause we loved and lost" would be told. He was respectful (perhaps sarcastically) of Lee's memory, saying, "God forbid that I should say one word to detract from his great Merit," but Holmes coldly remarked that Lee's reputation now had the "opportuness of death." At the end of his letter, Holmes told Davis, "I am eaking out the sad reward of life in cheerfulness and labor[,] living only in the past."[9]

Holmes was allowed to stay on the Wetmore property and farm the land until 1871, when his daughter married William H. MacPherson, of Fayetteville. MacPherson and Elizabeth moved Holmes out of the farmhouse to their home shortly thereafter. He spent the rest of his life with them and his grandchildren, whom he described as "beautiful, well bred, well behaved." During his later years, he was described as "a saddened old man, gray and grim-visaged, worn and weary."[10] He thought often of his wife, buried so far away on Governors Island.

When Laura died in 1860, she was buried at the Fort Columbus graveyard. At that time and assuming that, eventually, he would rest by her side, Holmes placed a large stone marker on the grave. The stone had Laura's inscription and space for Holmes's name and dates to be added when the time came. Several years after the war, the United States government ordered the removal of all graves from Governors Island. During the 1870s, Holmes and Elizabeth made arrangements to move Laura's remains and the marker to Fayetteville. She was reburied at MacPherson Presbyterian Church.

In March 1877, the Forty-fourth Congress of the United States approved an act to remove "all the political disabilities imposed by the fourteenth amendment to the Constitution of the United States, upon Theophilus H. Holmes, a citizen of the state of North Carolina."[11] At the age of seventy-two, Holmes was pardoned.

He remained loyal to Jefferson Davis to the very end. Davis, like Holmes, had been blamed by many for the loss of the war. In 1879, Holmes wrote to Lucius Bellinger Northrup, former commissary general of the Confederacy, "As for Jefferson Davis[,] I look upon him as the great sacrifice of the age, his and not Lee's name should fill the hearts of the Southern people." In quoting parts of Holmes's letter to Davis, Northrop affectionately referred to Holmes as the "old paladin."[12]

Although Peter Mallett returned to New York City in 1868, the Holmes and Mallett families remained close. Holmes's son Gabriel married Peter Mallett's daughter Susan. The couple named their son Pierre Mallett Holmes.[13] Unlike so many of his former colleagues and adversaries, Holmes chose not to write about his wartime experiences. His comrades-in-arms died off one by one: Trans-Mississippi nemesis Sterling Price in 1867; Samuel Cooper, his friend and the highest-ranking general in the Confederate army, in 1876. Both Price and Smith died in poverty, broken by the war. Holmes, completely deaf and in declining health, contented himself with his family and his memories.

The solitude imposed by his deafness allowed, perhaps compelled, Holmes to consider the triumphs and tragedies of his life, his own bitterness and joy. He was an unremarkable scholar, but at West Point he had made a lifelong friend of Jefferson Davis. Davis defended Holmes well past the time anyone cared. On the frontier, in the miserable swamps of Florida, on the heights of Monterrey, and in the Confederate army, Holmes led some of the finest soldiers America ever produced. His life with Laura was joyous, but they buried two children at distant army posts. Laura was taken from him when he needed her most, as his nation and career were tearing apart. His death-wish during the battle of Helena was, instead, visited upon his son, Theo, in Virginia, but his daughter, Elizabeth, surrounded him with loving grandchildren.

In his last days, the old general's mind drifted away from the wars that had defined his life. His thoughts returned to peaceful army posts in the West. He dreamed of the years with Laura on America's endless frontier. Once again, a garrison flag floated in the golden afternoon sun. Again, he could hear the fort's musicians playing the evening retreat. The soldiers of his regiment were perfectly aligned in their formation. Officers stood in front of their companies. They saluted as the flag was lowered. Holmes saluted his flag and his regiment. Laura gave him a loving smile. Their children played in the gentle breeze, at the base of the flagpole, under the flowing colors of red, white, and blue.

11

Beyond the Reach of
Censure or Praise

Theophilus Hunter Holmes died on June 21, 1880, at the age of seventy-five. In their summations of his life, his admirers focused on his personal virtues. Two weeks after his death, a Raleigh *Observer* editorial described Holmes as "simple in his tastes, brave, true, and just in his deportment ... a splendid example of an unpretentious North Carolina patriot and gentleman."[1]

In 1892, North Carolina historian and Confederate veteran Samuel A. Ashe wrote that Holmes, in his last years, was a "Christian gentleman ... without guile ... setting an example of personal labor and industry and frugality ... under the crushing yoke of misfortune."[2] Holmes's misfortune was the contrast between the Holmes of promise and the Holmes of achievement. He had walked among the giants of his day, Zachary Taylor, Winfield Scott, Jefferson Davis, and Robert E. Lee, but he failed to share in their glory.

Recalling wartime controversy and post-war criticism leveled at Holmes, Jefferson Davis wrote, " I, who knew him from our school-boy days, who served with him in garrison and in the field, and with pride, watched him as he gallantly led a storming party up a rocky height at Monterrey, and was intimately acquainted with his whole character during our sectional war, bear a willing testimony to the purity, self-abnegation, generosity, fidelity, and gallantry, which characterized him as a man and a soldier.... He has passed beyond the reach of censure or of praise."[3]

Davis outlived Robert E. Lee and wrote the book Holmes suggested, *Rise and Fall of the Confederate Government*. Published in 1881, the book refuted much of the criticism of Davis, the Confederacy, and Holmes. *Rise and Fall* was virtually ignored in the North but well received in the South.[4] Nonetheless, Southerners revered Lee's words and deeds more than Davis's. Davis was more controversial and less beloved than Lee. Lee and Holmes were never close during the war and disagreed often. In 1862, at the beginning of Lee's march to fame, Holmes was sent to a backwater of the war. Generals who remained in Lee's army after the Peninsular Campaign, some of only moderate ability, are widely known by virtue of their association with Lee. After the war, Lee rarely, if ever, spoke of Holmes.

Holmes's detractors used him as a convenient scapegoat for lost opportunities at First Manassas and in the Peninsular Campaign. They blamed him for the loss of Vicksburg and the Trans-Mississippi. Before the war ended, Gen. P. G. T. Beauregard wrote

"Epitaph of the Confederate States." He declared that the Confederacy was being "murdered by Jefferson Davis—aided and abetted" by other members of his administration. Among the Confederacy's "pallbearers" listed by Beauregard, General Holmes's name was prominent.[5]

Subsequent writers diminished Holmes further. At least one historian, Gen. Thomas Hindman's son Briscoe, tried to rebuild Hindman's wartime record at Holmes's expense. He circulated the story that the battle of Prairie Grove "was won by the Confederate army ... until General Holmes ordered General Hindman to withdraw his army from the field.... Had he [General Hindman] been left to carry out his own campaign, he would have either annihilated Blount's retreating army or destroyed its efficiency for a long time to come."[6] By the early 20th century, Theophilus Holmes, one of only eighteen Confederate lieutenant generals, had faded into obscurity.[7]

In June 1929, the 39th Reunion of the United Confederate Veterans was held in Charlotte, North Carolina. Thousands of former Confederate soldiers attended the week-long event. Confederate heritage groups at the reunion included the Confederated Southern Memorial Association, the United Daughters of the Confederacy, the Children of the Confederacy, and the Sons of Confederate Veterans. The sixty-four-page official program of the reunion featured dozens of photographs and full-page articles including "North Carolina in the Confederacy," "Important Events of North Carolina, 1861–1865," and "Some of North Carolina's Famous Generals." The program did not mention General Theophilus Hunter Holmes.[8]

Appendices

A. Confederate Artillery at Helena

Historian Cliff "Rudy" Shultz, cites archeological evidence from the Helena battlefield that supports the conclusion that Confederate artillerymen were forced from their guns before they could support the infantry attacks. The crew of at least one Confederate gun, serving with General Walker's command, dug earthworks to protect their position, but likely never fired a shot before being forced to withdraw. During the 1970s, Shultz and other battlefield archaeologists found unfired Confederate Archer shells in a depression (likely an entrenched artillery position) on the battlefield approximately five hundred yards north of Union rifle pits in front of Union Battery A on Rightor Hill. The area is well within range of Battery A. This position was also within range of Union artillery and infantry along the river bank. The position and immediate area were found to be heavily sprinkled with Union artillery shells and fragments, as well as musket and rifle bullets. Implying a hasty withdrawal, a sword and Enfield rifle, apparently left by the gun crew, were found close by. No fired Archer shells have been found on the battlefield within the range of this position.

B. 68th North Carolina Troops: Weapons and Equipment

The inspection report of the 68th North Carolina Troops taken at Weldon on June 1, 1864, gives a fascinating glimpse of a late-war North Carolina infantry regiment. The unit had a difficult organizational period between October 1863, and January 20, 1864, when it was formally designated as the 68th North Carolina Troops. At Weldon, the regiment had more than five hundred men. All ten companies were armed with Enfield rifles and accouterments, consisting of a bayonet and scabbard, cartridge box and shoulder belt, percussion cap box, and a waist belt. The regiment's uniforms were described as "good."[1]

C. Confederate Reserves: A Comparison of Several States

Author William Fox's *Regimental Losses* defines the term "military population" in the Civil War as the number of white males between the ages of eighteen and forty-five. The number includes men unfit for military duty as well as those who were physically capable of service.[2] For the purpose of comparing General Holmes's organization of North Carolina's Reserves with those in South Carolina, Virginia, and Georgia, the number of Reserves raised under the February 1864 Confederate conscription law can be calculated as a percentage of each state's 1861 military population.

Clark's *Histories* states that 10,088 North Carolina Junior and Senior Reserves had entered the Confederate army by November 19, 1864.[3] The 8th N.C. Reserve Regiment (Seniors) was organized after that date. Broadfoot's *Confederate State Roster* for North Carolina lists approximately 10,230 North Carolina Junior and Senior Reserves as having been enrolled by the end of the war. This number is 8.86 percent of North Carolina's 1861 military population of 115,369. North Carolina had a state militia, Home Guard, and a number of local defense companies raised under various Confederate and state laws. These troops were not included in North Carolina's total for the purpose of this comparison.

South Carolina's Reserve General James Chesnut raised approximately forty-seven hundred Reserves before the state came under Union control. A June 23, 1864, report from Chesnut states that he had thirty-seven companies, totaling twenty-three hundred men, on that date. (This is an average of sixty-five men per company. In maintaining sixty-five men per company, it is likely that a total of approximately one hundred men served in any given Reserve company during its existence.) Confederate regulations required a minimum of sixty-four men in Reserve infantry companies.[4] Dr. Robert S. Seigler's excellent work, *South Carolina's Military Organizations During the War Between the States*, v. 4, lists eight battalions, totaling forty-seven companies, of South Carolina Reserves raised under the February 1864 conscription act. Using one hundred men as the average for all forty-seven companies yields a total of 4,700 men. The four Reserve Battalions listed in Broadfoot's roster contain approximately 2,160 names or 540 men per battalion. South Carolina's military population in 1861 was 55,046. Using the above figures, General Chesnut organized 8.54 percent of the state's 1861 military population as Reserves under the February 1864 law. In September of the same year, South Carolina created a reserve militia force, called "Junior Reserves," of men, age sixteen to sixty, not already in the army. (Broadfoot's South Carolina roster includes these regiments.) For the purpose of this comparison, these men cannot be counted because they were state militia, not raised under the 1864 law, and not officially part of the Confederate army. (Mr. Knudsen, Dr. Seigler, Mr. Long, and Mr. Brasington generously assisted in gathering the figures for South Carolina. They have respectfully reserved the option of disputing the author's conclusions.)

Virginia's military population in 1861 was 196,587. The number of men documented in *Reserves: The Virginia Regimental History Series*, 13,713, means that 6.97 percent of the state's military population were assembled by General Kemper. (Broadfoot's numbers for Virginia are lower.) Numerous other Reserve units were organized by various officers in Virginia. Some were nominally commanded by General Kemper, but as in the case of North and South Carolina, these troops were not organized under the February 1864 law. Many of these organizations were disbanded or consolidated with other units. Including these troops in the Virginia roster yields an estimated 17,000 to 18,000 Reserves.[5]

In compliance with the February 1864 law, Georgia's general of the Reserves, Thomas Howell Cobb, assembled approximately 7,400 Reserves or 6.66 percent of the state's 1861 military population of 111,005. Broadfoot's *Roster* lists approximately 7,390 names. Mr. Alan Pitts, an expert on Georgia troops, estimates 7,500 Reserves for Georgia.

Chapter Notes

The following shortened titles of frequently cited sources are used in these notes:

Confederate Service Records— United States War Department. *Compiled Service Records of Confederate Soldiers Who Served During the Civil War.* Record Group 109. National Archives, Washington, D.C. Accessed through www.fold3.com unless otherwise noted.

Duke— Duke University Rare Book, Manuscript, and Special Collections. Durham, North Carolina.

NCTAR— Brown, Matthew, Michael W. Coffey, Louis H. Manarin, Weymouth T. Jordan Jr., et al., eds. *North Carolina Troops 1861–1865: A Roster.* 18 vols. to date. Raleigh: Division of Archives and History, North Carolina Department of Cultural Resources, 1966 to present.

OR— United States War Department. *The War of the Rebellion: A Compilation of the Official Records of the Union and Confederate Armies.* 128 vols. Harrisburg, PA: Government Printing Office, 1885; reprint National Historical Society, 1971.

OR Supplement— Hewett, Janet B., ed. *Supplement to the Official Records of the Union and Confederate Armies.* Facsimile ed. Wilmington: Broadfoot, 1999.

Introduction

1. David J. Coles, David Stephen Heidler, and Jeanne T. Heidler, eds., *Encyclopedia of the American Civil War*, vol. 2, p. 990.

2. Mark K. Christ, ed., *Rugged and Sublime*, p. 45; William C. Davis, ed., *The Confederate General*, p. 117.

3. Christ, *Rugged and Sublime*, p. 60.

4. John H. Eicher and David J. Eicher, eds., *Civil War High Commands*, p. 808.

Chapter 1

1. Holmes family papers; Oscar M. Bizzell, *The Heritage of Sampson County, North Carolina*, item 351.

2. Holmes family papers.

3. Bizzell, *Heritage of Sampson County*, item 351;

Louis Spilman, "North Carolina's Paladin: Theophilus Hunter Holmes."

4. Albert Castel, "Theophilus Hunter Holmes: Pallbearer of the Confederacy," *Civil War Times Illustrated* 14, no. 4 (July 1977): 11.

5. U.S. Military and Naval Academies, Cadet Records and Applications, 1805–1908, Daniel to Calhoun, June 2, 1824, accessed through ancestry.com.

6. U.S. Military and Naval Academies, Cadet Records and Applications, 1805–1908, accessed through ancestry.com, November 20, 2010.

7. U.S. Military Academy, "Roll of the Cadets Arranged According to Merit in Conduct for the Year Ending 30th June 1829," pp. 6–7.

8. Albert E. Church, *Personal Reminiscences of the Military Academy from 1824 to 1831*, p. 7.

9. Douglas Southall Freeman, *Robert E. Lee: A Biography*, vol. 1, p. 51.

10. Church, *Personal Reminiscences*, p. 11.

11. Hudson Strode, *Jefferson Davis, American Patriot, 1808–1861*, pp. 33–34.

12. Church, *Personal Reminiscences*, p. 32.

13. Clement Eaton, *Jefferson Davis*, p. 13; Strode, *Jefferson Davis, American Patriot*, p. 33.

14. Church, *Personal Reminiscences*, p. 11.

15. Strode, *Jefferson Davis, American Patriot*, p. 34.

16. Church, *Personal Reminiscences*, pp. 48–49.

17. Strode, *Jefferson Davis, American Patriot*, pp. 34–35.

18. Ibid., p. 35.

19. Church, *Personal Reminiscences*, p. 60.

20. Strode, *Jefferson Davis, American Patriot*, pp. 40–41; Eaton, *Jefferson Davis*, p. 14.

21. U.S. Military Academy, "Roll of the Cadets," p. 22.

22. John C. McManus, *American Courage, American Carnage*, pp. 19–20.

23. John Missall and Mary Lou Missall, *The Seminole Wars, America's Longest Indian Conflict*, pp. 6, 39; Chris Kimball, *Timeline of Events and Battles of the Florida Seminole Wars*, p. 12.

24. Kimball, *Timeline of Events*, p. 18; Missall, *Seminole Wars*, p. 26.

25. Kimball, *Timeline of Events*, p. 17; Grant Fore-

man, *Indian Removal: The Emigration of the Five Civilized Tribes of Indians*, pp. 316–317.

26. John C. White, *American Military Strategy During the Second Seminole War*, p. 8; Kimball, *Timeline of Events*, p. 18.

27. Kimball, *Timeline of Events*, pp. 19–20.

28. Holmes family papers.

29. Ronald N. Wall, "Fort Smith, Arkansas: The Beginning."

30. Ibid.

31. Ibid.

32. Oklahoma Historical Society, "Fort Gibson."

33. Ibid.

Chapter 2

1. Martin Dugard, *The Training Ground: Grant, Lee, Sherman, and Davis in the Mexican War, 1846–1858*, p. 31.

2. McManus, *American Courage*, p. 44.

3. Foreman, *Indian Removal*, p. 193.

4. Washington Irving, *A Tour on the Prairies*, p. 1.

5. *Chronicles of Oklahoma* 19, no. 2, p. 123.

6. Ibid., pp. 122–123.

7. *Chronicles of Oklahoma* 19, no. 2, p. 123; vol. 5, no. 3, pp. 333–347.

8. *Chronicles of Oklahoma* 5, no. 3, pp. 333–347.

9. Ibid.

10. George Croghan and Francis Paul Prucha, eds., *Army Life on the Western Frontier*, p. 58.

11. Grant Foreman, "Fort Gibson: A Brief History."

12. *Returns of the 7th U.S. Infantry, January 1832 through December 1850.*

13. Ibid.

14. Carolyn Thomas Foreman, "Lieutenant-General Theophilus Hunter Holmes, C.S.A., Founder of Fort Holmes," *Chronicles of Oklahoma* 35, no. 4, p. 426.

15. J. Patrick Hughes, "Forts and Camps in Oklahoma Before the Civil War," pp. 39–40.

16. Fran Cook, *Acho: Flower of the Prairie*, p. 29.

17. *Returns of the 7th U.S. Infantry.*

18. *Chronicles of Oklahoma* 18, no. 4, pp. 315–316.

19. *Fort Gibson Orders and Letters Book.*

20. Ibid., entries for November 10–11, 1834.

21. Jefferson Davis, *Papers of Jefferson Davis*, vol. 1, p. 399.

22. Ibid., pp. 358, 381.

23. Mark M. Boatner, *Civil War Dictionary*, p. 225.

24. Irving, *Tour on the Prairies*, p. 1.

25. Foreman, *Indian Removal*, pp. 140–141.

26. Ibid.

27. Ibid., pp. 141–142, 148, 152.

28. Ibid., pp. 154–156.

29. Ibid., p. 157.

30. Ibid., pp. 178–179.

31. Ibid., p. 193.

32. Ibid., p. 209.

33. Ibid., p. 226.

34. Winfield Scott, *Memoirs of Lieutenant General Winfield Scott*, vol. 1, pp. 318–319.

35. Foreman, *Indian Removal*, pp. 286–290.

36. Ibid., map insert between pages 384 and 385.

37. Grant Foreman, *The Five Civilized Tribes*, pp. 281–282.

38. *Chronicles of Oklahoma* 18, no. 4, pp. 317–318.

39. Missall, *Seminole Wars*, pp. 54, 63–64.

40. Ibid., pp. 63–64.

41. Ibid., pp. 86.

42. Ibid., pp. 90.

43. Ibid., pp. 94–97; Kimball, *Timeline of Events*, p. 25.

44. Ethan Allen Hitchcock, *Fifty Years in Camp and Field: Diary of Major General Ethan Allen Hitchcock, U.S.A.*, p. 120.

45. Kimball, *Timeline of Events*, p. 27.

46. Ibid., pp. 30–33.

47. Anthony F.C. Wallace, *The Long Bitter Trail*, pp. 99–100.

48. Kimball, *Timeline of Events*, p. 36.

49. Ibid., p. 36.

50. Charles J. Kapler, *Indian Affairs: Laws and Treaties*, vol. 2, *Treaties*.

51. Ibid.

52. Eicher and Eicher, *Civil War High Commands*, p. 301.

Chapter 3

1. *Chronicles of Oklahoma* 18, no. 4, p. 321.

2. Ibid., p. 322.

3. *Returns of the 7th U.S. Infantry*; Florida Historical Society, http://myfloridahistory.org/ accessed July 8, 2010; Kimball, *Timeline of Events*, p. 37.

4. *Returns of the 7th U.S. Infantry*; Chris Kimball, "Tour of the Florida Territory During the Florida Seminole Wars: 1792–1859."

5. McManus, *American Courage*, pp. 52–53; *Chronicles of Oklahoma* 18, no. 4, p. 323.

6. McManus, *American Courage*, pp. 52–53; *Chronicles of Oklahoma* 18, no. 4, p. 323; Kimball, *Timeline of Events*, p. 38.

7. *Returns of the 7th U.S. Infantry.*

8. McManus, *American Courage*, pp. 55–57.

9. Ibid., pp. 55–57.

10. *Chronicles of Oklahoma* 18, no. 4, p. 323; Kimball, *Timeline of Events*, p. 38.

11. *Returns of the 7th U.S. Infantry.*

12. McManus, *American Courage*, pp. 57–59; Kimball, *Timeline of Events*, p. 39.

13. McManus, *American Courage*, p. 58.

14. *Returns of the 7th U.S. Infantry.*

15. Ibid.; Holmes family records.

16. White, *American Military Strategy*, p. 47.

17. *Returns of the 7th U.S. Infantry.*

18. Kimball, *Timeline of Events*, p. 42.

19. Ibid., p. 42.

20. *Returns of the 7th U.S. Infantry.*

21. *Chronicles of Oklahoma* 18, no. 4, p. 325; McManus, *American Courage*, p. 50. The totals vary among the sources. McManus puts the number of 7th Infantry deaths due to disease at ninety.

22. Missall, *Seminole Wars*, p. 296; John K. Mahon, *History of the Second Seminole War, 1835–1842*, pp. 321.

23. Foreman, *Indian Removal*, p. 380.

24. *Returns of the 7th U.S. Infantry.*

25. Mary Maria Holmes is buried at Chalmette National Cemetery, St. Bernard Parish, New Orleans, plot section 99, grave #54.

26. Croghan and Prucha, ed., *Army Life*, p. 68.

27. *Returns of the 7th U.S. Infantry.*

28. Sharyn Kane and Richard Keeton, *Fort Brown, Texas: A New Frontier*, p. 2.

29. Harbert Davenport and Craig H. Roell, "Goliad Massacre," *Handbook of Texas Online*, p. 1, accessed June 12, 2011.

30. Stephen A. Carney, "Guns Along the Rio Grande, Palo Alto and Resaca de la Palma," p. 3.

31. John Corey Henshaw, *Recollections of the War with Mexico*, p. 37; David Nevin, ed., *The Mexican War*, p. 13.

32. Nevin, *Mexican War*, p. 22.

33. Felice Flanery Lewis, *Trailing Clouds of Glory*, p. 37.

34. Nevin, *Mexican War*, p. 13.

35. Kane and Keeton, *Fort Brown*, pp. 2–3.

36. McManus, *American Courage*, pp. 65–66.

37. Robert Selph Henry, *The Story of the Mexican War*, p. 45.

38. Kane and Keeton, *Fort Brown*, pp. 3–4.

39. Ibid., p. 4.

40. McManus, *American Courage*, p. 67.

41. Nevin, *Mexican War*, p. 35.

42. Edgar S. Hawkins, "Captain Edgar S. Hawkins, at Fort Taylor (a.k.a. Fort Texas), to W.W.S. Bliss, Assistant Adjutant-General, Army of Occupation, Texas."

43. McManus, *American Courage*, p. 69.

44. Hawkins, "Captain Edgar S. Hawkins, at Fort Taylor."

45. Henshaw, *Recollections*, p. 55.

46. Lewis, *Trailing Clouds of Glory*, p. 71–72.

47. Henshaw, *Recollections*, p. 59.

48. Ibid., pp. 60–61.

49. Kane and Keeton, *Fort Brown*, p. 5.

50. Hawkins, "Captain Edgar S. Hawkins, at Fort Taylor."

51. Henshaw, *Recollections*, p. 62.

52. Ibid., p. 63.

53. Kane and Keeton, *Fort Brown*, p. 6.

54. Nevin, *Mexican War*, p. 38.

55. Ibid., p. 39.

56. Ibid.

57. Ibid.

58. Ibid.

59. Ibid., pp. 39, 42.

60. Carney, "Guns Along the Rio Grande, Palo Alto and Resaca de la Palma," pp. 22, 24–25.

61. Carney, "Guns Along the Rio Grande," p. 22.

62. Ibid.

63. Ibid.

64. Ibid., p. 24.

65. Ibid., pp. 24–25.

66. Ibid.

67. Nevin, *Mexican War*, p. 43; Carney, "Guns Along the Rio Grande," p. 25.

68. Carney, "Guns Along the Rio Grande," p. 26.

69. Kane and Keeton, *Fort Brown*, p. 6.

70. Nevin, *Mexican War*, p. 43; Carney, "Guns Along the Rio Grande," p. 25; McManus, *American Courage*, p. 76.

71. Nevin, *Mexican War*, p. 43.

72. *Returns of the 7th U.S. Infantry*; Carney, "Guns Along the Rio Grande," p. 25; Nevin, *Mexican War*, p. 57.

73. Nevin, *Mexican War*, pp. 57–58.

74. Ibid., pp. 58, 60.

75. Timothy D. Johnson, *A Gallant Little Army*, p. 5.

76. Johnson, *Gallant Little Army*, p. 12.

77. Nevin, *Mexican War*, p. 60.

78. Red Reeder, *The Story of the Mexican War*, p. 62; Nevin, *Mexican War*, pp. 60–62.

79. Reeder, *Story of the Mexican War*, p. 62.

80. Ibid., pp. 61, 63; Nevin, *Mexican War*, p. 64.

81. Nevin, *Mexican War*, p. 65; Reeder, *Story of the Mexican War*, p. 67.

82. Henshaw, *Recollections*, p. 80.

83. McManus, *American Courage*, p. 82; Reeder, *Story of the Mexican War*, p. 71.

84. Henshaw, *Recollections*, p. 80.

85. Reeder, *Story of the Mexican War*, p. 65; Boatner, *Civil War Dictionary*, p. 530.

86. Henshaw, *Recollections*, pp. 80–81; McManus, *American Courage*, p. 83; Nevin, *Mexican War*, pp. 66–67.

87. McManus, *American Courage*, p. 85; Nevin, *Mexican War*, pp. 66–67; Henshaw, *Recollections*, pp. 80–81.

88. Henshaw, *Recollections*, pp. 80–81.

89. Ibid., p. 81.

90. Ibid., p. 82; McManus, *American Courage*, p. 87.

91. Henshaw, *Recollections*, p. 82; McManus, *American Courage*, p. 87.

92. Henshaw, *Recollections*, p. 82.

93. McManus, *American Courage*, p. 87.

94. Henshaw, *Recollections*, p. 82.

95. Ibid., p. 86.

96. Nevin, *Mexican War*, p. 73.

97. Ibid., pp. 73, 76.

98. Ibid., p. 76.

99. Ibid.

100. McManus, *American Courage*, p. 88.

101. Nevin, *Mexican War*, p. 76; McManus, *American Courage*, pp. 88–89.

102. Henshaw, *Recollections*, p. 83.

103. Ibid.; McManus, *American Courage*, p. 89.

104. McManus, *American Courage*, p. 89.

105. Henshaw, *Recollections*, p. 84.

106. Ibid., p. 85.

107. McManus, *American Courage*, p. 90; Nevin, *Mexican War*, p. 77.

108. Lewis, *Trailing Clouds of Glory*, p. 154.

109. McManus, *American Courage*, p. 91.

110. Ibid.

111. Ibid.

112. Henshaw, *Recollections*, p. 89.

113. Ibid., p. 88; Reeder, *Story of the Mexican War*, pp. 83–85.

114. McManus, *American Courage*, p. 92.

115. Nevin, *Mexican War*, p. 78; Reeder, *Story of the Mexican War*, p. 58.

116. Johnson, *Gallant Little Army*, p. 14.

117. Ibid., p. 15.

118. Ibid.

119. Ibid., p. 17.

120. Henshaw, *Recollections*, pp. 105–106.

121. Ibid.

122. Ibid., p. 108.

123. Reeder, *Story of the Mexican War*, pp. 105–108.

124. Kevin Dougherty, *Civil War Leadership and Mexican War Experience*, p. 133–136.

125. Reeder, *Story of the Mexican War*, p. 123.

126. Ibid., p. 124.

127. Johnson, *Gallant Little Army*, pp. 9–10.

128. McManus, *American Courage*, p. 94.

129. Nevin, *Mexican War*, p. 139; Johnson, *Gallant Little Army*, p. 21.

130. Nevin, *Mexican War*, p. 139; Henshaw, *Recollections*, p. 114.

131. Henry, *Story of the Mexican War*, p. 265.

132. Ibid., pp. 265–266.

133. McManus, *American Courage*, p. 94.

134. Ibid., p. 95.

135. Reeder, *Story of the Mexican War*, p. 128.

136. Ibid., p. 129.

137. Broadside issued by General Worth, May 27, 1847 (Early American History Store, Ebay item #370467663158, accessed December 17, 2010).

138. James K. Polk, *A Compilation of the Messages and Papers of the Presidents*, part 5, "Memo to the United States Senate, March 2, 1847," accessed February 17, 2011.

139. Johnson, *Gallant Little Army*, pp. 86–89.

140. T.F. Rodenbough and W.L. Haskin, eds., *The Army of the United States: Historical Sketches of Staff and Line with Portraits of Generals-In-Chief*; A.B. Johnson, "The Seventh Regiment of Infantry," p. 499.

141. Rodenbough and Haskin, *Army of the United States*; Johnson, "The Seventh Regiment of Infantry," p. 500.

142. *Niles Weekly Register*, Aug. 3, 1848.

143. Elizabeth MacPherson, "Old Times in the South," undated, p. 1, Holmes family papers.

Chapter 4

1. Elizabeth Hinsdale MacPherson, "Old Times in the South," undated, p. 1, Holmes family papers.

2. Foreman, *Five Civilized Tribes*, p. 251.

3. *Returns of the 7th U.S. Infantry*.

4. Hughes, "Forts and Camps in Oklahoma," p. 57; Foreman, *Five Civilized Tribes*, pp. 141, 139n.

5. MacPherson, "Old Times in the South," p. 1.

6. National Park Service. "Commanding Officers 1833–1871."

7. Henshaw, *Recollections*, pp. 24, 79, 191.

8. Spilman, "North Carolina's Paladin," p. 4; MacPherson, "Old Times In the South," p. 1.

9. Ancestry.com Operations, U.S. Military and Naval Academies, Cadet Records and Applications, 1805–1908 (database on-line).

10. Ibid.

11. Ibid.

12. Castel, "Theophilus Hunter Holmes," p. 11.

13. Typed copy of a letter from Holmes to Lydia Wetmore, February 12, 1861, Holmes family papers.

14. *New York Times*, February 16, 1861; typed copy of a letter from Holmes to Lydia Wetmore, February 12, 1861, Spilman family papers; 1860 U.S. census,www.fold3.com, image #54797303.

15. *OR*, Series I, vol. 1, pp. 113, 119.

16. Ibid., p. 114.

17. Ibid., p. 131.

18. *New York Times*, January 14, 1861.

19. *OR*, Series I, vol. 1, p. 10.

20. Alfred H. Guernsey and Henry M. Alden, eds., *Harper's Pictorial History of the Civil War*, p. 36.

21. Eric C. Caren, *Civil War Extra*, vol. 1, p. 34; *Daily Advocate*, January 12, 1861, article dated January 9, 1861.

22. John Wagman, ed., *Civil War Front Pages*; Richmond *Daily Dispatch*, January 12, 1861.

23. *OR*, Series I, vol. 1, p. 10.

24. Caren, *Civil War Extra*, vol. 1, p. 34.

25. John G. Barrett, *The Civil War in North Carolina*, p. 9.

26. Ibid., pp. 6–8.

27. *New York Times*, January 23, 1861, p. and February 16, 1861.

28. *OR*, Series I, vol. 51, part 1, p. 316.

29. *OR*, Series I, vol. 1, pp. 236, 240, 245, 251.

30. *New York Times*, April 8, 1861.

31. *OR, Navy*, series 1, vol. 4, pp. 223–225.

32. *New York Times*, April 11, 1861. Major Samuel P. Heintzelman assumed command at the post (see Cullum, *Register of Officers and Graduates of the United States Military Academy*, vol. 1, p. 372). Heintzelman's appointment was temporary. "Col. Smith" had been previously scheduled to replace Holmes in June, suggesting that Holmes's original intention was to complete his thirty-sixth year of service in the U.S. Army (see *New York Times*, April 11, 1861). Historian Edmond Smith gives the date of Heintzelman's assumption of command as April 14, 1861 (see Edmond B. Smith, *Governors Island: Its Military History Under Three Flags*, p. 212). Many sources cite April 22 as Holmes's resignation date. By then, he had traveled to North Carolina and Montgomery, Alabama, and was returning to North Carolina.

33. John B. Jones, *A Rebel War Clerk's Diary*, v. 1, p. 15.

34. Ibid.

35. T.H. Holmes Collection, Southern Historical Society Papers, T.H. Holmes file #2457, #349-z, University of North Carolina, Chapel Hill.

36. *OR*, Series III, vol. 1, p. 72.

37. *OR*, Series I, vol. 51, part 2, p. 12.

38. Noble J. Tolbert, *Papers of John W. Ellis*, vol. 2, pp. 614, 660, 686; *OR*, Series I, vol. 51, part 2, p. 23.

39. Boatner, *Civil War Dictionary*, p. 70.

40. Barrett, *Civil War*, p. 15.

41. "North Carolina. Convention, 1861–1862. North Carolina Military Board," North Carolina Collection, University of North Carolina at Chapel Hill, vol. 1, pp. 51–56. Promotions and assignments of veteran officers like Holmes came at a dizzying pace during the first months of the war.

42. United States War Department, *Compiled Service Records of Confederate Soldiers Who Served During the Civil War*, Record Group 109 (cited hereafter as *Confederate Service Records*), www.fold3.com, image #68815955; North Carolina Department of Cultural Resources Office of Archives and History, "Fort Fisher: Civil War — National Historic Landmark."

43. "North Carolina. Convention 1861–1862. North Carolina Military Board," North Carolina Collection, University of North Carolina at Chapel Hill, vol. 1, pp. 51–56, communications between Holmes, Whiting, Governor Ellis, R.H. Riddick, Colonel Hook and Colonel Morris, April 28–May 28, 1861; Tolbert, *Papers of John W. Ellis*, p. 743.

44. *OR*, Series IV, vol. 1, p. 336.

45. Captain Hill to Ochiltree, May 24, 1861, in *Correspondence of General T.H. Holmes*, War Department Collection of Confederate Records, Chapter II, Vol. 358, RG 109, National Archives, Washington, D.C.

46. Holmes to Governor Ellis, May 16, 1861, in *Correspondence of General T.H. Holmes*, War Department Collection of Confederate Records, Chapter II, Vol. 358, RG 109, National Archives, Washington, D.C..

47. Ibid.

48. *OR*, Series I, vol. 51, part 2, pp. 116, 125; *OR*, Series I, vol. 2, p. 907; Boatner, *Civil War Dictionary*, p. 406.

49. Peter D. Skirbunt, "Washington Secured: Breaking the Confederate Blockade of the Potomac, 1861–1862," pp. 1, 3, 4.

50. E.B. Long, *Civil War Day by Day*, p. 81; Skirbunt, "Washington Secured," p. 7.

51. T.H. Holmes Collection, *Duke*.

52. Ibid.

53. Ibid. The term "file closers" refers to lieutenants and sergeants who march in a line behind their companies during an attack and maintain the company's formation.

54. *Daily Dispatch*, Richmond, June 20, 1861,; *Richmond Daily Dispatch 1860–1865*, http://dlxs.richmond.edu/d/ddr/, accessed June 21, 2011.

55. *OR*, Series I, vol. 2, pp. 929, 932.

56. Ibid., pp. 133–134, 136–138.

57. *OR*, Series I, vol. 51, part 2, p. 142.

58. *OR*, Series I, vol. 2, p. 941.

59. Ibid., pp. 933, 959, 961, 973, 974, 976, 979.

60. Holmes to Beauregard, June 13, 1861, bMS Am 1649.24 [416], Frederick M. Dearborn Collection, Houghton Library, Harvard University.

61. *Confederate Service Records*, fold3.com, image #73181643; Ellis died suddenly on July 7 and was replaced by Speaker of the Senate Henry T. Clark.

62. E.B. Long, *Civil War Day by Day*, p. 88.

63. James M. Lundberg, "On to Richmond! Or Not."

64. E.B. Long, *Civil War Day by Day*, pp. 88, 94–96.

65. Ibid., pp. 94–96.

66. *OR*, Series I, vol. 2, pp. 439–440.

Chapter 5

1. *OR*, Series I, vol. 2, pp. 980, 565.

2. Richmond *Daily Dispatch*, August 16, 1861; Bradley M. Gottfried, *The Maps of First Bull Run*, p. 29; *OR*, Series I, vol. 2, p. 565.

3. E.B. Long, *Civil War Day by Day*, p. 98.

4. *OR*, Series I, vol. 2, p. 565.

5. Ibid.

6. Richmond *Daily Dispatch*, August 5, 1861.

7. *OR*, Series I, vol. 2, p. 565.

8. Robert U. Johnson and Clarence E. Buell, eds., *Battles and Leaders of the Civil War*, vol. 1, pp. 259–260; *OR*, Series I, vol. 2, pp. 565–566.

9. *OR*, Series I, vol. 5, pp. 801–802.

10. Aubrey Lee Brooks and Hugh T. Lefler, eds., *The Papers of Walter Clark*, vol. 1, pp. 55–56; Richard N. Current, *Encyclopedia of the Confederacy*, p. 585.

11. Boatner, *Civil War Dictionary*, p. 406; *OR*, Series I, vol. 5, p. 913.

12. *OR*, Series I, vol. 5, p. 913.

13. *OR*, Series I, vol. 51, part 2, pp. 357–58; Boatner, *Civil War Dictionary*, p. 849; Holmes announced Walker's promotion and new assignment on January 13, 1862, in District General Order No. 3. George Picket was promoted to brigadier general at about the same time. Eleanor Brockenbrough Library, Museum of the Confederacy, Richmond, Virginia.

14. *Fayetteville (North Carolina) Observer*, June 21, 1961.

15. *OR*, Series I, vol. 51, part 2, p. 360; Holmes to Johnston, October 28, 1861, bMS Am 1649.24 [418], Frederick M. Dearborn Collection, Houghton Library, Harvard University.

16. *OR*, Series I, vol. 5, p. 967.

17. *NCTAR*, vol. 7, p. 1.

18. *OR*, Series I, vol. 11, part 3, p. 423.

19. Frederick S. Haydon, *Military Ballooning During the Early Civil War*, pp. 123–124.

20. *New York Times*, December 15, 1861.

21. A.G. Thompson to M.C. Thompson, April 9, 1863.

22. Haydon, *Military Ballooning*, p. 358.

23. *OR*, Series I, vol. 5, p. 993.

24. Richmond *Daily Dispatch*, December 25, 1861.

25. Holmes to Swain, January 21, 1862, in *Documenting the American South*, digital library, collection #40005, University of North Carolina, Chapel Hill.

26. Ibid.

27. Circular issued on December 24, 1861, Eleanor Brockenbrough Library, The Museum of the Confederacy, Richmond, Virginia.

28. Richmond *Daily Dispatch*, January 6. and March 14, 1862.

29. Richmond *Daily Dispatch*, March 14, 1862; *New York Times*, March 21, 1862.

30. General Order, January 11, 1862, Eleanor S. Brockenbrough Library, Museum of the Confederacy.

31. Richmond *Daily Dispatch*, January 27, 1862, and January 28, 1862.

32. *Confederate Service Records*, www.fold3.com, image #71803734.

33. Paul D. Escott, ed., *North Carolina Yeoman: The Diary of Basil Armstrong Thomasson, 1853–1862*, p. 322; *Daily Bulletin*, Charlotte, February 1, 1862, p. and April 1, 1862.

34. *Confederate Service Records*, www.fold3.com, image #71803734.

35. Ibid., images #71803714, #71803330.

36. Ibid., image #64986823.

37. "Theophilus H. Holmes," *35th Georgia in Vir-*

ginia, http://www.chrisanddavid.com/georgia/Virginia.html, accessed June 28, 2011.

38. Barrett, *Civil War*, pp. 36–37, 46.

39. Boatner, *Civil War Dictionary*, pp. 701, 108.

40. Richard A. Sauers, *The Battle of New Bern and Related Sites in Craven County, N.C., 1861–1865*, pp. 3–7.

41. Ibid., pp. 9, 11.

42. Ibid., p. 6.

43. *NCTAR*, vol. 7, p. 455.

44. Sauers, *Battle of New Bern*, p. 7.

45. Walter J. Clark, *Histories of the Several Regiments and Battalions from North Carolina in the Great War*, vol. 4, p. 647.

46. Sauers, *Battle of New Bern*, pp. 13, 15.

47. Ibid., p. 15.

48. *OR*, Series I, vol. 9, pp. 267–268.

49. Clark, *Histories*, vol. 4, p. 647.

50. *NCTAR*, vol. 9, p. 354.

51. Sauers, *Battle of New Bern*, pp. 17, 19.

52. Ibid., pp. 21, 23.

53. *OR*, Series I, vol. 11, part 3, p. 392.

54. *OR*, Series I, vol. 9, pp. 450–451.

55. *OR*, Series I, vol. 51, part 2, p. 497.

56. *OR*, Series I, vol. 9, p. 455.

57. Ibid., p. 452.

58. Ibid.

59. Ibid., p. 461.

60. Ibid., p. 456.

61. Clark, *Histories*, vol. 4, p. 646.

62. *OR*, Series I, vol. 9, p. 454.

63. Ibid., pp. 453–455, 462.

64. Ibid., p. 461.

65. *OR*, Series I, vol. 51, part 2, p. 540.

66. David A. Norris, "For the Benefit of Our Gallant Volunteers," *North Carolina Historical Review* 75, no. 3 (July 1998): 318; Sidney Ann Wilson and George A. Thomas, *Personae: The History of Peace College*, p. 6.

67. *OR*, Series I, vol. 9, p. 458.

68. Barrett, *Civil War*, pp. 116, 119.

69. *OR*, Series, I, vol. 9, p. 459.

70. Ibid., pp. 459–460.

71. Ibid., pp. 305–306.

72. Boatner, *Civil War Dictionary*, p. 632; *OR*, Series, I, vol. 9, pp. 461–462, 465.

73. Albert Burton Moore, *Conscription and Conflict in the Confederacy*, p. 360.

74. Ibid., p. 14.

75. Boatner, *Civil War Dictionary*, p. 756.

76. *OR*, Series IV, vol. 1, p. 1095.

77. A.B. Moore, *Conscription and Conflict*, pp. 356–357; *OR*, Series III, vol. 1, p. 1094.

78. *OR Supplement*, vol. 2, serial 94, p. 247.

79. *NCTAR*, vol. 9, p. 245.

80. *OR*, Series I, vol. 9, p. 465.

81. *Confederate Service Records*, www.fold3.com, image #71803813.

82. Barrett, *Civil War*, pp. 121–22.

83. *OR*, Series I, vol. 9, pp. 455, 469.

84. *OR*, Series I, vol. 11, part 3, p. 501.

85. Ibid., p. 512.

86. *OR*, Series I, vol. 14, p. 541.

87. *OR*, Series I, vol. 11, part 3, pp. 536–537.

88. Ibid., pp. 559, 568.

89. E.B. Long, *Civil War Day by Day*, pp. 218–220; Boatner, *Civil War Dictionary*, p. 273.

90. *OR*, Series I, vol. 11, part 3, pp. 568–569.

91. Ibid., p. 607.

92. E.B. Long, *Civil War Day by Day*, p. 237.

93. *OR*, Series I, vol. 11, part 3, p. 610.

94. *OR*, Series I, vol. 9, p. 475; *OR*, Series I, vol. 11, part 3, p. 611.

95. *OR*, Series I, vol. 11, part 3, p. 619.

96. Ibid., pp. 618–623.

97. Richard Taylor, *Destruction and Reconstruction*, p. 105.

98. *OR*, Series I, vol. 11, part 3, p. 623.

99. *OR*, Series I, vol. 11, part 2, pp. 488, 906.

100. Ibid., p. 907.

101. Ibid.

102. Ibid., pp. 906–907.

103. Douglas Southall Freeman, *Lee's Lieutenants*, vol. 1, p. 582; Benson J. Lossing, *Pictorial History of the Civil War in the United States of America*, vol. 2, p. 431.

104. *OR*, Series I, vol. 11, part 2, p. 907.

105. Boatner, *Civil War Dictionary*, p. 504; Freeman, *Lee's Lieutenants*, vol. 1, p. 589.

106. Freeman, *Lee's Lieutenants*, vol. 1, p. 583; *OR*, Series I, vol. 11, p. 907; Stephen W. Sears, *To the Gates of Richmond: The Peninsula Campaign*, p. 290.

107. Freeman, *Lee's Lieutenants*, vol. 1, p. 585; John S. Salmon, *The Official Virginia Civil War Battlefield Guide*, p. 116.

108. *OR*, Series I, vol. 11, part 3, p. 238; vol. 11, part 2, p. 227.

109. *OR*, Series I, vol. 11, part 1, p. 257.

110. Richmond *Daily Dispatch*, July 2, 1862; *OR*, Series I, vol. 11, part 3, p. 625.

111. *OR*, Series I, vol. 11, part 2, pp. 257–258.

112. *OR*, Series I, vol. 11, p. 2, p. 910.

113. *NCTAR*, vol. 12, pp. 140–141.

114. Ibid.

115. *NCTAR*, vol. 17, p. 6. Throughout the war, D.H. Hill was known for his derisive and insulting remarks. Some scholars regard the incident as apocryphal.

116. *OR*, Series I, vol. 11, part 2, p. 675.

117. Sears, *To the Gates of Richmond*, pp. 292, 293; Freeman, *Lee's Lieutenants*, vol. 1, pp. 582–583.

118. Clark, *Histories*, vol. 4, p. 501.

119. *OR*, Series I, vol. 11, part 2, p. 908.

120. *New York Times*, May 3, 1863.

121. Boatner, *Civil War Dictionary*, pp. 506–507.

122. Ibid., p. 506.

123. *OR*, Series I, vol. 11, part 1, p. 256.

124. *OR*, Series I, vol. 11, part 2, p. 350.

125. Freeman, *Lee's Lieutenants*, vol. 1, p. 587.

126. Ibid., p. 604.

127. Ibid., p. 574.

128. *OR*, Series I, vol. 11, part 2, p. 666.

129. Gary Gallagher, ed., *The Richmond Campaign of 1862*, p. 109. In Gallagher's work, historian Peter S. Charmichael blames much of the campaign's failure on Magruder and mentions no failures by Holmes. Likewise, Douglas Southall Freeman did not consider Holmes responsible "for serious failure" (*Lee's Lieutenants*, vol. 1, p. 614).

130. *OR*, Series I, vol. 11, part 2, p. 495.

131. Sears, *To the Gates of Richmond*, p. 343.

132. Albert Castel, *General Sterling Price and the Civil War in the West*, p. 141.

133. Freeman, *Lee's Lieutenants*, vol. 1, p. 585n; Gary W. Gallagher, *Fighting for the Confederacy: The Personal Recollections of General Edward Porter Alexander*, p. 106.

134. Jefferson Davis, *The Rise and Fall of the Confederate Government*, vol. 2, p. 122.

135. Ibid., pp. 122–123.

136. Ibid., p. 123.

137. Jefferson Davis, *Papers*, vol. 8, p. 439.

138. Strode, *Jefferson Davis: Confederate President*, p. 282.

139. Ibid., p. 283.

140. *OR*, Series I, vol. 9, p. 461.

141. Jefferson Davis, *Papers*, vol. 8, p. 276.

142. Barrett, *Civil War*, p. 136.

143. *OR*, Series I, vol. 11, part 3, p. 641.

144. *OR*, Series I, vol. 9, p. 476; vol. 11, part 3, pp. 643.

145. Castel, *General Sterling Price*, p. 91; John N. Edwards, *Shelby And His Men; or, The War in the West*, pp. 106–107.

146. *OR*, Series I, vol. 11, part 3, pp. 540, 551.

147. Castel, *General Sterling Price*, p. 91; Edwards, *Shelby And His Men*, pp. 106–107.

148. Stephen W. Woodworth, *Jefferson Davis and His Generals*, pp. 150–152.

149. *OR*, Series I, vol. 53, p. 817.

150. *OR*, Series I, vol. 13, p. 860.

Chapter 6

1. Holmes to Randolph, July 18, 1862, in *Correspondence of General T.H. Holmes*, War Department Collection of Confederate Records, Chapter II, Vol. 358, RG 109, National Archives, Washington, D.C.

2. Ibid.

3. Ibid.

4. *Confederate Service Records*, www.fold3.com, image #71803330.

5. Holmes to Randolph, July 18, 1862, in *Correspondence of General T.H. Holmes*, War Department

Collection of Confederate Records, Chapter II, Vol. 358, RG 109, National Archives, Washington, D.C.

6. Archer Jones, *Confederate Strategy from Shiloh to Vicksburg*, p. 19; *OR*, Series I, vol. 53, p. 881.

7. A. Jones, *Confederate Strategy*, pp. 25–26.

8. *Richmond Examiner*, January 8, 1862,

9. Anne J. Bailey, "The Role of the Trans-Mississippi Region," p. 1.

10. Doyle Taylor, "A Brief Analysis of Arkansas, General Holmes, and the Trans-Mississippi," p. 1.

11. W.W. Heartsill and Irwin Bell Wiley, eds., *Fourteen Hundred and 91 Days in the Confederate Army*, p. 81.

12. Bailey, "Role of the Trans-Mississippi," p. 2.

13. *Southern Historical Society Papers* 49, p. 124.

14. Bailey, "Role of the Trans-Mississippi," p. 2.

15. Boatner, *Civil War Dictionary*, p. 13.

16. Ibid., p. 845.

17. Ibid., pp. 627–628.

18. A. Jones, *Confederate Strategy*, p. 53.

19. Mark Swanson and Jacqueline D. Langley, *Atlas of the Civil War*, pp. 34–40; Boatner, *Civil War Dictionary*, p. 756.

20. William R. Geise, "A Study of Organization and Command in the Trans-Mississippi West," part 5, "A New Command," *Military History of Texas and the Southwest*:38.

21. Taylor, "Brief Analysis of Arkansas," p. 5.

22. A.B. Moore, *Conscription and Conflict*, p. 359.

23. Taylor, "Brief Analysis of Arkansas," p. 2; Christ, *Rugged and Sublime*, p. 38.

24. Ibid., pp. 2–3.

25. Boatner, *Civil War Dictionary*, p. 402; E.B. Long, *Civil War Day by Day*, p. 219.

26. Swanson and Langley, *Atlas of the Civil War*, p. 42.

27. Taylor, "Brief Analysis of Arkansas," p. 4; Swanson and Langley, *Atlas of the Civil War*, pp. 40, 42, 44.

28. Boatner, *Civil War Dictionary*, p. 675.

29. Jefferson Davis, *Papers*, vol. 8, p. 456.

30. Swanson and Langley, *Atlas of the Civil War*, pp. 36–42: Boatner, *Civil War Dictionary*, p. 23.

31. Boatner, *Civil War Dictionary*, pp. 352–353.

32. *OR*, Series I, vol. 13, p. 860.

33. *Confederate Service Records*, www.fold3.com, image #64986848.

34. Shelby Foote, *The Civil War: A Narrative*, vol. 1, p. 783.

35. *OR*, Series I, vol. 13, p. 877; Current, *Encyclopedia of the Confederacy*, vol. 4, p. 1607.

36. Geise, William R. "General Holmes Fails to Create a Department," *Military History of Texas and the Southwest* 14 (1): 174.

37. Boatner, *Civil War Dictionary*, p. 402.

38. Christ, *Rugged and Sublime*, p. 46.

39. *OR*, Series I, vol. 15, pp. 789, 791.

40. *OR*, Series I, vol. 53, pp. 818, 819.

41. *OR*, Series I, vol. 9, p. 732; Boatner, *Civil War Dictionary*, p. 846.

42. Holmes to Cooper, Aug. 17, 1862, *Duke*.

43. Geise, "A Study of Organization and Command in the Trans-Mississippi West," part 4, "Hindman and Hebert Divide Command," p. 116.

44. *Weekly Arkansas Gazette*, Little Rock, August 30, 1862.

45. Holmes to Nelson, August, 21, 1862, in *Correspondence of General T.H. Holmes*, War Department Collection of Confederate Records, Chapter II, Vol. 358, RG 109, National Archives, Washington, D.C.

46. Ibid.

47. Holmes to Davis, August, 28, 1862, in *Correspondence of General T.H. Holmes*, War Department Collection of Confederate Records, Chapter II, Vol. 358, RG 109, National Archives, Washington, D.C.

48. Ibid.

49. Ibid.

50. *OR*, Series II, vol. 4, p. 492.

51. Ibid., pp. 492–493.

52. Ibid., p. 493.

53. Briscoe Hindman, "Thomas Carmichael Hindman," *Confederate Veteran* 38, no. 3 (March 1930): 101.

54. *OR*, Series II, vol. 4, p. 494.

55. Ibid.

56. Ibid., p. 495.

57. Holmes to Cooper, September 7, 1862, in *Correspondence of General T.H. Holmes*, War Department Collection of Confederate Records, Chapter II, Vol. 358, RG 109, National Archives, Washington, D.C.

58. *OR*, Series I, vol. 13, p. 897.

59. Holmes to Northrop, September 28, 1862, in *Correspondence of General T.H. Holmes*, War Department Collection of Confederate Records, Chapter II, Vol. 358, RG 109, National Archives, Washington, D.C.

60. *OR*, Series I, vol. 13, pp. 885–886.

61. Ibid., p. 915.

62. *OR Supplement*, vol. 2, serial 94, pp. 615–617.

63. Ibid., p. 617.

64. Ibid.

65. Ibid.

66. *OR*, Series I, vol. 13, p. 918; Geise, "Holmes, Arkansas and the Defense of the Lower River," *Military History of Texas and the Southwest* 14 (1978): 230.

67. *OR*, Series I, vol. 13, pp. 883–885.

68. "Camp Nelson Confederate Cemetery," *Encyclopedia of Arkansas History and Culture*, Central Arkansas Library System, http://www.encyclopediaofarkansas.net/encyclopedia/entry-detail.aspx?search=1&entryID=4275, accessed June 15, 2011.

69. *OR*, Series I, vol. 13, p. 887.

70. Boatner, *Civil War Dictionary*, p. 232.

71. Holmes to Hindman, August 27, 1862, P.W. Anderson Collection, Columbia University Library.

72. Holmes to Davis, November 9, 1862, in *Correspondence of General T.H. Holmes*, War Department Collection of Confederate Records, Chapter II, Vol. 358, RG 109, National Archives, Washington, D.C.; Jefferson Davis, *Papers*, vol. 8, p. 484. The other generals promoted were James Longstreet, Leonidas Polk, William J. Hardee, and Thomas J. Jackson.

73. Swanson and Langley, *Atlas of the Civil War*, p. 50.

Chapter 7

1. *OR*, Series I, vol. 13, pp. 889–890.

2. Ibid., p. 918.

3. Ibid., p. 926; Bruce Catton, *The Centennial History of the Civil War*, vol. 3, *Never Call Retreat*, pp. 10–12; Holmes to Pemberton, November 25, 1862, in *Correspondence of General T.H. Holmes*, War Department Collection of Confederate Records, Chapter II, Vol. 358, RG 109, National Archives, Washington, D.C.

4. *OR*, Series I, vol. 13, pp. 918–921.

5. *OR Supplement*, vol. 3, vol. 13, serial 19, pp. 59–62.

6. A. Jones, *Confederate Strategy*, pp. 96–98.

7. Holmes to Johnston, October 15, 1862, in *Correspondence of General T.H. Holmes*, War Department Collection of Confederate Records, Chapter II, Vol. 358, RG 109, National Archives, Washington, D.C.

8. Thomas L. Connelly, *Autumn of Glory*, p. 38.

9. Joseph E. Johnston, *Narrative of Military Operations Directed During the Civil War*, p. 153.

10. *OR*, Series I, vol. 13, p. 899.

11. Ibid., p. 914.

12. A. Jones, *Confederate Strategy*, pp. 89–90.

13. Boatner, *Civil War Dictionary*, pp. 730, 772. Gustavus W. Smith served as secretary of war between Randolph's resignation and Seddon's appointment.

14. Holmes to Samuel J. Hinsdale, November 9, 1862, in *Correspondence of General T.H. Holmes*, War Department Collection of Confederate Records, Chapter II, Vol. 358, RG 109, National Archives, Washington, D.C.

15. *OR*, Series I, vol. 13, pp. 918–919.

16. Albert Pike's letters to General Holmes, dated December 20, 1862, and April 20, 1863; Pike's Address to the Senators and Representatives of Arkansas in the Congress of the Confederate States, dated March 20, 1863, Virginia Historical Society, Richmond, Virginia.

17. Jefferson Davis, *Papers*, vol. 8, p. 361.

18. *OR*, Series I, vol. 17, part 2, p. 810.

19. Boatner, *Civil War Dictionary*, p. 871.

20. Ibid., pp. 967, 965.

21. Doyle Taylor, message to author, February 6, 2010.

22. Ibid.

23. Walter B. Cisco, *War Crimes Against Southern Citizens*, p. 24.

24. Ibid., p. 24.

25. *OR*, Series I, vol. 13, pp. 742–743.

26. Ibid., p. 727.

27. Foote, *The Civil War: A Narrative*, vol. 1, p. 783.

28. Holmes to Magruder, November 28, 1862, in *Correspondence of General T.H. Holmes*, War Department Collection of Confederate Records, Chapter II, Vol. 358, RG 109, National Archives, Washington, D.C.

29. *OR*, Series I, vol. 15, p. 882; Strode, *Jefferson Davis, Confederate President*, p. 333–334.

30. *OR*, Series I, vol. 15, p. 884; E.B. Long, *Civil War Day by Day*, p. 307; Swanson and Langley, *Atlas of the Civil War*, p. 56.

31. Peter Cozzens, "Hindman's Grand Delusion," *Civil War Times Illustrated*, October 2000, p. 32.

32. *OR*, Series I, vol. 22, part 1, pp. 138–143; Cozzens, "Hindman's Grand Delusion," pp. 34–35.

33. *The Southern Bivouac* 1, no. 4 (September 1885): 211.

34. Jefferson Davis, *Papers*, vol. 8, p. 585.

35. Cozzens, "Hindman's Grand Delusion," pp. 66–69; Geise, "Holmes, Arkansas, and Defense of the Lower River," p. 232.

36. Jefferson Davis, *Papers*, vol. 8, p. 585.

37. *OR Supplement*, vol. 2, serial 94, pp. 785–786.

38. Swanson and Langley, *Atlas of the Civil War*, p. 54; E.B. Long, *Civil War Day by Day*, pp. 300–303; Boatner, *Civil War Dictionary*, p. 871.

39. *OR*, Series I, vol. 15, p. 220; E.B. Long, *Civil War Day by Day*, p. 307.

40. Boatner, *Civil War Dictionary*, pp. 24–25; *The New York Herald*, January 21, 1863; Christ, *Rugged and Sublime*, p. 60.

41. Christ, *Rugged and Sublime*, pp. 60–61.

42. Mark K. Christ, *The Civil War in Arkansas, 1863*, pp. 44.

43. Ibid., p. 52; Boatner, *Civil War Dictionary*, p. 24–25.

44. John M. Harrell, "Arkansas," in *Confederate Military History*, vol. 10, ed. Clement A. Evans, p. 160.

45. Christ, *Rugged and Sublime*, pp. 62–63.

46. Ibid., p. 63.

47. Heartsill and Wiley, eds., *Fourteen Hundred and 91 Days*, p. 95.

48. *New York Herald*, January 21, 1863.

49. Heartsill and Wiley, eds., *Fourteen Hundred and 91 Days*, pp. 96, 98.

50. Harrell, "Arkansas," pp. 159–160; Heartsill and Wiley, eds., *Fourteen Hundred and 91 Days*, p. 98.

51. *OR*, Series I, vol. 17, part 1, p. 794. Other accounts of Deshler's surrender, including General Sherman's, indicate that General Churchill was brought up and personally ordered Deshler to end

the fighting (Christ, *Civil War in Arkansas,* p. 79; Harrell, "Arkansas," pp. 159–160).

52. Christ, *Civil War in Arkansas,* p. 77.
53. Harrell, "Arkansas," 160.
54. Heartsill and Wiley, eds., *Fourteen Hundred and 91 Days,* p. 114.
55. *OR,* Series I,vol. 17, part 1, p. 782.
56. *OR,* Series I, vol. 17, part 2, p. 571.
57. Ibid., pp. 783–784.
58. Christ, *Civil War in Arkansas,* p. 97.
59. Ibid., p. 99.
60. Ibid., pp. 98–99.
61. *OR,* Series I, vol. 53, pp. 846–847.
62. Ibid., p. 848.
63. *OR,* Series I, vol. 22, part 2, p. 802.
64. J.B. Jones, *Rebel War Clerk's Diary,* vol. 1, p. 292.
65. *OR,* Series I, vol. 13, p. 818; Series IV, vol. 1, p. 1176; Series IV, vol. 2, p. 278; Series IV, vol. 2, p. 530; Series IV, vol. 2, p. 615; Series I, vol. 22, part 1, p. 440; Series I, vol. 22, part 2, p. 1029; Series IV, vol. 2, p. 1073.
66. *OR,* Series IV, vol. 2, p. 380.
67. *OR,* Series I, vol. 9, pp. 735–736; Series I, vol. 13, p. 886.
68. Holmes to Major General Walker, February 18, 1863, in *Correspondence of General T.H. Holmes,* War Department Collection of Confederate Records, Chapter II, Vol. 358, RG 109, National Archives, Washington, D.C.
69. *OR,* Series I, vol. 22, part 1, pp. 138–139, 143–144.
70. Swanson and Langley, *Atlas of the Civil War,* pp. 45, 61.
71. Ibid., pp. 55.
72. *OR,* Series I, vol. 53, p. 848.
73. Ibid., p. 862.
74. Holmes to Davis, February 12, 1863, in *Correspondence of General T.H. Holmes,* War Department Collection of Confederate Records, Chapter II, Vol. 358, RG 109, National Archives, Washington, D.C.
75. *OR,* Series I, vol. 53, p. 848.
76. Flyer dated March 1863, Conf Pam 12mo 889 c-1, *Duke.*
77. *OR,* Series I, vol. 53, p. 862.
78. *OR,* Series I, vol. 15, p. 972; Series I, vol. 53, p. 850.
79. *OR,* Series I, vol. 22, part 2, p. 798.
80. Ibid., p. 871.
81. Current, *Encyclopedia of the Confederacy,* p. 1607.
82. General Court Martial, Order No. 26, dated January 28, 1865, at Washington, D.C., author's collection. Clifford was released in 1865 at the age of twenty-three. He was described as "big and very handsome" but the "meanest man anyone had ever met." While in prison, he killed a fellow prisoner, a Union soldier, by crushing his chest with the ball and

chain that Clifford was wearing. Clifford was shot and killed several years after the war by a sheriff "against whom he had a grudge" (William D. Huitt, "Descendants of Rebecca Huitt Carlin," *Carroll's Corner,* http://www.carrollscorner.net/Huitt3.htm, accessed May 12, 2011.

83. Richmond *Daily Dispatch,* April 22, 186.; *New York Times,* May 3, 1863.
84. Holmes to Elizabeth, March 29, 1863, [VOLUME OR COLLECTION], *Duke.*
85. Ibid.
86. *NCTAR,* vol. 10, p. 325.
87. Holmes to Davis, April 7, 1863, in *Correspondence of General T.H. Holmes,* War Department Collection of Confederate Records, Chapter II, Vol. 358, RG 109, National Archives, Washington, D.C.
88. Ibid., April 8, 1863.
89. William Glenn to Holmes, not dated, *Duke.*
90. Edward G. Gerdes, "Company I, 36th Arkansas Infantry Regiment, Confederate States of America, *Arkansas: Edward G. Gerdes Civil War Home Page,* http://www.couchgenweb.com/civilwar/36coi.html, accessed June15, 2011.
91. Elmo Ingenthron, "Civil War Atrocities in the Upper White River Valley," *White River Valley Historical Quarterly* 1, no. 4 (Summer 1962).
92. *OR,* Series I, vol. 22, part 2, pp. 871–872.
93. Holmes to Colonel R.W. Johnson, Confederate Senate, February 16, 1863, in *Correspondence of General T.H. Holmes,* War Department Collection of Confederate Records, Chapter II, Vol. 358, RG 109, National Archives, Washington, D.C.
94. *OR,* Series I, vol. 22, part 1, pp. 310–312.
95. Ibid., pp. 310–312.
96. Ibid., pp. 285–286.
97. Ibid., pp. 255, 286.
98. Ibid., p. 287.
99. Christ, *Civil War in Arkansas,* p. 105.
100. *OR,* vol. 24, part 2, p. 460.

Chapter 8

1. Christ, *Civil War in Arkansas,* pp. 104–105.
2. Gregory J.W. Urwin, "A Very Disastrous Defeat: The Battle of Helena Arkansas," *North & South: The Official Magazine of the Civil War Society,* December 2002, pp. 26–39.
3. *OR,* Series I, vol. 22, part 1, p. 407.
4. Christ, *Civil War in Arkansas,* p. 105.
5. Woodworth, *Jefferson Davis and His Generals,* p. 150; Castel, *General Sterling Price,* p. 132–133.
6. Castel, *General Sterling Price,* pp. 132–134, 138–139; E.B. Long, *Civil War Day by Day,* p. 324.
7. Castel, *General Sterling Price,* p. 142.
8. *Confederate Service Records,* www.fold3.com image, #73181832. He may have been using an ambulance in this manner since March 1862, when he was transferred back to North Carolina. On the tenth

of that month, Major Burton requisitioned an ambulance, two mules, and harnesses. Other officers had used this type of conveyance since before the war and often modified the interiors of the vehicles to suit their needs (Percival G. Lowe, *Five Years a Dragoon*, p. 48).

9. *OR*, Series I, vol. 22, part 2, p. 863.
10. Ibid., pp. 866–868.
11. Castel, *General Sterling Price*, p. 144.
12. Richmond *Daily Dispatch*, June 30, 1863, quoting a letter printed in the *Mississippian*.
13. *OR*, Series I, vol. 22, part 2, p. 412; Series I, vol. 22, part 1, p. 436.
14. *OR*, Series I, vol. 22, part 2, p. 877.
15. Ashe, "Theophilus Hunter Holmes," p. 3, Holmes family papers; Edwin Cole Bearss, *Unvexed to the Sea: The Campaign for Vicksburg*, vol. 3, p. 1213.
16. Castel, *General Sterling Price*, pp. 144, 145.
17. Bearss, *Unvexed to the Sea*, vol. 3, p. 1216.
18. *OR*, Series I, vol. 22, part 1, p. 409.
19. *OR*, Series I, vol. 22, part 2, p. 890; Series I, vol. 22, part 1, p. 409.
20. *OR*, Series I, vol. 22, part 1, pp. 409–410.
21. Holmes to Davis, July 14, 1863, in *Correspondence of General T.H. Holmes*, War Department Collection of Confederate Records, Chapter II, Vol. 358, RG 109, National Archives, Washington, D.C.
22. Christ, *Civil War in Arkansas*, p. 113.
23. *OR*, Series I, vol. 22, part 1, pp. 387–388.
24. Ibid., p. 394.
25. Ibid., p. 430.
26. Ibid., p. 424.
27. Ibid., p. 436.
28. Ibid., pp. 433, 436–437.
29. Ibid., p. 424.
30. Holmes to Davis, July 14, 1863, in *Correspondence of General T.H. Holmes*, War Department Collection of Confederate Records, Chapter II, Vol. 358, RG 109, National Archives, Washington, D.C.
31. *OR*, Series I, vol. 22, part 1, p. 413.
32. Dr. R.J. Bell Diary, typed transcription, Missouri Historical Society, p. 14; *OR*, Series I, vol. 22, part 1, p. 413.
33. *OR*, Series I, vol. 22, part 1, p. 413.
34. Ibid., p. 414.
35. Holmes to Davis, July 14, 1863, T. H. Holmes Papers, *Duke*.
36. Albert G. Foster, "On Picket Duty before the Battle of Helena," from an original dated June 26, 1902, *Twenty-Eighth Wisconsin Volunteer Infantry*, accessed May 12, 2011.
37. *OR*, Series I, vol. 22, part 1, p. 414.
38. Ibid.; Christ, *Rugged and Sublime*, p. 84.
39. *OR*, Series I, vol. 22, part 1, p. 422; Castel, *General Sterling Price*, p. 148.
40. Holmes to Davis, July 14, 1863, T.H. Holmes Collection, *Duke*.
41. *OR*, Series I, vol. 22, part 1, pp. 400–401, 425.

42. *Southern Historical Papers* 24: 199. These men were likely shot by sergeants and lieutenants, "file closers," who were acting on orders from General Holmes. Holmes had issued similar orders to his troops when he was a brigade commander in 1861 (draft of General Order No. 2, paragraph 4, Holmes Papers, *Duke*).
43. *Southern Historical Papers* 24: 199.
44. *OR*, Series I, vol. 22, part 1, p. 433.
45. Ibid., p. 430.
46. Ibid., p. 411.
47. *OR*, Series I, vol. 24, part 3, p. 492.
48. Thomas Holcomb Papers, #605, Private Collections, North Carolina Archives.
49. *OR*, Series I, vol. 22, part 1, p. 386.
50. Ibid., p. 387.
51. Ibid., p. 412.
52. Ibid., p. 389.
53. Bearss, *Unvexed to the Sea*, vol. 3, pp. 1240–1241.
54. *OR*, Series I, vol. 22, part 2, p. 899.
55. Edwin C. Bearss, "The Battle of Helena, July 4, 1863," *Arkansas Historical Quarterly* 20 (Autumn 1961): 293.
56. Ibid.
57. *OR*, Series I, vol. 22, part 1, p. 406.
58. Steven Davis, "The Timberclad Tyler," *Civil War Times*, February 2005, p. 80.
59. *New York Times*, August 9, 1863, quoting the *Little Rock True Democrat*, July 8, 1863.
60. Bearss, "The Battle of Helena," p. 293.
61. Holmes to Davis, July 14, 1863, *Duke*; *OR*, Series I, vol. 22, part 1, p. 438.
62. *OR*, Series I, vol. 22, part 1, p. 437.
63. Boatner, *Civil War Dictionary*, p. 885.
64. *OR*, Series I, vol. 22, part 1, p. 408.
65. Castel, *General Sterling Price*, p. 283.
66. *OR*, Series I, vol. 51, part 2, p. 1005.
67. "The Letters of Newton Scott," letter dated July 6, 1863, *The Patriot Files*, http://www.patriotfiles.com/index.php?name=News&file=article&sid=456, accessed May 14, 2011.
68. *OR*, Series I, vol. 22, part 2, p. 459; *Harpers Weekly*, August 29, 1863.
69. Richmond *Daily Dispatch*, August 20 and 26, 1863.
70. Harold B. Simpson, *Simpson Speaks on History*, p. 66; *OR*, Series I, vol. 22, part 2, p. 1130.
71. Richmond *Daily Dispatch*, August 15, 1863.
72. Christ, *Rugged and Sublime*, p. 84.
73. Edwards, *Shelby and His Men*, p. 169–170.
74. *New York Times*, August 9, 1863; *Confederate Service Records*, www.fold3.com, image #71803558.
75. Holmes to Davis, July 14, 1863, in *Correspondence of General T.H. Holmes*, War Department Collection of Confederate Records, Chapter II, Vol. 358, RG 109, National Archives, Washington, D.C.; *OR*, Series I, vol. 22, part 1, p. 411.

76. Johnson and Buell, *Battles and Leaders*, vol. 3, p. 456; *OR*, Series I, vol. 22, part 2, p. 942.
77. Samuel Ashe, untitled article, p. 4, Holmes family papers.
78. R.J. Bell diary, transcript, p. 27, Missouri History Museum.
79. Castel, *General Sterling Price*, pp. 282–283.
80. *OR*, Series I, vol. 13, p. 881.
81. *New York Times*, August 30, 1863.
82. *OR*, Series I, vol. 22, part 2, p. 1049.
83. Ibid., p. 1050.
84. Castel, *General Sterling Price*, p. 281.
85. *OR*, Series I, vol. 22, part 1, pp. 521–520.
86. *OR*, Series I, vol. 22, part 2, pp. 941–942.
87. Castel, *General Sterling Price*, pp. 153–154.
88. *OR*, Series I, vol. 22, part 2, pp. 991–992.
89. Castel, *General Sterling Price*, pp. 156, 158.
90. *OR* Series I, vol. 22, part 1, pp. 477, 480, 521–522.
91. Castel, *General Sterling Price*, pp. 158–159.
92. *OR*, Series I, vol. 53, p. 897.
93. Jefferson Davis, *Papers*, vol. 10, p. 82.
94. *OR*, Series I, vol. 22, part 1, p. 480.
95. *OR*, Series I, vol. 22, part 2, pp. 1023–1024.
96. Holmes to Northrop, September 29, 1863, in *Correspondence of General T.H. Holmes*, War Department Collection of Confederate Records, Chapter II, Vol. 358, RG 109, National Archives, Washington, D.C.; *OR*, Series I, vol. 22, part 2, pp. 1027, 1029.
97. Boatner, *Civil War Dictionary*, p. 237.
98. *OR*, Series I, vol. 22, part 2, pp. 1028–1029.
99. John C. Moore, *Confederate Military History of Missouri*, p. 119.
100. Holmes to Smith, October 20, 1863, in *Correspondence of General T.H. Holmes*, War Department Collection of Confederate Records, Chapter II, Vol. 358, RG 109, National Archives, Washington, D.C.
101. Holmes to Kirby Smith, October 20, 1863, in *Correspondence of General T.H. Holmes*, War Department Collection of Confederate Records, Chapter II, Vol. 358, RG 109, National Archives, Washington, D.C.
102. *OR*, Series I, vol. 22, part 2, p. 1049.
103. Ibid., p. 1055.
104. Ibid., pp. 1064, 1074.
105. Ibid., pp. 1030, 1036.
106. Ibid., p. 1072.
107. Ibid., p. 1045.
108. Christ, *Rugged and Sublime*, pp. 99–102.
109. *OR*, Series I, vol. 22, part 2, pp. 1060–1061.
110. Ibid., p. 1084.
111. Ibid., p. 1082.
112. Holmes to Smith, October 19, 1863, in *Correspondence of General T.H. Holmes*, War Department Collection of Confederate Records, Chapter II, Vol. 358, RG 109, National Archives, Washington, D.C.
113. Holmes to Flanagin, December 22, 1863, in *Correspondence of General T.H. Holmes*, War Department Collection of Confederate Records, Chapter II,

Vol. 358, RG 109, National Archives, Washington, D.C.
114. *OR*, Series I, vol. 22, part 2, p. 1127.
115. Holmes to Davis, December 24, 1863, Frederick M. Dearborn Collection, Houghton Library, Harvard University.
116. Current, *Encyclopedia of the Confederacy*, vol. 4, pp. 1609–1610; Robert L. Kerby, *Kirby Smith's Confederacy*, p. 284; Boatner, *Civil War Dictionary*, p. 685.
117. Kerby, *Kirby Smith's Confederacy*, pp. 284, 288.
118. Ibid., p. 288.
119. Holmes to Smith, February 20, 1864, in *Correspondence of General T.H. Holmes*, War Department Collection of Confederate Records, Chapter II, Vol. 358, RG 109, National Archives, Washington, D.C.
120. *Confederate Service Records*, www.fold3.com, image #153593522; District of Arkansas Special Orders, no. 56, Feb. 25, 1864, *Duke*; *OR Supplement*, vol. 73, p. 616; *OR*, Series I, vol. 34, part 2, p. 935.
121. *OR*, Series I, vol. 34, part 2, pp. 896. At some point, Davis may have told Holmes about Smith's letter.
122. *OR*, Series I, vol. 34, part 2, p. 935; Holmes to Kirby Smith, February 1, 1864, in *Correspondence of General T.H. Holmes*, War Department Collection of Confederate Records, Chapter II, Vol. 358, RG 109, National Archives, Washington, D.C.
123. Holmes to Brigadier General William R. Boggs, February 28, 1864, in *Correspondence of General T.H. Holmes*, War Department Collection of Confederate Records, Chapter II, Vol. 358, RG 109, National Archives, Washington, D.C.
124. *OR*, Series I, vol. 34, part 2, p. 1021.
125. Holmes to Kirby Smith, March 8, 1864, in *Correspondence of General T.H. Holmes*, War Department Collection of Confederate Records, Chapter II, Vol. 358, RG 109, National Archives, Washington, D.C.
126. *OR*, Series I, vol. 34, part 2, p. 1035.
127. Current, *Encyclopedia of the Confederacy*, vol. 4, p. 1610.
128. Kerby, *Kirby Smith's Confederacy*, p. 289; *OR*, Series I, vol. 34, part 2, p. 1047.
129. *OR*, Series I, vol. 34, part 2, p. 1034.
130. Ibid., p. 1047.
131. Elizabeth Hinsdale MacPherson, "Old Times in the South," p. 2.
132. Boatner, *Civil War Dictionary*, pp. 685–689.
133. Ibid., p. 689.
134. *OR*, Series I, vol. 52, part 2, pp. 397–399.
135. *OR*, Series I, vol. 53, p. 836.
136. *OR*, Series I, vol. 26, part 2, p. 41.
137. Current, *Encyclopedia of the Confederacy*, vol. 4, p. 1608.
138. Taylor, "Brief Analysis of Arkansas," p. 10; Swanson and Langley, *Atlas of the Civil War*, p. 112.
139. *OR*, Series I, vol. 22, part 2, p. 1130.